This Damnable Dilemma

By DAVID NYPAVER

To my wife, Deb,
who is absolute proof
that a sure path to a happy life
is to marry well.

PROLOGUE

I cannot recall ever hearing him enter.

Such a small thing but now that I've had time to ponder it, that was a clue. When penitents leave my confessional, they often hold the door for the next person. "Midwest nice" maybe, or perhaps the natural goodwill that flows from forgiveness. Yet even if he entered silently, anonymous confession in my church building requires the use of an old, wooden kneeler that creaks at the weight of a second-grader. It didn't creak under him.

All I heard was, "Bless me, Father, for I have sinned." He knew what he was doing. Once you say those seven words, you begin a process that locks your confession in a vault no cop, no court, not even the pope himself can open. Cynics may scoff but this is fact. It's the famous Seal of the Confessional.

The Church's Code of Canon Law, like most legal systems, is verbose, complex, and frequently vague. But when it comes to the seal, canon law is ominously concise and clear:

> *"The sacramental seal is inviolable; therefore it is absolutely forbidden for a confessor to betray in any way a penitent in words or in any manner for any reason."*
>
> *Code of Canon Law*
> *Can. 983§1*

Did you catch the trinity of any's in that sentence? They form an unassailable NO for every hypothetical you can think up. The Church takes the seal so seriously that priests have been martyred for their silence, the last one in Mexico in the 1920s.

Why such inflexibility? Because a priest who purposefully breaks the seal puts at risk the faith of the world's 1.3 billion Catholics by undermining a sacrament instituted by the Savior himself.

For such a crime the Church imposes its harshest punishment: excommunication. To someone outside our faith this probably doesn't sound like much of a threat. So, they threw you out, so what? Just dust off your resume and see if the Episcopalians are hiring.

But to Catholic clergy, it is a catastrophe beyond thought. Excommunication means banishment not only from the priesthood, but from a faith at the center of my being. I could no longer receive the Eucharist. Confession would be barred to me, so no absolution for this and all other mortal sins I would commit in my remaining, despairing days. We all recall that Jesus told his disciples "whosoever sins you forgive are forgiven," but forget that He added: "…and whosoever sins you retain, they are retained." Enchained in my spiritual crimes, what hope could I have of escaping damnation?

The Penitent understood this when he entered my confessional. He knew I could not report his gruesome deeds without betraying my faith and possibly imperiling the souls of millions. But if I do not report him, he'll return with even more horrors to tell.

This is my damnable dilemma. A predicament so hellish I now agree with Fr. Mwangi: it is not of human design.

CHAPTER 1

St. Al's is not the kind of place you'd expect a thing like this to happen, though I'd hate to live anywhere it would. Buried deep in the suburbs of Cleveland, St. Alphonsus Liguori is a pleasant community that I call my Goldilocks parish. Not nearly as big as the downtown church that was my first assignment, nor as small as my next post, St. George's out in the sticks. How small was that? A parishioner once asked how I liked the sweet corn I had for dinner the previous night. I hadn't mentioned my meal, and she cheerfully explained that a friend of a friend told her he'd seen me buying ears at the farmer's market. That's a bit too cozy for my liking.

St. Al's was just right. You don't see it from busy Manchester Street because the church sits down-slope from the road with a scattering of pines and shrubs filtering out most of the noise. A large, masonry sign proclaims the church's name and Mass times, as well as a small placard with my title and name: Pastor: Fr. Thomas P. Pastor. Yeah, believe me I know. Sometimes I wish my Polish grandfather hadn't shortened our surname of Pastorczak. The senior citizens and kids enjoy calling me Pastor Pastor. It was fun at first, then it got old, then it got real old. Now I don't even notice.

The rectory where I live stands beside the church and it, too, is screened from neighboring houses by pine trees.

We have an elementary and middle school, Holy Spirit
Academy, situated on Manchester Street for easier access
by parents and buses. There's a good-sized, fenced-in
grassy playground behind it, a couple of basketball
courts, and a large parking lot shared by the school and
church.

St. Al's is blessed with healthy finances, largely thanks
to my predecessor, Fr. Scarpelli. A pastor for many years,
he was quite the dynamo back in the day. Scarpelli was
first-generation American and shrewdly leveraged the
loyalties of ethnic families. A St. Patrick's Day never
passed without a boisterous corned-beef and cabbage
dinner; in August he chartered buses to ferry
parishioners to the magnificent celebration of the Feast of
the Assumption in Cleveland's Little Italy; locals enjoyed
beer and brats at a modest Oktoberfest each September;
and the Eastern European families received *oplatki* wafers
for Christmas Eve dinner. These activities made St. Al's a
fixture in the traditions and lives of parish families, who
responded with pride and fidelity. When the diocese
decreed that our school consolidate with two others, St.
Al's was the largest and most vibrant by far, so the others
were merged into it.

Time, however, takes its toll. Scarpelli entered his 70s
gracefully enough but faltered as the years passed. Well-
established church committees had to run themselves
while youth and music ministry leaders chafed under
Scarpelli's dismissive "We don't need any of that
nonsense." Never the world's greatest homilist, the old
fellow sedated parishioners with mumbled, meandering
sermons. He eventually retired to an apartment close to
Lake Erie, but every year on his ordination anniversary

we brought him out for a Mass and dinner to re-connect with older parishioners. If I ever get a tattoo saying, "No good deed goes unpunished," Scarpelli will be the reason.

By the time I arrived, it was with streaks of premature gray on my 39-year-old head, but after doddering Scarpelli the parishioners boasted of the "young priest" St. Al's had somehow scored. It probably helped that I occasionally jumped into the kids' soccer games during recess, led retirees on hikes at the Metroparks, and convened a monthly "holy smoke" scripture-study at a local cigar lounge. That last one also allows me to enjoy a cigarette or two without disapproving frowns. I try to engage with all the parish ministries, clubs, and activities, and it seems to have paid off. Our registry is growing and Sunday collections are good, though not as robust as before the pandemic. Several priest friends at other parishes aren't nearly so lucky.

The church building was constructed 50 years ago, and updated in 2000 with the addition of office space and a media center. It reflects the transition in Church architecture from medieval-style fortresses to modern, overturned arks with flowing lines, airy and bright interiors, and ranks of pews forming a semi-circle around the sanctuary. Above and behind the altar hangs an eight-foot crucifix with a stylized "Risen Christ" corpus. It is suspended by intersecting steel cables, as though the Romans had invented an additional torture. At more than one Mass, standing beneath that ponderous cross, I've wondered when those cables were last inspected.

The modern design included confessionals built to accommodate changes wrought by the Second Vatican

Council. For the first time in over a thousand years penitents had a choice: the traditional anonymity of kneeling behind a screen, or the therapy-session style of sitting face-to-face with a hopefully sympathetic confessor. St. Al's has two confessionals, one on either side of the building, accessed from inside the church. The small rooms are painted a warm shade of cream and generously lit by stained-glass windows or fluorescent lights, depending on the time of day.

A wall divides each confessional room nearly in two, with a narrow opening for the penitent to walk through if he or she wishes to sit with the priest. There they find nestled in a corner a pair of chairs not unlike those in a doctor's waiting room. Between them stands a small table with a figurine of the Good Shepherd, and a box of tissues. Both confessionals serve double duty as storage space, with cabinets and stacks of cardboard boxes filled with missalettes, Christmas decorations, candles and other odds and ends. The two rooms are much the same, but for some reason the visiting-priest confessional has a little-used door at the back that opens illogically onto a mulched flower bed facing the parking lot. I wonder if it was a fire-code thing. The confessional with my name has no such backdoor, but often includes its own unique feature: Bongo, known to me as the RLD – Rotten Little Dog. More about him later.

If a penitent chooses to confess anonymously, he or she remains on the other side of the wall. More like a small nook, this area is furnished with only a wooden kneeler, above which is a circular opening in the wall about two-feet in diameter and screened by a tightly woven mat of red glass beads (1970s construction,

7

remember? Groovy.) The hip décor is ruined by an old wall-phone next to the opening, and a small, black plastic sign with white lettering directing penitents to, "Use phone if hard of hearing."

My chair on the other side of the wall is positioned next to the screen. The glass beads effectively transfer voices while rendering penitents as mere silhouettes. Which they did for him.

When he spoke on that sunny afternoon, backlit by the window's glow, all I saw was a vague, dark shadow within a circle of red.

CHAPTER 2

"Bless me, Father, for I have sinned."

I startled at the sudden voice, slid a folded sticky-note into the book on my lap and waited. It was one of those warm, gorgeous afternoons you get in early October, and for a while there came nothing but the distant drone of a lawnmower. Apparently he needed a nudge, so I asked how long since his last confession.

"Ah," the man half-groaned. "Long time. Years."

"Well, welcome back, brother," I said. When a penitent measures the gap in years, the confessions tend to be either short, or really, really long. I glanced at my watch and saw I had only 30 minutes until my meeting with the principal at the school. Hopefully his confession would be the short kind. "Our Lord rejoices at your return," I added.

"Yeah," came a weak reply before more silence. I gave him a moment then murmured, "Whenever you're ready..."

He began in a conversational tone, not the usual half-whisper of most penitents, and methodically organized his sins based on the Ten Commandments. For example, instead of saying "I took the Lord's name in vain," he said "I have broken the second commandment many, many times." That method of confessing was common among my grandparents' generation, but these days I doubt many people can even recite the Decalogue, let alone apply it. This man also used the Catholic numbering system for the commandments rather than the more common Protestant version.

He seemed deliberately vague in describing his sins, but that is hardly unusual. Confession enables you to face your transgressions and recognize your vulnerability to particular sins. It's similar to therapy, and the church practiced it for centuries before Freud made it a thing. But achieving self-awareness requires specifics. Men seem to struggle with that more than women, and are sometimes resentful when I explain they must say more than "I got mad and did some bad stuff." That's how this guy was, though he got plenty precise later.

"I have broken the sixth commandment in thoughts and deeds many times —"

"Again, you need to be more specific," I prompted.

"Well, pornography, and um, masturbation."

"How much porn?"

"What, over all these years? There's no way —"

"No, let's say recently. In the past week or month."

He thought about it. "I still couldn't guess. I mean I'm on my phone and computer all day for work, so it's easy to slip some in. Daily, just about."

"How much time do you spend with it?"

"At work only a half-hour or two. At night, maybe a couple of hours."

Woof, that was a lot. "OK," I replied. "Any other sins of the flesh?"

"Uh-huh. Fornication."

This was getting more serious. "Are you married?"

"Yeah."

"So, sex outside of marriage?"

He let out a sigh. "Mmm-hmmm. With hookers."

"OK, that's adultery, not just fornication. How often?"

"Once a month, I guess. Sometimes a little more often."

"When was the last time?"

"Tuesday."

"Is your wife aware of this?"

"No, not about the hookers. She knows about the porn and doesn't care. I got her to watch it with me a few times, but it doesn't do much for her."

I winced and made a mental note to circle back and explain how grievous it is to deliberately draw others into sin.

"Do you use condoms when you're with the women?"

"Yeah," he said. "Most hookers carry rubb– condoms and make you put one on, but sometimes with the younger ones, if they seem fresher and clean, I might pay extra to skip that."

His voice had become nonchalant, and a sadness weighed down on me like the lead X-ray apron they drape on you at the dentist office.

"My brother," I said, "you and I are children of God, made in His image, and so are these women who sell their bodies to you in real life as well as in videos. They're our sisters. Each of us carries God within us, and when we disrespect one another, we are disrespecting our Creator who loves us, who died for us."

"I know," he said slowly. "That's why I'm here. I need to stop."

My heart picked up at this first hint of remorse and resolve. "I am so glad to hear it," I said. "Christ is delighted, too, that you've turned your back to sin. OK, let's consider some steps to help you out of this darkness. Obviously, the adultery must stop immediately. But let's also focus on the porn, because that's a particularly insidious sin. It's easy to rationalize away, but it's like a slow-acting poison to your soul, and can lead to more serious sins, like the adultery. You sound intelligent, so I'm sure you know about filters you can install—"

"Before we talk about those, can I get to one other thing?" he asked.

I hesitated. Sometimes when a penitent doesn't want to face an embarrassing or deeply ingrained sin, he'll try to keep moving and hope the confessor doesn't address it. I know because I've used that tactic myself in confession. Human nature.

"We have plenty of time, and can get to the other stuff," I said, "but this seems central to what's keeping you from God—"

"Probably not as much as the other."

That set me back a step. I wasn't sure where he was going with this, so I conceded. "OK, let's talk about the other thing."

"Well," he took a breath. "I've broken the fifth commandment."

I knew what he meant but hoped he had misunderstood or misapplied that grimmest of God's laws. It was my turn to hesitate so long that he prompted me with a whispered, "Father?"

"By, ah, by saying that," I stammered, "do you mean...?"

"I have killed," he said.

A chill wiggled down my spine. I'm not sure if it was because of the weight of those words, or because he spoke them with no more emotion than saying "Gesundheit."

CHAPTER 3

"Are you talking about an animal?" I offered.

"No. A woman."

"Was this an accident?"

"No," came the voice from the other side of the red screen. "Well, maybe. I don't know. I didn't mean to kill her...not at first. I didn't start with the intention, but – I guess it became murder. Or manslaughter, I don't know."

Probably in every seminary around the world, in every course on canon law and confession, someone asks the Big One: "What if a penitent confesses to murder?" Now here I sat, on a bright October afternoon with a book in my lap, facing that very circumstance.

"Tell me what happened. Start at the beginning," I said calmly, ignoring a dread congealing in my gut like cold, wet cement.

He took another deep breath, and it let out in a shaky whoosh.

"It was Tuesday night. I went into the city looking for a hooker. One came up to my truck on East 55th, asked if I wanted to party. She looked like a skag whore–"

"A what?"

"Skag whore. That's what they call heroin addicts who hook. I guess 'skag' is slang for heroin. I wouldn't know, I don't mess with the stuff. I'm kind of particular about women. I don't go for the old or fat or ugly ones, I try to stick to the younger, you know, attractive types. But I had something in mind and junkies are so desperate for cash they're usually up for anything. So we agreed on a price, she got in, and we drove to some warehouses down by the port. I found a spot in the shadows, no security cameras around, and got out my wallet. This was for, um, oral sex. I asked if I could choke her while she did it."

"You wanted to *choke* her?" I could not keep the astonishment out of my voice.

"It's a thing now," he protested. "All the kids, the Millennials and Gen Zs, are into it. I don't even have to go to fetish pages for it anymore, it's on all the porn sites. And I did ask her, I didn't just reach down and grab. In fact, I agreed to double the price."

"All right," I said. "Go on."

"Well," I saw the shadow shift as he looked up at the stained-glass window. "That's how it happened. It got out of control. This was the first time I'd done the choking thing. I mean, I'd fantasized about it a lot."

"About choking a woman during sex, or choking another person in general?"

He said nothing.

"This is the time to get it out," I said gently, leaning toward the screen. "Bring it out of the darkness, into the light."

"Both," he said so softly I could barely hear him.

"Didn't she struggle?"

"Toward the end. Maybe I thought she was faking so I would finish faster, but it drove me on instead. I don't, I don't think it was me in control at that time."

"Did she cry out or say anything to stop you?"

His voice was very small. "She couldn't."

"Did you try to revive her?" I asked. "Maybe she passed out, but wasn't completely gone. I've read that–"

"No, she was gone," he cut me off, certainty in his words. "I didn't let go for a long time. Um, I kept squeezing her throat while I used my other hand to, you know..." I heard his breath catch. "Oh my God. What do I do now?"

"Where is she?" I asked.

"I buried her. Very deep, no shallow grave, so nothing's going to get to her."

I shook my head though he couldn't see it. "OK, you must restore her body to her family. You know that, right? She's someone's daughter. She may be someone's mother, or sister or aunt."

"You're saying I have to turn myself in?"

"I think you know in your heart you must. The darkness that welled up within you is still only a small thing. The rest of your soul recoils at what happened, I can hear it in your voice."

He was silent until a soft moan came through the red glass beads. "My life is over."

"Not at all," I said. "We're going to save your life, your immortal life. And your mortal one may not be as bad as you think. You'll get the mental health services you need. And I'll be there for you the entire way. If you'd like, I can even go with you to the police, and speak on your behalf. I'll tell them of your remorse."

"If I do that, they'll put me in prison," he said. "Everybody will know. My wife, my family, everyone at work…"

"It'll be hard, there's no way around it," I said. "But you sound like a man who has accomplished hard things in your life. Take courage from that, and from the understanding that others have walked this path before you. And you will have the grace and mercy of the Holy Spirit to strengthen you. It can be done. You will have help, I promise you."

On the other side of the beads his silhouette slumped out of sight as he dropped his head onto his hands. "Oh my God, my God, my God," he muttered softly. Well, at least he's pointing in the right direction, I thought.

"Here's how this works," I said. "I can't say anything to anyone about what you've just confessed. I can't even acknowledge you came here. If you want me to go with you, you need to see me outside of the sacrament. Come to the rectory, or even wait for me here in the church after we're done, and tell me everything about the woman again. Then I can help you."

"But I already told you…"

"I can't say anything to anyone about this. That's the seal of the confessional. I couldn't even bring it up with you, if I knew who you were. This whole conversation has really been between you and God. I'm just like a translator. This is your secret with Him."

"So, going to the police is my penance?"

"No," I said. "I can't force you, it must be a voluntary act. A very, very, very necessary one, but it must be voluntary. And you must tell them where she is, right away. We need to minimize the pain of this tragedy as much as possible."

"I should probably get a lawyer before I go to the cops," he said, defeat in his voice.

"That would be wise, but don't let it distract or delay you. Get one today. I don't know how, but I'm sure it's a lot easier than we might think. But get moving, because the Enemy is moving, too. He's not happy you're here, and he'll try to dissuade you from doing what's right. The longer you delay, the more time you give him to prey on your mind."

"'K," came the murmur. "So, what happens next?"

"I'll give you your penance, and you'll say an Act of Contrition – I can help you with it – and then I'll absolve you of your sins."

"What's the penance?" he asked, a hint of dread in his words.

Guide me, I prayed silently. Show me how to help him.

"Given how the Enemy has blinded you to the humanity and spiritual kinship you share with women, I think you really need the aid of our Holy Mother. Asking for her help will raise your respect and appreciation for women. Do you have a rosary?"

"No."

"You can pick them up almost anywhere for noth–." Inspiration seized me. "Tell you what. I'll loan you mine. I'll toss it around the corner. Take it and bring it back when you get your own. But use mine for now. Go online, there're lots of how-to sites for praying the rosary. The Marians of the Immaculate Conception have a good one. Say the rosary daily, it will be a source of great strength for you."

"That's my penance?" he asked.

"No," I said. "It's a strong recommendation." I pulled my rosary from my pocket and looking at the glossy black beads and bright silver crucifix, I felt a twinge of reluctance to part with it. But I got myself up and went to the doorway. The temptation was strong, so incredibly strong, to look around the wall, but I put my face against it and with my left hand tossed the beads into the room. For all I knew, they wrapped around his ear.

"Your penance," I said as I returned to my chair, "is to fast for ten days. That means a small meal like a piece of fruit for breakfast, maybe a small salad at lunch, then a regular meal for dinner. No snacks in between. And no meat during this fast."

He coughed, or maybe it was a scoff, and added, "That sounds like something my doctor would recommend. I mean it's a good practice, I know, but I don't see how this—"

"I wasn't finished," I said. "Every time you get a craving or feel a hunger pang, I want you to visualize the woman you killed. Think about her face. Then say a prayer for her soul, for whatever family she left behind, and for what you need to do. It doesn't have to be elaborate, something as simple as 'Dear God, may she rest with You in heaven, and grant her family and loved ones comfort and care. Give me the strength to do what's right.' That's it. Do that every time you feel hungry, and as long as you're feeling hungry. Stop what you're doing and say that prayer, or something very similar."

The intent, of course, is for the penance to haunt him day and night. With every stomach rumble or slavering at a burger commercial on TV, every time he stopped himself from opening the fridge or pantry, his crime would come to mind. Not only would it confront him, but remind him of his duty to act. If that would not compel him to go to the police, I couldn't think of anything that would.

"My brother, know that I will pray for you. In fact, I will commit right now to saying an additional rosary twice a day for you until we speak again. And I will do a fast as well, to ask God to give you strength and courage to go to the authorities."

He was quiet a moment, and asked in a hesitant voice, "So, I'm forgiven?"

"First say an Act of Contrition. Do you remember how?"

"Not really, no."

"I'll say each line and you repeat it. Think about the words as you say them. OK, it goes like this, "Oh my God, I am heartily sorry for having offended thee…""

He recited them well, and it sure sounded like he meant them. When I said the words of absolution, I heard a sigh on the other side.

"Go in peace, my brother," I said, "but remember, though your sins are forgiven, a heavy responsibility weighs on your shoulders. Go directly and do the things we talked about."

"I will, Father," he said meekly. "Thank you."

I heard the door handle turn and waited for the latch to catch again. I closed my eyes but before I could enter prayer, the door reopened and after a moment there came a soft, feminine groan. Several long seconds later, the four-pronged, rubber-tipped feet of a bronzed aluminum cane swung through the doorway. It was followed by an iron-haired matron in a long, brown autumn coat, a luggage-sized purse hanging from one gnarled hand and an oxygen bottle nestled in something like a second purse strapped over her shoulder. Transparent tubes led to a set of green cannulas under her bulbous nose.

I smiled a greeting as she dropped into the chair beside me and let out a dramatic, "Ooohhh." Her purse thumped onto the floor, she shifted the cane to her other hand and extended a fist to me.

"Here," she huffed, cramming a lot of disapproval into that small syllable. "I picked this up off the floor in the other room."

And into my hand she dropped my rosary.

CHAPTER 4

When I stepped out of the confessional, I found only two women kneeling among the pews and no one outside. That afternoon I checked my email at least a dozen times before it dawned on me I hadn't given him any contact info. My brooding conscience evoked mental images of "the Penitent," as I thought of him, sitting handcuffed in a police station wondering what happened to his pastoral support. More agonizing were thoughts of his victim, a tormented soul driven by addiction to take a desperate and ultimately fatal risk. She was buried deep, the Penitent had emphasized. Why? More digging meant more danger of discovery. Had he made this extra effort out of remorse, a good sign for redemption? Or had he dug a deep grave in advance, in which case it was premeditated. "Lord, what have I gotten myself into?" I muttered.

For the rest of Friday, I could think of almost nothing else. I should have rescheduled the meeting with Miss Challey, the 30-ish principal of the grade school. So distracted was I that she easily maneuvered me into teaching next spring's First-Communion classes for second-graders. God help me, I even agreed to bring Bongo, which shows how detached my brain had become.

Fortunately, we had a wedding on Saturday afternoon, followed almost immediately by the beginning of the weekend Masses. Sunday was its usual blur, with the added duties of a trip to an assisted-living facility because the Eucharistic minister who usually went to Green Knoll Village called in sick and all the others weren't available. Probably watching the Browns game.

I was busy, but not enough to totally occupy my mind. Repeated checks of my email and local news websites turned up nothing, and the probability loomed that the Penitent had surrendered not to the police, but to his own fears. I hadn't forgotten my promise to fast for him, and on Saturday night pondered what kind. Our Lord told his disciples some demons gain such a strong hold onto their victim's souls that prayer and fasting are required to cast them out. The monstrosity of the Penitent's confession led me to conclude that my usual fast of no-beer/no-snacks wouldn't cut it. I had almost decided to join the Penitent in giving up meat when the Holy Spirit intervened. I knew the inspiration was from Him because it hit me like a 95-mph fastball: cigarettes. I'd had the habit since high school, tried multiple times to quit but never succeeded. I'd beaten it down to about a third of a pack a day, but that's as far as the beast would retreat. Ten days without a smoke. Oh well, desperate times call for insanely stupid promises.

Sunday proved both good and bad: tough because I started my fast, but busy enough to distract me. By Monday afternoon, though, the first, familiar jangling of nicotine-deprived nerves appeared. Still no call or email from the Penitent, and nothing in the news about his killing although sadly there were plenty of others. I was feeling pretty low by sunset when I climbed into my old Nissan Versa and backed out of the rectory's garage. This was the second Monday of the month, which meant a Tulip night. A very bad time to give up smokes. I said a quick prayer of gratitude that at least God hadn't inspired me give up bourbon, too.

CHAPTER 5

I'm not sure who first called us the Tulips. It must have been another seminarian because we kept the faculty in the dark about our little gatherings. The seminary doesn't ban alcohol, but draws a hard line at drunkenness.

Not that we got "buttered," as Fr. Beech called it. One night long ago, a study session among four of us ended with a game of euchre. It was a great way to unwind, and so we concluded all our study sessions with a game or two. At some point someone observed "you know what else facilitates relaxation? Whiskey." Bourbon, to be specific. To avoid trouble, we made a fast rule that you only got one glass. And because we were seminarians, we debated excessively over the definition of "a glass." Mike settled it the following session by bringing a set of four Glencairn whiskey glasses and a bottle of Cave Hill Rabbit Hole. Those lovely, fragile, tulip-shaped glasses concentrate the bourbon aroma, and bestow on the drinker the air of a discriminating connoisseur rather than a mere boozer. What college student could resist? We became the Tulips.

In addition to me there was long-tall Mike Flynn, the oldest of us at 46 and an attorney before he accepted his vocation and entered the seminary; Auggie Krauss, once an all-state tight end with Hollywood looks, who spoiled his mother's dreams of grandchildren and his father's boasts of financial success when he left a promising career in engineering for the priesthood; and Jim Olecki, short, nerdy, and gentle, and probably the best priest among us.

After ordination we drifted into our parish identities: Fr. Flynn, Rev. Augustus Krauss, Fr. Jim, and last and probably least, me as Pastor Pastor. But we all treasured memories of those late-night theological debates/euchre matches, fueled by exhaustion, holy zeal, and Kentucky's finest. So much so that even after ordination and assignments that scattered us across the diocese, we made the second Monday of every month a Tulip Dinner. Hosting duties rotated and the previous month's euchre losers brought dinner or paid for carry-out.

At first, it morphed into a kind of support group. We shared the excitement and wonder of our callings, along with the difficulties and realities of the priesthood. Nowadays as we sip, shuffle and call trump, the talk flows around parish drudgery, diocesan gossip, and family issues.

I was the last to show up at St. Barbara's, Mike's parish, and the others were already offering opinions on tonight's bourbon sampling: Angel's Envy. I placed a blue plastic grocery bag with Cheetos and pretzels on the kitchen counter when Auggie called out "What'd you do with the dog? Didn't shoot it, did ya?"

"Get thee behind me, Satan," I grumbled.

So here's the story with Bongo. I have several nieces and one of them, Lauren, is an Army nurse. She was stationed in Tennessee when her unit was deployed to

Germany and she had to find a home for her beagle. Her mom is my sister, Terry, with whom I am very tight. The youngest of five kids, we're what folks call Irish twins; her birthday is in January and mine is in November of the same year. We differ in a lot of ways, are similar in others, and have always had each other's back. When Terry asked me to take the dog, I tried to beg off, but knew she was in a bind. T is crazy about dogs and hated the idea of a pet shelter. And several priests I know own dogs to diminish the loneliness that comes with the vocation. In a fit of weakness, familial love, and inexcusable stupidity, I said yes. Worst. Decision. Ever.

A beagle is, perhaps, the most stubborn animal the Lord created. Uber-athletic Lauren took him on early morning runs, so Bongo was accustomed to his breakfast at 4:30 a.m. His vocalization range is broader than an opera star's. Bongo howls, bays, barks, yips, and whines. He scratches woodwork and furniture. I can't talk anyone into walking him because…well, he's a beagle. He will drag you in the direction of any scent that bisects his path, regardless of property, traffic, or obstacles. If he smells rabbit, everyone in a two-block area is treated to his deep-throated baying, a kind of wrenching, below-the-diaphragm eruption that sounds like someone kicked him in the stomach. And there's another reason hounds are considered outdoor dogs. Once while working on a homily in my office, I turned in time to see him cock his leg against a filing cabinet, and as God is my witness, he kept those brown eyes on me the whole time he let fly. There are spray bottles of Resolve Pet Stain Remover in three rooms of the rectory. Even my Croatian housekeeper, Sophie, uses his nickname though she skips the acronym and calls him "Rotten Leetle Dog."

The guys had called in an order for Thai food, and set up the cards while we waited for Door Dash. A tumbler of ice water and a tulip glass with about two fingers of amber liquid already waited for me at my chair, so I took a seat. I hadn't even raised the liquor to my lips when Jim asked, "Why do you keep that dog if it's making you miserable?"

"My sister would kill me if I got rid of it. And it can be sweet at times. I just wish it wasn't such a pain in the ass."

"The dog's bored," said Auggie as Jim dealt cards. "It's a hound, a field dog. My uncle bred them, sold 'em mostly to hunters. He always told people who bought them as pets, 'If you're gonna keep it indoors, you gotta wear it out. A tired beagle is a good beagle."

"Then I'm in trouble," I said. I put an imaginary phone to my ear. "So sorry about your dying mother, I'm skipping hospice rounds today because I need to play with my dog."

"You've got a school," Jim said. "Let the kids play with it."

Mike laughed. "Liability issues out the wazoo." We all nodded in deference to his legal expertise and habit of usually being right. "Anyway," he said, nodding at the queen of hearts showing on top of the deck, "pick it up and Auggie, you stay home."

"Seriously?" Jim whined. "You're gonna do this right out of the gate?"

"Yup," Mike grinned.

"Ya know," Auggie said and dutifully scooped up the tricks as Mike bulldozed our cards with both bowers and trump to spare. "My uncle did this thing that might work for you, Tom. He taught the pups to track by soaking a lure in rabbit scent and attached it to his four-wheeler. Then he dragged it all around a big, old meadow, doing zigzags and such. Afterall, a beagle is nothing more than a nose with legs. Those dogs love that. They absolutely wear themselves out following the track. Make a big circle or a figure 8 and they'll stay busy for most of the afternoon. Your church has that big fenced-in lawn with all those shrubs. Maybe ask your maintenance guys to tie one to their riding mower."

I considered it. A few retirees from the parish made-up a volunteer grounds crew, and the idea sounded like something that might amuse them. Auggie fiddled with his cell phone and turned the screen toward me. "You can get a lure kit from Amazon for fifteen bucks. Why not?" I nodded as Mike rolled us up and showed four clubs on his score cards.

"This might be an early night," he said.

"Somebody give him another drink," I muttered.

"To the victors go the spoils," Mike replied and held his empty glass to me. "Go get me my spoils."

I couldn't help but laugh and rose to fetch his bourbon. Ever since the Penitent showed up in my confessional, a funk as dense as a Cleveland sky in December had descended on me. But now, in this company of old friends, those clouds parted and some light shone through. I should have known it was a sucker hole. As I returned with Mike's glass, Jim glanced up and spoke.

"Sooooo," he drew the single syllable out in a long, tantalizing sound. "Anyone hear about the new IBS update?"

Had we been doctors or nurses or pretty much anyone else we'd have thought he was talking about irritable bowel syndrome. But to priests of our diocese, an "IBS update" meant an announcement from His Excellency, Bishop Emilio Reyes Bodillo Sanchez, who began every letter, every email, and probably every Mother's Day card with "I, Bishop Sanchez..." That the acronym also applied to a colon-clutching malady was just an appropriate coincidence.

"Expect a new episcopal missive, maybe this week," Jim continued. "Supposedly there's a congresswoman up for re-election who is about to propose legislation targeting us." That got everybody's attention, including mine. "Well, it's all clergy, really. She wants to expand our role as mandated reporters of child abuse to now include any crime resulting in death. And here's the kicker," Jim paused for effect. "Her proposal states, quote: with no exemptions based on doctrine, policy, or tradition. End quote."

"Get out," Auggie said. "They expect us to break the seal?"

"Never happen," Mike tossed in. "Even if it became law – and I can't see how it would – the Church would challenge it before the ink was dry. They'd get a judge to order a stay, and an appeals court would quash it." He waved his hand to swat the very idea away. "It's basic First Amendment stuff. She's grandstanding to energize her base."

"I dunno," Jim said. "Look what's been going on at the state level. In the past couple of years there's been, what? Three, four state legislatures with bills to force us to violate the seal under certain conditions. Utah, Vermont…I forget the other ones."

Mike shrugged it off by saying those also were tied up in court. Jim whipped out his cell phone to contradict him, Mike and Auggie got out theirs, too, and the debate was on. The discussion fully restored my gloom. That's why pilots call those breaks in the clouds 'sucker holes.' They suck you in with false hope, then close in around you. I got up and watered my tulip with more Angel's Envy.

"Anyway," Jim continued. "My guy in the diocese office says IBS plans to make a splash. He's hoping to beat the Conference of Bishops to the punch and publicly direct his priests to ignore this law. That'll get Rome's attention. Which they say has been his goal ever since he got here."

"More power to him," Mike said. "The sooner they notice him, the sooner he moves on and we get a new fanny in the bishop's chair."

The discussion went on for another 10 minutes, but I stayed out of it. We took a break when dinner came, and they still chewed on that bone throughout the meal. When we got back to euchre, it was my turn to deal and as I shuffled I desperately tried to think of a new topic of discussion. I didn't think fast enough.

"Speaking of the seal," Auggie said, reaching into his shirt pocket, "it's been a long time since we've had a PeniTest. And I'm feelin' lucky."

I groaned inside while the others laughed. To everyone's amazement, Auggie produced a Sailor Pro Gear fountain pen, elegant with a glossy black coating banded in gold. You must understand that in addition to

31

being bourbon snobs, three of the four Tulips were hopeless pen nerds, me among them. Only Jim was immune to the allure of these functional works of art, but his nerd bona fides exceeded ours. In fact, his love of all things Star Wars got him in trouble once when the auxiliary bishop learned he had persuaded his organist to play the Imperial March, Darth Vader's theme music, as the recessional after a Mass.

Such was our madness as stylophiles that we had to put a $200 limit on pens wagered in the PeniTest. The practice had begun shortly after our ordinations. While playing euchre one night, somebody said he'd recently heard a humdinger of a confession. Another person – it might have been Auggie, I really don't remember – said he'd gotten a wild one, too. And the first guy wagered a new fountain pen that his story would top the other. We were dying of curiosity, but leery of breaking the seal. It was Lawyer Mike, of course, who thought up loopholes we made into rules. Number One, no details that could in any way identify the penitents. Number Two, there had to be some theological or evangelical merit to the story. Can't be lurid tales just for the sake of titillation. And Number Three, if more than one guy had a story, we'd have a contest: each man wagers a pen, and all four of us voted on which was best. We called it the PeniTest. I confess that I invented that groaner, but in my defense, bourbon was involved.

At first it was a regular thing, and some good came of it. There was one situation involving the sin of sloth that all four of us eventually worked into our homilies, with appropriate care taken so the penitent could never recognize themselves in it. But over time, the PeniTest faded. Maybe as we matured in the priesthood, our need for advice or counsel diminished. Or it could simply be that the overwhelming majority of confessions are repetitious, boring, and banal. I know people avoid confession because they're afraid I'll remember them, and think less of them or be shocked by what they say. They don't get that listening to people's failings and sins is depressing. It's the healing part of the sacrament that attracts and affects most priests. The sins are the dreck you try to forget. It's like asking a dermatologist about his most memorable pustule. You don't want think about it. But as I learned a few days ago, sometimes you can't help but remember.

Auggie held the pen up for all to see before laying it on the table in front of him. Jim dug into his shirt pocket. "OK, I'll put up um…I've got this…well, it says Wells Fargo on the side," he said to a chorus of groans. "I didn't know we were gonna do this," he objected. "I'd have brought a good one. Wait a minute," he added. He went to his coat hanging over a chair and produced his checkbook. Jim flipped it open and pulled out another plastic pen, provoking another round of guffaws. "My cousin is a graphic designer and she gave me this. It's a…" he rolled it in his fingers and frowned at the Japanese characters. Then he looked at the top and declared triumphantly, "it's a 0.03 tip. Super, ultra, extra, optimum point. I use it for my checkbook register because you can write in like 3-point type."

He handed it to me, and I shrugged and passed it to Mike. He took a longer moment, scratched his cheek, and said, "I didn't know they made anything smaller than point-oh-five millimeters. Does it write?" With a flourish,

Jim scratched out his signature, and after a brief debate, his wager was accepted.

"You're the challenger, you go first," Auggie said.

Jim paused, bowed his head to arrange his words. I've got to say that Jim is good, even better than Mike, at phrasing his words delicately and diplomatically.

"The penitent suffered a public insult at a family gathering. It bothered —" he stopped himself, careful of pronoun use "it bothered the penitent very much, but there was no retaliation. The insulter and insultee later found themselves in the kitchen preparing a traditional meal, and the insulter asked the insultee to fill a measuring cup with cornstarch for the gravy, which was somehow pivotal for the meal's success. The measuring cup, however, got filled with baking powder instead of cornstarch. The substitution was not discovered until the meal was served and the gravy turned out bitter. Crazy bitter. As in inedible. As in, people scraping their plates into the trash. Disaster for the host, who also was the insulter. The penitent quietly discovered the substitution, but rinsed out the measuring cup to destroy the evidence. And consequently, allowed the host to suffer a loss of reputation."

"I'm about ready to throw that cheap-ass pen of yours out the window," Mike cut in.

Jim closed his eyes and raised his hand. "Here's the conundrum: the penitent does not recall deliberately making the substitution of baking powder for cornstarch, but admits to stewing over the insult at the time and was in a 'spirit of revenge,' and thus, while fantasizing about pay-back, in fact, achieved it. So...for an act to be a sin, it must be a deliberate choice. But if one indulgently places oneself in a mindset of revenge, in circumstances where that revenge could be obtained, are they guilty of an evil act, even if the act takes place subconsciously?"

The room was surprisingly quiet with that unexpected poser. It took several minutes of discussion and sips from our tulip glasses to arrive at the communal decision that while indulging in evil thoughts is a venial sin, any unconscious acts cannot be connected to it. And, of course, the penitent should get a scolding for not fessing up.

Auggie quietly tapped his pen against the table and said, "I'm not sure I can beat that."

"It is not for you to decide," Mike said with mock pomposity. "Tell us your tale."

"I had a penitent who wanted to know if it's a sin to summon the devil in order to argue with him."

"What?"

"Yeah, this old guy heard something on EWTN about how Satan seeks the ruin of each individual soul. Not just collective, but personal. I guess he really stewed about it because he wanted to know why. His words were 'I wanna ask that S.O.B., what'd I ever do to you?' He was serious. Said he even asked at the library if they had books on how to summon the devil. Thank God no one ever showed him how to use a computer.

"I explained that summoning a demon is sorcery, which is way up there on the list of mortal sins. I think I scared him off the idea, but he got me thinking: how can we get people to appreciate Satan's danger in their lives if they can't grasp his motivation? How do we answer the guy's question; why does Lucifer have it in for each of us, in a way people can understand?"

"Cattle," Jim said flatly. "C.S. Lewis covered this perfectly in 'The Screwtape Letters.' The devils see us as cattle, or as he put it, we are 'bred for the table.' In hell they'll dine on our souls over, and over and over. How did he put it? Each of us would become 'A brimful, living chalice of despair, horror and astonishment' that demons can raise to their lips whenever they want."

Auggie shook his head. "Yeah, but even Lewis pointed out that few people believe in devils. He wrote that in the 1940s, and it's gotten way worse since then. Soul-devouring demons? Sounds like a spin-off of the Walking Dead. They just don't buy it. We need an explanation that the folks in the pews would find relatable."

"Something like the vindictive ex-spouse," Mike said softly. "We've all seen it, in our own lives or among others. A marriage breaks up in a fiery divorce, mom gets the kids. Let's say her ex can't hurt her directly – she's successful in her career, or has a new and better boyfriend, or maybe she's just bigger and meaner than him. So how does this vengeful bastard strike back at her? Simple: he hurts the kids. Inflicts psychological or emotional or even physical pain on the children. Or, even better in his mind, he turns the kids against their mother with lies and bribes. Either way, she suffers." Mike tapped his glass against his lower lip. "Might be too puerile for our brethren in the theology departments at Notre Dame or Catholic University, but for the folks out in the pews, it's relatable."

He looked around the table. "How do you inflict pain on an all-powerful god? Go after His children. He gave them free will and the opportunity to use it. So first you

36

turn God's children against Him. Then destroy them one by one."

We sipped our liquor and pondered that in silence. Finally, Auggie slid the elegant Sailor Pro Gear across the table to Mike, and Jim did the same with his plastic micro-point. Mike smiled and shook his head.

"Keep 'em. That's been buzzing in my head a long time. Real long. For some reason, it came together now."

Jim smiled with his usual, genuine warmth. "It was the Spirit," he said softly.

Mike made an embarrassed face, mumbled something that sounded like "I dunno" and swirled his liquor in the tulip glass. His eye caught mine and he turned to me.

"What's with you? You haven't said a word all night."

"And," Auggie said, waving a finger, "you haven't gone out for a smoke. You on the wagon again?"

"Just for a week or so. I already bought another carton to spark up when it's over."

"Why only a week?"

"I'm fasting."

"Special intention?" Jim asked.

"For a penitent," I said too quickly, regretting the words as soon as they tumbled out. Better switch to water, I thought, before the bourbon completely unlatches my tongue.

"Sounds serious," Auggie said.

"You could say that," I replied.

"What else could you say?" Mike asked without looking at me.

"Not much," I said. If I hadn't fogged my frontal cortex with liquor, I would have stopped right there. But I had, so I didn't.

"All I can tell you is…if they pass that law requiring us to report a fatal crime, I could go to prison."

Jim whistled and Auggie muttered, "No shit?"

I nodded and waited for someone to break the shocked silence.

Mike set his glass down and looked at me. "You know you gotta take this to the Wolfman."

"Yeah, I would," Auggie said. Jim nodded, then tried to shake something out of his mind, which must not have worked because he took a big sip from his glass.

They were right, but I had others to talk to first.

CHAPTER 6

It turned out that The Wolfman, known to the rest of the world as Fr. Kenneth Wulfram, senior moral theologian at St. Agnes' Seminary, would not return from a conference at Marquette University until the following Saturday. I could have learned that with a phone call, but by Tuesday morning my angst had browbeaten me into driving to his seminary office.

"Can you get him a message, Dolores?" I asked, standing as a supplicant before his administrative assistant. A bulky, 60-ish woman with well-coifed hair, Dolores gave me a respectful but flat stare through her gold-trimmed, brow line glasses. She had long ago found a way to balance her instinctive, cradle-Catholic deference to priests with a senior admin's stony obstinance. The party-size bag of peanut M&Ms in her desk drawer probably helped.

"I'm sorry, Fr. Pastor, he left instructions for no interruptions. Do you want an appointment with him for…" she turned, reached back to her computer and tapped a keyboard, "…next Wednesday afternoon?"

My head shook involuntarily. "I really need to see him. Any availabilities on Saturday?"

A few more clicks on her keyboard and she shrugged. "His flight leaves Milwaukee at 7 p.m., and even if it's on time he won't get in until late. He's got lectures Monday morning, so he'll want Sunday to rest and prep. He's booked solid until Wednesday."

I've been told my face is not the ugliest in the world, and in favorable light retains a shadow of its boyish charm. If you've got a decent card, you play it. I heaved a deep sigh and gave my best impression of a puppy waiting at the window for the school bus to bring the kids back. God bless her, Dolores wears many hats but first and foremost, she's a mom. She sighed, blinked, then looked up at me.

"Email him," she said. "He's checking those. Tell him you talked with me and I'll find a time on Sunday if he agrees. And copy me on everything."

"You are a life-saver, Dolores," I said. Funny how our subconscious works its way into our phrasing.

Back on the street the wind blew past with sufficient force and chill to make me look in the direction of Lake Erie. Sure enough, a wall of grey clouds loomed over the telephone wires and rooftops. Autumn's overdue arrival would delight Northeast Ohio's many cold-weather fans, who resented sipping long-awaited pumpkin-spice lattes while wearing shorts and T-shirts instead of sweaters and down vests.

I got into my Nissan and started it, and given the depressing frequency of car-jackings in Cleveland, locked my doors. Before throwing the car into gear I thumbed the call button on my steering wheel, announced "Terry," and waited for my sister's phone to ring. It went to voicemail instead so I cancelled the call and pulled into traffic.

When Terry doesn't pick up it usually means she's with someone for work. Our running gag is it's hard for her to answer a smart phone when she's got an informant pinned up against an alley wall, the guy's shirt bunched up in her fist. Terry used to explain that when you can't reach an insurance investigator, 9 times out of 10 it's because the phone is silenced to allow for concentration while reading policies, records, or spreadsheets. But she finally figured out that to a parish priest, any profession with the word "investigator" in the title sounds thrillingly exotic, so now she plays along.

On the other hand, if Terry wanted to throw somebody up against a wall I wouldn't bet against her. We often said our bodies were switched for our genders: I inherited Mom's slender, tall figure and Terry got Dad's stout, big-boned frame. Not ideal for either of us during our tender teen years, but it proved advantageous for Terry when she joined the Army. Her robust physique, as well as her smarts and ambition propelled her to the rank of warrant officer in the Army Criminal Investigative Division. Its acronym is a constant source of amusement for our brother, John, who never tires of delivering the line "Terry used to be on ACID." She had planned on making a career of it until little Lauren bloomed inside her womb. We never heard much about the daddy, other than his lack of interest in marriage or fatherhood. So single-mom Terry left the military, briefly considered work as a cop, and eventually settled into the comparatively dull but routine life of insurance investigation. Nonetheless, she bought a Sig Sauer P320, a 9mm semi-auto just like the one she carried for ACID, and got a carry permit.

That was another big difference between us. Christ could have been looking at me when He said the meek shall inherit the earth. Terry, on the other hand, was more Old Testament. I can imagine her joy-riding a chariot over the rubble of Jericho. In a situation where I would turn the other cheek, Terry would pull on sparring gloves.

But we had our similarities, too. For one, I doubt any brother and sister could be more devoted to one another. I helped her weather the teary storms of high school when guys dumped her or she dumped them. When her Army lover abandoned her at news of the pregnancy, I left school for two weeks and drove to Colorado to be with her. I think if I hadn't, she might have made a decision she'd regret the rest of her life. She didn't that time, but certainly did a few years later by marrying a boat salesman named Carl. That short-lived civil union led to a lot of well-earned regret, but it also produced Cammie, Terry's other kid and my godchild.

For her part, T stood by me when Mom's death and doubts about my vocation sent me spiraling into a depression that required therapy and pharmaceuticals to escape. I don't talk much about that time in my life. Even with my faith, the therapist, and the drugs, if Terry hadn't been there for me…let's just say the black dogs, as the Roman poet Horace called depression, might have pulled me down for good. And Terry shone an additional ray of light into my life by asking me to be Cammie's godfather. It was great fun while she was a kid. Now that she's a 14-year-old, in-your-face teen-ager, I have developed a deeper appreciation for the gift of celibacy.

Another connection Terry and I share is a fondness for target shooting we inherited from Dad. He took each of his five kids to the gully on the farm to teach the basics of firearm safety and shooting, but only Terry and I really liked it, which seemed to tickle the old man. Some of my most cherished childhood memories are of making pop cans dance with BB guns while our noses dripped in the frigid winter air, or of oven-hot August afternoons when we shot our .22 rifles into the gully wall just to make puffs of dry dirt like in Westerns. Shortly before Dad passed a year and a half ago, Terry and I were with him in his bedroom and he verbally bequeathed his gun collections to us. Our other siblings couldn't care less. Dad had motioned to Terry and told her to take the firearms because "you know guns better than most men and in your line of work, you might need 'em." He looked at me and said, "Tommy, a priest has no business with a gun. You get the toys."

So among my possessions is a tub with what looks like an arsenal, but not a single firearm among them. They're all air guns. There are WWII rifles, handguns, a submachine gun, cowboy revolvers, and a lever-action rifle. There's a huge, black, malevolent-looking beast with a massive scope and bipod legs folded under the barrel, the kind of rifle an assassin in a spy movie might wield. I wonder how my parishioners would react if they knew Pastor Pastor had a makeshift shooting range in the rectory basement. It's only a box stuffed with rags and a target taped to the front. There's something Zen-like about clearing your mind of everything, modulating your breathing, focusing on the front sight, and gently squeezing the trigger until you get a sound no louder than a stapler. If all goes well, a little hole appears on or near the bullseye. Dad sunk good money into some of his air guns, and they have more accuracy in them than I have in me. I mess with them when I feel lonely for the old man, or need something to supplement prayer in calming my mind. The only people who know about my basement range are Terry and Sophie. The housekeeper's response at its discovery was to shrug and say, "Like leetle kid in Christmas movie. You shoot your eye out." Then she shook a finger, scowled, and said, "God's punishment."

By the time I got back to my office in the rectory, I was tempted to go down to my little range and fling some pellets, but a check of my schedule showed only 15 minutes until a counseling session with a middle-aged couple concerning their teenaged child. Often these sessions were about a) our kid is gay, what should we do, b) our kid is doing drugs, what should we do, c) our kid won't go to church anymore, what should we do, or d) all of the above. Lucky for me, the answer to all of those is "Show them how much you love them."

Ticking off my to-dos before the session made me think of my usual pre-meeting smoke, which summoned a nicotine craving so intense my gut clenched up. Thank God (and I mean that literally), my cell went off and I snatched it up, thinking it might be Terry. Even as I lifted the phone, I realized from the tone it wasn't a call but a news alert. My throat tightened as I thought this might be about the Penitent or the prostitute he'd killed. Instead, it was about a truck accident tying up I-71 in both directions. Still, I hadn't checked the news feeds since early this morning, and it was possible something might have happened that I hadn't seen. I looked at my counseling binder, decided since I didn't know why they were coming in, I'd best play it by ear. Something else nagged at my conscience, and when it hit me, I shook my head in frustration at my forgetfulness. I grabbed a pen and a piece of junk mail on my desk and scribbled in the margin "Email wolfy ASAP." Geez I was getting scatterbrained. I wanted so much to light up.

Instead, I picked up my phone, scrolled to my news feed, and down the rabbit hole I went.

CHAPTER 7

Terry called at about 7:45 a.m. Wednesday as I was finishing up in the sacristy after early Mass. This was one of those times when we're worlds apart, me in the serenity and solitude of the church, my sister grinding through rush hour and salting her end of the conversation with gems like, "Nice signal, jerk" or "What the fudge are you waiting for?" (She doesn't say "fudge.") Long ago our family invented the phrase "Terry Time" to explain her usual tardiness for everything from dinners and movies to weddings and baptisms. You'd think a person with a military background would be more prompt.

Anyway, her news wasn't great. She was tied up in a civil suit her company had leveled against a medical practice. I tried to follow along as she wove through traffic and the intricacies of insurance filing protocols and requirements, but she lost me with all the acronyms and jargon. What I gleaned from her monologue was that she and another insurance investigator would give depositions this week, and needed to remain handy to answer any additional questions.

I had hoped to get one-on-one time with Terry for advice I might share with the Penitent on the smartest way to turn oneself in to the police. My sister had contacts in Cleveland PD, the Cuyahoga County sheriff's office, and some of the suburban police departments. Of course, an actual police detective or a criminal lawyer would be a far better resource for such information, but I don't run into many of those in the Altar & Rosary Society, or at scripture study.

"Tell you what," Terry said to my request for a meet-up. "Cammie is going camping with friends this weekend, so I'm free."

"Yeah, but I'm not," I replied. "Remember what mom used to say, 'My boy Tommy is a priest, so he only works one day a week.' I don't think I can shake loose any time before late afternoon on Sunday."

"What about Saturday?"

"Got Mass at 5, but we don't have any weddings, so late morning looks good. Lunch, too."

"Moron!" she shouted. "Sorry, not you, some guy in a Mercedes. Yeah, that would work. Hey, why don't we meet at the farm and go down to the gully and launch bullets? Loser buys lunch."

"Sure. Don't bring much money, I'll order something light."

"Ha, ha," she replied. "I'll bring the Ruger and the Smith. We can trade off halfway through, like last time."

We chatted a bit about family and Cammie's latest shenanigans (pink and purple hair). Terry got to her office, finishing our conversation. I lingered at the sacristy window, first scanning the overcast sky, then the autumn colors defiantly splashing beauty into the world. A maple tree practically glowed yellow, spreading its golden splendor in a circle on the lawn. Other trees remained deep green save for splotches of orange, red and brown high up on their canopy, as though some careless giant had brushed past with open cans of paint. The burning bushes that lined the school lived up to their name in deep shades of burgundy and crimson. I said a small prayer of gratitude for this grandeur, and then remembered my pledge to the Penitent. Retrieving my rosary from my pocket, I got down on the kneeler in the sacristy, and recalled that today being Wednesday, the rosary meditation would be the Glorious Mysteries. Thinking of that wonderous golden tree outside, I couldn't help but smile and whisper, "Sounds right to me," and raised the small crucifix to my lips to begin the prayer with a kiss.

Afterwards, I got back to the rectory in time for a commotion in the kitchen. Bongo was yelling his head off, and even delivered one of those awful, baying howls. Sophie responded with a fiery stream of Croatian that did not sound complimentary. When I stepped in, I found her holding a flat, blue-and-white Amazon plastic bag over her head while Bongo stood on hind legs, forelegs clawing on her hip. I grabbed his collar and pulled him back, panting and straining for another go at Sophie and the bag. Despite his constant protests, I dragged the RLD to his crate in the hallway and once inside, threw the black-out cover over it to shut him up. It didn't work.

"What did you buy now?" Sophie shouted at me over Bongo's barking. "A dead cat?" Honestly, I couldn't recall what I had ordered, so I found the perforated tab and opened it up.

"Wow, it's the lure. This got here quick." Sophie stared and shook her head in disgust at the cartoon dog prancing across the top of the packaging. I explained as briefly as I could above Bongo's yapping that this was intended to tire him out.

"Should buy rope to shut his fat mouth," she grumbled. An ear-splitting bay from the crate deepened her scowl. She flung a finger at the wall beside us and bellowed, "Put in garage, so he don't smell it no more." I meekly did as I was told. Who says priests can't relate to married men. The funny thing was, several deep sniffs of the package revealed nothing more than the solvent stink of plastic. A beagle's nose is supernatural.

In the comparative quiet of my office, I fired up my laptop. As I waited for the software to boot up, I sat back in my chair, thinking how best to phrase the email. Wulfram was not only a former faculty member, but the spiritual advisor and confessor to me and the other Tulips. I don't know why he took a shine to us, but it's easy enough to understand why we loved the man. His courses in moral theology engaged us, drew us in, and deepened our appreciation for the omnipresent love of God. He's not the stereotype of a theologian. I remember my first day in his class, expected a pinch-faced, wizened gnome with wire-rimmed glasses hovering over an open book. Instead, the man who came in and stood between the desk and white board looked like a guy you'd see pulling drafts at a local craft brewery. He was big, with shaggy brown hair that flowed into a beard any Amish elder would approve. Unlike most other faculty, Wulfram did not wear a Roman collar, but left his black shirt open at the throat. The fabric sloped out to cover a substantial belly and disappear into a black leather belt cinched with a big oval buckle displaying three crosses in bas-relief.

He spoke with a voice deep and strong, but never forceful. One the first day of class he asked simply, "What is theology?" Somebody tossed out a grandiose explanation, to which Wulfram merely blinked. Another guy, perhaps thinking he had the all-purpose answer because he used it in nearly every class said simply, "Love." Wulfram didn't correct him, just asked, "Anybody else?" He turned to the white board, and in blue marker wrote Theo-logy. He tapped a finger against the first half. "God" someone said. Wulfram nodded and pointed to the latter half. "Study" came the answer and he shook his head slowly. "Reason," I ventured. Wulfram gave a slight nod and put his hands on the lectern.

"God and reason. The unknowable, and the path to knowledge. For the rest of this class, I want you to silently ponder, meditate if you like, on that paradox. But begin with a prayer of thanksgiving for the gift of reason, and humbly ask Our Father to what purpose it was given us." And with that, he walked out of the room.

I can't say Wulfram was the reason I became a priest, but he sure helped keep me from becoming a not-a-priest. When the doubts came in my middle year, followed by anxiety and depression, he stepped up to keep me from washing out. And I think he saw how the Tulips rallied behind me, as we later did with Auggie when he had his crisis. After our ordination, Jim was the first to ask Wulfram to become his spiritual advisor and confessor, followed by the rest of us. I can't imagine how or why Wulfram found time for all of us, but he did.

I stared at the white blaze of my Gmail screen, wondering what approach would most likely get me onto his calendar for Sunday. I had to give him the gist of it without any details, which meant despite Dolores' instructions I could not copy her on this. That made it even more important to craft a first sentence sure to draw him into the rest, considering all the email he probably had to go through. I mulled it, then the Holy Spirit nudged my stuck, nicotine-starved brain and the answer suddenly became dazzlingly clear.

"Dear Ken," I wrote. "I don't know what to do."

CHAPTER 8

Thursday had been blustery but bright, flapping the gold, crimson, and brown leaves on the trees like hundreds of tiny pennants. During the night, however, the winds rose and temperatures dropped, and Friday dawned as a declaration that summer was truly done and gone, and only cold, dark months lay ahead. Occasional gusts rattled chilly rain off the stained-glass windows in my confessional and made a soft whistle where the lower louvers didn't fit tight. I guess it had drawn my attention, because I didn't hear him come in. I'm sure that must have been why.

"Bless me father, for I have sinned."

The voice caught me by surprise and I couldn't be certain it was the Penitent. His next words removed all doubt.

"It's been a week since my last confession," he deadpanned. Priests are expected to forget penitents the moment they leave the confessional, and I flatter myself that I've gotten pretty good at it. But that wasn't possible in this situation. Excitement and, yes, pity, rose in my heart. It was him, and I heard in his voice a shameful admission of failure.

"Why do you seek God's mercy so soon?"

"Two things," he said. "First, you know who I am?"

I'm not supposed to acknowledge it, but to lie under these circumstances would profane this sacred space. "Yes," I replied.

There was a long pause, but I waited. Let him come to it in his own time.

"I couldn't do it," he said at last. "I sat in my truck in the parking lot, and almost came back in to wait for you. Honest to God, I had my hand on the door latch, but...I couldn't.

"When I was a kid, one afternoon me and a buddy got caught trespassing in an empty office building. The cops took us to their station and put us in separate cells while they called our parents and the owner. It was this little township jail, and the middle of a weekday so there was nobody else there. But I remember how freaked out I was by something on the wall. Somebody had written in pencil, 'Bikers are the best people,' but they spelled it p-e-p-l. There was a little dried blood, too, probably from road rash or a busted lip. But that phrase scared me to death. It still does. That's who you find in those cages. Ignorant, violent thugs you can't reason with. They grew up in horrible situations, which made them meaner and harder than I'll ever be. They would eat me alive."

"How old were you?"

"Thirteen, I think."

"And how old are you now?"

"32."

I nodded. Without the sun to backlight him, all I saw was the solid circle of red beads, so I imagined him, head hanging in despair.

"You're older now, and you've made your way in the world. You're a smart guy, I can hear it. And remember, you're not doing this as punishment, you're doing this to save yourself. To save your soul. Atonement is part of the healing process. Like physical therapy after a surgery or injury. It hurts, it's unpleasant, it can feel like torture and you'd rather do anything else. But it's crucial for healing, just like the penance I gave you. How's that going?"

"Tough," he admitted. "I've never fasted before."

"Not even on Ash Wednesday or Good Friday?"

"Well, yeah, of course," he countered a little too quickly. "I meant a long, sustained fast. And I've, uh, slipped up a few times."

"That's OK, as long as you get back on it. Did you resume your the fast?"

"I did. I've got three days left."

Well, if he's keeping count he's probably keeping up, I thought. "And the prayer? When you get hunger pains or cravings?"

"Yeah, I'm doin' it." He said, again a bit hastily. Before I could ask him to recite his prayer, he switched gears on me.

"I gotta ask. Are you really fasting, too? For me?"

"I am."

"You mean you haven't had meat for a week?"

I couldn't help but chuckle. "No, it's not that kind of fast, although now I wish I had given up food instead. I gave up cigarettes."

"Oh," he said, disappointment in his voice. Obviously a non-smoker.

"Let's get back to your prayers for your victim. How

often are you saying them?"

"At least a couple dozen times every day," he said.

"Good, very good. Recite it, please."

He hesitated. "I made up my own prayer. You said that would be OK."

"Sure," I replied. "Let's hear it."

Again, he faltered then took a breath and released it. "God, forgive me for my sin. I hope she's up there with You right now. Amen."

Hmmm. He'd turned it around to focus on himself, his victim added like a postscript. And no mention of her family. No wonder it wasn't having the effect I'd hoped.

"I think we can do better," I said.

"Yeah, we definitely need to."

I tilted my head. "Why definitely?"

"Remember, I said there are two things that brought me here today. The first is I failed to turn myself in."

Deep in the corridors of my soul a siren began to wail, and with it a great resistance to go further. But as his confessor I could not leave it be. And so, squeezing my eyes shut like a man expecting a blow to the face, I asked for the second reason.

"It happened again," he said.

CHAPTER 9

I probably sat shaking my head in dismay for a full five seconds. "What happened again?" I asked, knowing full well what he meant.

"Another one. Another girl."

"You mean you had sex with another prostitute?"

"Well, yeah, we did that, too."

Too. Like an afterthought. Like a secondary pleasure. Which maybe it was.

I closed my eyes and bowed my head, not caring if he could see my shadow move. "Why?"

A deep sigh came from the other side of the wall. "I guess I thought...I thought maybe there was another way out. If I could be with a hooker and keep things under control, maybe it isn't necessary to go to the police."

I must have groaned out loud because he hurried to continue.

A few inarticulate syllables sputtered out, followed by, "She's gone. I-I can't bring her back. I am so sorry and if I could switch places with her I would. And I'm not saying I would never contact her family, if she has one – you probably don't know, being a priest, but a lot of hookers don't have families or are on the outs with them and neither side is interested in the other. But I would try," he insisted. "I have resources and I'm good at finding information, so maybe in a year or so, I would reach out to them. Anonymously. But they would know what happened to her and where she is." He added with a touch of self-congratulation, "And they could get closure."

"Alright," I stopped him. "Tell me about what happened. When was this?"

"Tuesday night. I was—"

"Tell me about the girl," I said. "Did she give you a name?"

"No. Most times they don't, and when they do it's fake."

"What did she look like?"

"Average height, I guess. Black. Not much in the chest but she had hips and a big—"

"I mean her face. What did she look like?"

He said nothing for a long time. "She was a black chick, ya know. I dunno. What are you looking for?"

My god, my sweet god, my mind screamed. He can't even recall her face.

"She was young, I could see that," he offered. "Wore a lot of make-up, had a lot of piercings in her ear, and acne on her shoulders. But you know, they hit puberty real young in the hood, so, I don't know for sure. If you ask 'em, they all swear they're 18 or 19."

"So, how did—what happened? The same thing?"

"Pretty much," he acknowledged.

"What do you mean, pretty much? You said you were trying to replicate what happened before to see if you could defeat the compulsion."

"Yeah, that's what happened. She approached my

truck, we agreed on a price and she got in. I went to a different place, a little nook inside of an alley."

"Did you ask her about choking?"

"No," he said. "I didn't bring it up because I thought if I didn't suggest it, the compulsion as you called it, wouldn't happen."

"Were you thinking of it as you looked for a girl?"

"No. Well, I mean, I couldn't keep it out of my head, but I wasn't indulging in it. I wasn't fantasizing like the last time. I tried to block it out."

A glimmer. The faint flicker of hope in this feral darkness.

"What happened?"

Another sigh. "I dunno. I think maybe the motion as she was doing me triggered it. I had a hand on the back of her head, and the other on her shoulder. I remember putting both hands on her shoulders, and um…"

"And what?"

"The thing inside me broke through. Like a pit bull blowing through a screen door. I pushed her back, she asked something about cops, and then my hands were on her throat. She might have been young but she knew what was happening. She scratched my hands and wrists. And she was smart, too, she tried to get at my…ya know, genitals, but got tangled up in my clothes. If it wasn't for that she probably would have gotten loose." He hurriedly added, "I wish she would have, it'd be worth the pain."

"Did you try to stop yourself?"

"I think," he said hesitantly, "yeah, I think part of me, on the inside, was trying to make me stop but, it was too late."

"What happened after?" I asked.

"I cried," he said. "Right there in the truck. With her head on my lap, almost like a kid asleep. I couldn't believe this had happened again. I thought for sure I'd be able to manage it."

He stopped. I think he was waiting for me, and I waited for him. Finally, he spoke.

"So, what now?"

And then I talked. I'll bet I talked for 10 minutes. I hope no one was waiting next in line for the confessional because there wouldn't be a next that Friday. I tried to explain to him that, just as a prosecutor can bring a variety of charges from one incident, a variety of sins applied to his situation: refusing to aid the families of the first victim; reneging on our agreement to turn himself in; putting himself in an occasion of sin to "test" himself; using another child of God as a mere tool to try to help himself; and those are just the preliminaries to the mortal sins of adultery and murder.

The first time he came to me I used the soft touch, the emphasis on healing. It's what the Church teaches. But I wanted so much to go Old Testament on him. Haul out everything I could remember from Genesis and Leviticus and Exodus, every "he who sheds the blood of man shall have his blood shed by man." Somehow I kept it together, although I did lose it when I asked where the body was.

"She's like the other. Buried real deep, I promise," his voice strengthened with conviction. "In fact, I can guarantee you nothing is going to get to her."

"You don't get points for that," I practically shouted. "That's not something to be proud of."

He was silent so long I thought he might have left as quietly as he had arrived. Then came the soft, chastened voice.

"No absolution?"

I had never refused absolution to anyone. I'll bet there are 90-year-old priests who have never refused God's mercy to a sinner. But I didn't know what to say. For absolution to be granted, the sinner must demonstrate the Three Rs: regret for the sin, renunciation of the attraction to the sin, and resolve to at least try to avoid the sin. Those are generally covered in the Act of Contrition. But in this case…

"Are you going to turn yourself in?" I asked.

"I want to. I really do. But I'm scared. I know that makes me a coward, but I can't help it any more than I can help the other thing. If the police came to me, I wouldn't deny a thing. I'd, I'd…I'd take them to the bodies."

I reminded him, I argued with him, I pleaded with him, to see me outside the confessional, beyond the bonds of the sacramental seal, to tell me about the killings. Then I could take all that out of his hands. I'd make arrangements for him to turn himself in or for the cops to pick him up. I'd be with him on the whole journey. But it was like we were fencing, he blocked every move, every suggestion with some technicality or imagined difficulty or his trump card, "I'm too scared."

"I guess until I turn myself in, this sin hangs around my neck," he said morosely. Man, this guy knew what buttons to push.

"I admit I am in unfamiliar waters here," I said. "Will you give me permission to take this to my spiritual advisor, keeping the seal intact so it can't be traced back to you? Frankly I need guidance on how to help you."

The Penitent thought about it. "Would your spiritual advisor have to abide by the seal, too?"

"Yes, he would," I assured him. "And he won't have any information at all about who you are." For that matter, neither did I. The Penitent could stand in front of me in line at Chipotle's and I'd have no idea it was him.

"In that case, yes, you have permission. But Father?"

"Yes?"

"Is there no way I could have absolution now?"

What was I supposed to do? Tell him to go to hell? Figuratively and literally?

"Do you regret these sins?" I asked.

"How can you ask that?" he said in exasperation. "I'm here, kneeling against a wall, pouring my heart out about the most shameful, terrible thing a person could do. Why do I have this, this cancer on my soul? Why me? Why does God let this horrible craving exist in me? If this was something I could cut off, I'd grab a meat cleaver and blowtorch the minute I got home."

"Alright, alright," I mumbled. "Do you renounce the glamor of this evil?

He huffed out a scoff. "Glamor? You have no idea how awful this is. There's nothing appealing about a dead body. Did you know they empty their bowels and bladder when they die? The whole time, from beginning to end, you feel like you're in some kind of sewer. You're disgusted and ashamed and want to scream—"

"Ok, Ok," I soothed. "And what about resolve? I thought we were there the last time."

"I thought we were, too," he said miserably. "I am a

coward, add that to my list of sins. But I feel like I'm at the finish line. I'm right there, but I'm bogged down by fear. I need a friendly hand to reach out, grab my shirt and yank me across."

"Promise me," I said. "Promise me you will avoid all prostitutes, all pornography, especially the violent stuff. Promise me you will pray for God's help."

"I will. Oh my god, Father, I absolutely will."

"Well, start by not taking His name in vain," I muttered.

"Right, right."

I looked up in my confessional. The Holy Spirit wasn't floating around the fluorescent lights. No thumbs-up or thumbs-down emoji appeared miraculously in the air. I closed my eyes and asked Him, what would You do?

"Father?" he asked in response to my silence.

"Your penance is to continue the fast for an additional two weeks. And we're going to change the prayer you say so the focus is on the women and their families, not on you. And I want you to pray to St. Michael the Archangel – a lot. First thing in the morning, before you get out of bed, and the last thing before you turn out the lights at night, and at least a dozen times during the day. His prayer is all over the Internet, it's easy to find. Ask him to intercede for you for courage to go to the authorities, and to defend you if the compulsions return."

"I will. I will, Father."

"We must shut this down right now. I'll speak with my spiritual advisor this weekend. You don't have to wait until next Friday for us to talk. Send me a text or call me, my contact info is on our website. It's in the church bulletin, too, grab one on your way out. We can arrange a private conversation outside the sacrament. Anywhere, anytime."

"Yes, Father. Thank you so much."

"Ok. Let me hear an Act of Contrition."

CHAPTER 10

I should have fasted from food instead of cigarettes. Perhaps then I wouldn't have thrown up Friday night. Three times in fact. That's a record, if you don't count the flu or weekends during my freshman year in college.

Maybe it was nicotine withdrawal. Maybe it was worry because the Wolfman hadn't replied to my email. Maybe it was food poisoning, though I'd barely eaten during the day and skipped supper.

Or maybe it was those ghastly mental images, stereotypes of prostitutes I'd seen in movies, but with bruises on their throats and dirt and twigs in their hair. They stood on a corner, the Caucasian with arms crossed under her breasts, while the Black victim had her hand placed on a cocked hip. Both faces were studies in resentment. They didn't speak, they didn't have to. They just stared at me, the accusation fierce in their eyes. How dare you? How dare you grant him absolution for taking our lives?

I'd made it through the day by keeping my mind occupied, and with prayer, almost constant prayer. I prayed in my car on the way to the hospital for sick visitations, I prayed over the salad I forced down for lunch, I prayed on my knees with my head in the commode. And in the end, He answered me.

I was in my office, door closed, the dimmer on the

overhead light set to something like Barely Discernable Twilight. Instead of sitting at my desk I perched in a visitor's chair off to the side, with one foot on the edge of my desk so I could push the chair back on its two back legs and rock. I felt...beset. That's the best I can describe it. Nicotine cravings buzzed my brain like mental mosquitoes, and long-forgotten symptoms of anxiety returned; pounding heartbeat, tight breathing, unrelenting restlessness, a sense of impending catastrophe. And always my mind slid back to the victims. Buried deep he said. Did he at least cover them with a blanket or something, or did he just pack dirt tight against their faces? There would be worms, wouldn't there? And ants. Maybe beetles. I had to shake my head to get the images out.

The hell with this, I decided, I gotta have a smoke. It's been almost a week, close enough. Plus, I've spoken to the Penitent again, so my fast is declared over. I let my foot slide down the side of the desk and my chair dropped onto its front legs. As it did, my eyes went to the framed print on my wall. It was a classic rendition of the Good Shepherd. A clean-robed Christ with neatly trimmed beard and wide, satisfied smile walking down a delightful path in a beautiful, sunny, green meadow, shepherd's staff in hand. His other arm cradled an immaculate white lamb that calmly stared at the viewer with a vacant, "What? Me worry?" look.

The print was an ordination gift from my brother James and his wife, Marjorie. When I had unwrapped it, James helpfully pointed out that our family name meant "shepherd" or "herder" in Polish. Like I hadn't heard that story half a million times before. And though I preferred more historically accurate depictions of Christ with Semitic features, brown skin, and dark eyes, I'd displayed this one at each of the parishes I'd been assigned to. Kind of a family keepsake.

In my dark mood I stared at the print and thought how badly the artist had missed the mark. For starters the shepherd wouldn't carry the stupid animal, he'd probably have a rope or cord around its neck and be leading it. And if I was that shepherd, I wouldn't have a beatific smile on my face but a scowl as black as a Galilean night. His feet probably ached, he'd be thirsty, hungry, and dusty, and probably fretting over how many of the flock were still where he left them.

During His ministry Christ had thrown plenty of curveballs at his disciples that overturned their worldview: love thy enemy; the rich have a hard time entering heaven; and God seeks to forgive, not punish. But the parable of a shepherd leaving his flock to seek a lost lamb would not seem wrong in that ancient, pastoral culture. In fact, it might have gotten a "Duh," reaction. Maybe Jesus was asking, 'If a sheep goes astray, *doesn't* a shepherd leave the flock to go and find the lost one?' And his audience might have shrugged and said, "Well, yeah, of course he would. You can't write off a sheep just because it wanders off. They're idiots, that's what they do. So you go look for it. You go because every lamb has value, even the dumbest ones that deserve to be turned into wolf chow. Even ones who wander into a darkness so foul and deep it may transform them into something hideous. They are still God's lambs, and a shepherd's job is to try to recover them.

I wish I could say that realization swept away all the

anxiety, all the nicotine creepy-crawlies, all the angst. They didn't go away, but I felt less guilt-ridden for granting him absolution. Some part of him remained a lost sheep, and I could not abandon him to the darkness.

I went to my filing cabinet where I'd stashed the carton of smokes. I took it into my bathroom, turned on the water in the tub and tore open the cardboard. "And the king ordered the ships burned, so the men could not hope for retreat," I recited as I pulled out and mashed each pack to help the water penetrate the cellophane and crumbled them for good measure. Afterwards I went into the dark kitchen and tossed about $60 worth of ruined tobacco into the trash can. The fast, and my pursuit of that lost sheep, would continue.

And God be praised, the minute my head hit the pillow I went out like a light.

CHAPTER 11

"C'mon, already. That tuna can isn't gonna grow any bigger."

"Aim and claim," I murmured, "Don't spray and pray."

"Funny attitude coming from a priest," my sister replied.

The brisk Saturday morning was cold enough in the countryside to see our breath on the air, but the walk from our cars down to the gully had warmed us. Terry carried the range bag with the guns, ammo, hearing protection and other odds and ends. I had a plastic bag with cans I'd pilfered from the church's recycling dumpster.

I took one more breath and raised the gun. The Smith & Wesson Victory has a nice balance and Terry knew it suited my bullseye-style of shooting more so than the Ruger Mark IV. She was the tactical shooter, gun held in both hands, arms extended, knees flexed, torso slightly forward. Despite the extra pounds that padded her hips since her Army days, she still looked like the military cop she used to be. I, on the other hand, stood erect with my left hand parked in my trouser pocket and my extended gun arm slowly and casually dropping into position. I probably looked like a farmer pointing out yonder to where the salt lick ought to go.

But when the trigger broke, the sideways tuna can didn't just tumble off the splintered, wooden post, it leapt off, spinning madly as though caught in a tornado. The 40-grain slug had slapped it exactly on its bottom edge. As I intended.

"Such a show-off," Terry muttered.

"Clean livin' sister. That's the ticket."

"Yeah right," she said as we began to pack up. "OK, I know you want to hear it. You cleaned my clock. Still Mr. Lights Out, huh?"

It was an old joke in my family. Most folks think the expression comes from basketball, but it's much older. Back in the days of black powder and muzzleloaders, if a guy was a fantastic marksman it was said his shot could blow out a candle and never touch the wax. As a teen-ager I became obsessed with the idea, and spent a fortune on ammo and tea lights. But I finally did it with my dad's Browning. In front of Terry and my brothers. And because I was a jerk, I did it a second time, extinguishing three candles in a row. Nobody bothered to point out that if the trajectory of the slug is flat enough, if you extinguished one candle you could put out a dozen if you lined them up properly. But for several weeks afterwards, I was Mr. Lights Out. Then came the day in gym class they put a basketball in my hands. Nobody ever called me Mr. Lights Out after that.

"I'll bet you're going to shooting matches again."

"Like I have time," I scoffed. I popped out the gun's magazine, racked the slide a few times to clear it, and looked the Smith over. "If you ever think of selling this thing, let me know first," I said, and added, "I'm serious, Terry."

She shrugged. "Take it. I never shoot it, and this way it stays in the family." I protested and insisted on paying her, but Terry wouldn't hear of it as we packed up. We got to the cars, she dug in the trunk to find the Smith's hard plastic carrying case and handed it to me. "Just promise if you ever decide you don't want it, you'll give it back."

"You bet. Thanks, T. It's kind of nice to have one of the old man's boom sticks."

Terry scrunched up her nose. "He's probably up there frowning, sayin' 'I told those two knuckleheads a priest has no business with a gun.'"

"If he only knew," I muttered. In the early morning hours I had awoken with the Penitent on my mind, and the two phantom victims paid my conscience a visit in the sacristy during prayers after the 7 a.m. Mass. The darkness stayed with me on the drive here, and it wasn't until I got out of the car and gave Terry a hug before that monkey slipped off my back. Shooting usually clears my mind. The concentration, the crack of the pistols, and the banter with Terry raised my spirits. But now as we stood at the cars, that damned ape climbed back on. Sensitive as always, Terry picked up on my mood.

"Somethin' wrong?"

"No," I shrugged. "Why do you ask?"

"Oh, come on, Tommy. Like I can't tell when something's eating at you."

I shook my head, then to throw her off, I brightened. "Speaking of eating, where are you buying me brunch today?"

"How about Nemo's?"

"That's a bar," I objected.

"They serve breakfasts now, too. The food is good, and nobody said you had to start drinkin' at," she pulled her cell out of her jeans. "Jesus, it's almost noon."

We stowed the gear in the back of her Ford, and as I head toward my car I turned and yelled, "I'll follow you."

"Use your GPS, you luddite."

"Drive like a normal human being and I'll be fine." A thought occurred to me. "Hey should we stop at the house and thank John again for letting us shoot here today?"

"He left early this morning," Terry said as she opened her car door. "Poultry auction in Geauga County. I'll call to see if he's done and wants to meet us."

I started my motor and waited for Terry to back up. The thought flit through my head: a priest, a lady cop and a chicken farmer walk into a bar. A month ago I would have woven a joke around that concept. Now the only thing that came to me was a bleak indifference.

*　*　*

My phone pinged with an email alert while I drove, so as soon as I found a parking spot at the far end of Nemo's lot, I checked. It was the Wolfman.

"Hey Tom. Good to hear from you. Sorry I've been out of touch. Can you come to the seminary tomorrow at 3 p.m.? This may need canonical law expertise, and instead of involving the other faculty, there's a visiting priest here with that background. I'd like to ask him to sit

in. Let me know if this works.
All God's Blessings
Ken"

I thumbed out a quick reply saying I'd be there and hit send, sat for a moment and stared at the phone's screen resting against my steering wheel. Canonical law? Don't involve the other faculty? This was not reassuring. Had I screwed up? Was I too easy on the Penitent, because it was really starting to feel that way. Should I have pressed him to turn himself in, or at the very least give up the victim's location, before offering absolution? What was the Wolfman going to say when I told him the Penitent had done it again, and another girl was dead? And I had granted absolution...again.

I dropped my head onto my chest and began to pray. "This is too much for me. I'm not the one to handle–"

A sharp knock on my window jerked me out of my reverie, almost literally. My head snapped up and I think I twisted my whole body to see Terry's face staring at me. I had assumed she'd gone into the restaurant, but she'd come looking for me first. I jammed the phone in my pocket, popped the seat belt and opened my door.

"You OK? You gotta go somewhere?" she asked, staring at me. Her sisterly familiarity, overlaid with a cop's inherent suspicion, made it tough to hide things from her. And I knew that look. She was scrutinizing me the way an accountant examines his restaurant check before paying.

"No, I'm–, I'm alright. Just stuff. Church stuff."

"You can go if you need. We can do lunch another time."

"No, no. You're not getting out of this bet," I said.

"You're buying lunch and I feel hungry," and gave my slightly queasy stomach a couple of hearty pats. "Is John joining us?"

"Nah, he's still at the auction."

Nemo's is a neighborhood bar with pub grub good enough to generate revenue that almost matched that of the liquor license. Almost. The stools lining the bar were all occupied as were several tables. Terry spotted the last open booth and we slid in just as a party of four appeared in the doorway behind us.

We'd missed the breakfast menu, so I ordered a burger and when the server asked, "Anything to drink?" I thought that sounded pretty good.

"You got Warsteiner on draft?" She nodded and so did I. "Make it a tall."

Terry got a Coke and after the server left, said, "Somebody else doing the 5 o'clock Mass today?"

"Flag is down somewhere in the world," I shot back and hooked a thumb toward the row of backs on the stools. "Ask those guys."

"The flag never goes up for them," Terry mumbled. We talked about her daughter, Lauren, and how she was doing oversees. Then Terry told me about Cammie's latest phase, the "I hate you, Mom" attitude. "I don't remember Lauren being such a jerk at that age, but maybe she was and I forgot," she said.

"That's probably good policy," I offered.

"Cammie looks for fights. She and her friends are now fashionably woke, so everyone outside their circle are liars, racists, fascists, homophobes…" Terry waved a hand in the air.

"Maybe I could talk with her? Take her to a movie like

I used to?"

"Oh my God, Tommy, are you that out of touch?" Terry gave a belly laugh. "First of all, they don't go to movies anymore, they just get together and stream them. Second, the kind of movies they watch would turn your stomach with all the gore and guts. And third," she sipped on her straw, "don't flatter yourself, you're on the list with the rest of us dinosaurs."

"*Moi*?" I asked with fake offense. "Nah, not dear old Uncle Tommy. She's got no beef with me. I never made her do homework or said she couldn't go out. Seriously, I could talk with her, if you'd like."

"Seriously," Terry repeated back at me. "You're not Uncle Tommy anymore. You're 'my uncle the priest.' Believe me, I've overheard her jokes."

That took me aback. "Really? Like what?"

"Nothin'," she said, leaning back in her seat.

"No come on. What'd she say?"

"It's nothing," Terry shook her head. She saw the look on my face, probably the hurt, and rolled her eyes. "Typical teen bullshit. You know, 'priests and altar boys' stuff. It's nothing personal."

'Course not. You develop a thick skin as a priest when you hear that crud on the news or in TV shows and movies. It doesn't matter how much the Church does to stamp out this crime, how much compensation is paid, or how many studies show that pedophilia is more common among public school teachers than among the clergy. You know and are resigned to the fact that weak comics, lazy scriptwriters, and activists of every sort will always resort to the trope. But coming from your own family, from a kid who stood beside me putting dinner rolls on paper plates at the soup kitchen, that one hit a nerve.

The Warsteiner went down a little too smoothly, and the snarky thought bubbled in my brain that maybe if Terry darkened a church door occasionally her daughter might not be skipping down this particular road when, blessedly, the food arrived. I said a quick grace and we silently dug in. Nemo's really puts together a great bacon-and-cheese burger, and I'd just chomped out a mouthful when our server approached. I motioned to her and pointed at my nearly empty glass. "Another Warsteiner?" she asked, and I nodded and gestured apologetically at my bulging cheeks. She giggled and asked, "Tall?" and again I nodded. Terry cocked her head at me, and I managed to tuck the bolus far enough into my cheek to get out, "I'll pay for the beers."

Another eye-roll. Lunch went on as we returned to the neutral ground of our sister Mary's hip surgery and brother John's tenuous grip on the farm's finances.

I was feeling pleasantly buzzed and enjoyed the absence of anxiety so much I ordered a third beer, although Terry's "Tommy!" stampeded me into making it a short, then changed it back to a tall light beer. Some guys get mean when they drink, some get silly, others become weepy, and some can't stop their mouths from running. I am in the last category. As I sipped what I resolved to be my final beer for lunch, I blurted out a thought flitting in the back of my mind.

"You do surveillance work, don't ya?"

Terry shrugged. "Not much anymore. I used to back when I wore digies. Why? Need something?"

Putting on what I thought was a good show of nonchalance, I said, "Well, we still stream Masses online like we did during COVID. I was wondering if the same equipment could be used for security. Like, could we leave it on all the time?"

Terry made a face and shook her head. "I doubt it. I don't know much about the hardware but I doubt it's made for that. Your church doesn't have security cameras?" I shook my head. "You should. Thefts from churches are uncommon, but it happens every now and then. I'm thinking more about vandalism. That's a thing now, ya know. You'd probably get a break on your insurance premiums if you installed something."

"Ah, I'd have to take an expense like that to the parish finance committee. The diocese doesn't have the dough or the interest to spring for that," I mumbled into my glass. "So you think vandalism is a concern?" Before she had a chance to answer, I blustered on. "Did ya hear that from the cops? I imagine you've got friends on the police force. You guys talk about stuff."

"Sure. I know people."

If it weren't for the quart of good German lager in my belly I would have noticed Terry shift from sister-mode into investigator-mode. But I was too impressed with my own slyness in manipulating the conversation to realize she had a critical eye on me.

"If there was stuff going on, ya know, that they aren't telling the news guys, you might hear about it?"

"We're not that tight," Terry said, "We share information sometimes, mostly me feeding them stuff when they ask. But I know people at a few of the cop shops. Why are you interested? Have you heard something?"

"Yeah, right. Like Jeffrey Dahmer came to me for

confession." Jesus Christ, I thought in a panic, did that just fly out of my mouth?

"I'm just wondering," I hurriedly slurred. "You know, I watch those crime shows like *Dateline* and *20/20*, and wonder about stuff." I rolled the bottom of my glass around on the table, making the straw-colored liquid ride the inside. "Like, when there's a bad winter storm or freeze coming, they go to the street people and warn them to head into the shelters, right? Or if a gang is hitting retail stores they go and talk to those guys, right? Let them know to be on their guard."

"Sure, I suppose they do," Terry said. While I was watching the beer in my glass, my sister was probably watching me.

"So, I'm just sayin', if there was a danger to, you know, street hustlers, or street people in general, if the cops knew they might warn those folks to be more careful than usual, wouldn't they?"

"What did you hear?" she asked with more of an edge than I was used to from her.

I shook my head wordlessly.

"You heard something and it's got you worried," she said.

I shook my head more vigorously because that always convinces people, right?

"Even if I did, and I'm not saying I did, but even if," I said. "I couldn't…"

"Tommy," Terry said and put her hand on the top of my glass to stop its rotation. "What's the matter? What's scarin' the hell out of you?"

I let go of the glass, folded my arms around myself, and chuckled. "You answered your own question," I said looking at the bar. When that got no response, I turned and saw her staring at me with sister's eyes.

"Something right out of hell, Terry. Right out of hell."

CHAPTER 12

They say the third day of smoking secession is the worst, since all the accumulated nicotine in your body has dissipated and withdrawal really kicks in. I don't know about others, but for me Sunday was the worst. It was one week since I'd started the fast, and Sunday afternoons were my usual tobacco bacchanalia. After Masses I'd carve out two hours or so to walk the parks or hang out at the cigar lounge, and burn through half a pack. Combine that established habit with the angst of meeting the Wolfman and his mystery guest, and you've created a howling need for nicotine.

Speaking of howling, Bongo was in his glory. The day after his lure arrived, I talked with Stan Schumacher about the rabbit track idea. Stan captains our retiree maintenance crew, and does most of the mowing himself. Short and thin, with a tightly trimmed white goatee, he heard me out and a big grin crossed his face. The first day he attached the lure to the back of his riding mower, and made a simple oval. Bongo spent a good half hour practically wearing out a path, baying and snuffing with glee. It rained on Friday, so Stan reapplied the lure with fiendish cunning, dragging the scent-soaked ball of fur about ten yards, then reeling it back in to pick it up, then driving to another area and repeating the process. Bongo was beside himself when released on the lawn. He zigzagged back and forth, baying excitedly when he hit the scent, then stopped, whipped his head back and forth so fast his floppy ears smacked his face. The dog wore an expression that seemed to say, "The damned things have learned how to fly!" That evening I found the little hound stretched out on the dining room floor where he remained until our bedtime routine.

Chalk up one small victory in those dark days. Sunday, however, was not literally dark. The cold front of the previous days had blown past, and Sunday brought back temperatures in the mid-60s with low humidity. Truly glorious weather. So nice I would have enjoyed the drive into the city had I not known what waited at the end. The Browns were playing an away game so traffic was light. The Cleveland skyline looked welcoming and Lake Erie's grey-green waters shimmered in the sunlight. I said a prayer of thanksgiving for the beauty and wonder of creation, and tried to ignore my anxiety. Whatever would happen in the Wolfman's office would happen. Let go and let God, as they say.

St. Agnes Seminary is a U-shaped, two-story, red-brick structure with an attached church anchoring one corner. Wulfram's office is located on the second floor, near a corner overlooking the parking lot. He must have seen me arrive because as I reached for the intercom button, a buzzer sounded and the lock mechanism clacked back. A bit unnerving, to say the least.

I climbed the steps to the second floor and walked the familiar path to his office. His door was open but I knocked anyway out of habit. The deference learned in the seminary never completely leaves you, and I waited until Wulfram stood up and waved me in.

"Tom, thanks for coming," he said before I could thank him first. "Come on in, and close the door." As I did, I saw the other man seated in one of Wulfram's brown leather chairs, and the intimidation factor leapt up several notches.

"As I mentioned in my email," Wulfram continued, "I thought we could use the advice of a sound canonist, so I asked Fr. Mwangi to join us."

Fr. Isaac Mwangi. I'd skimmed an article about him in the diocese monthly email but couldn't recall much, other than some gossip I'd heard. Hardline conservative, like a lot of the African clergy. That made him an odd fit with Wulfram, a humanist whose politics unapologetically leaned left. The speculation ran heavy that Mwangi was being groomed for a bishop's chair when he returned home.

As the man stood and extended his hand, Wulfram made the introductions. "Fr. Mwangi is from the Diocese of Ngong in Kenya. We're lucky to get him, even if it's just for a short while. He recently taught a course in canon law at the Gregorian Pontifical University in Rome."

The Cleveland diocese has grown increasingly diverse with the addition of Black, Hispanic, Korean, and Philippine parishioners, but the clergy has not yet caught up and remains about as colorful as a bowl of mashed potatoes. That made Fr. Mwangi exotic indeed. Slightly built, cool and relaxed, with skin tones so dark as to be almost purple on his cheeks and forehead. His black hair was trimmed short and tight to his head in exact, symmetrical lines. The clothing he wore was impeccable, and you could probably shave with the sharp creases on his suit trousers. Everything about Mwangi screamed precision, control, and austerity. Until he spoke.

"A pleasure to meet you, Father Pastor. I thank you for extending your trust to me." The unfamiliar accent lent a musical quality to his baritone voice, with enough lilt to his perfect English to draw you into every syllable. An air of serene confidence gave him an almost stately presence. Yup, I thought as I shook his warm, soft hand, this guy's going to wear a pointy hat someday. Somehow I felt both hope and wariness as Wulfram motioned us to sit.

"We've both read your email," Wulfram began, "but why don't you run through it for us again."

"Of course," I replied. "However, there's been further developments that complicate things."

Wulfram nodded and Mwangi, who sat with one leg crossed over the other, stared at his gleaming dress shoe.

"The Penitent returned to my confessional two days ago. He's taken another life."

That brought up Mwangi's head. He glanced at Wulfram then turned his head to me.

"Begin at the beginning. Omit nothing that does not infringe on the seal, including your ministrations."

It felt like I was back in the seminary, defending a thesis. I began as best I could with the Penitent's first confession, though already the non-murderous details had grown fuzzy. And I told them about the second confession and concluded by blurting out the questions that haunted me.

"Was I wrong? Should I not have granted him absolution? Should I have forced him to turn himself in first?

"We'll get to all that," Wulfram soothed. He combed his beard with his fingers. "How are you holding up, Tom?"

"I wish I'd chosen something else to fast from, instead of cigarettes," I said. Wulfram smiled but Mwangi continued to stare at his shoe and pursed his lips. "It's hard," I acknowledged. "I feel an enormous sense of guilt, particularly about the second girl."

Wulfram shrugged. "You had no reason to think he'd do it again. For all you knew he had turned himself in already, or was in the process of getting a lawyer. I think it's commendable that you have kept the man's reclamation as the object of your intentions." That got a slow nod out of Mwangi. "Under such circumstances it's understandable to be distracted from the purpose of reconciliation, but it sounds like you stayed on task. Your purpose is to bring him out of that darkness and back to Christ. But I want to go back to my original question, Tom. How are you handling this?"

I knew what he meant. I could see it on his face, and felt the same concern in my own heart.

"It's not like the other time, Ken. I'm managing. It's fine."

"You said you have scrutinized the news for reports of these crimes," Mwangi offered. "Has there been anything?"

"Nothing. Nothing at all."

"Any stories of missing people?"

I shook my head.

Wulfram scratched his forehead. "Tom, have you considered the possibility these crimes have not actually happened?"

I had not, and the suggestion made me blink.

"I don't...I...what?"

"There are psychiatric conditions, often a form of OCD, in which individuals become convinced they've committed a crime when in fact they haven't. And that's only one possibility. Another is he's lying. Created these out of whole cloth for the purpose of self-aggrandizement. He wishes to be seen as dangerous, a man of consequence."

"To what end?" I interrupted. "Who am I going tell? And besides, I don't know his identity at all. I couldn't even guess at it." Wulfram opened his mouth to speak but I cut him off with a raised hand. "I understand the need to consider all possibilities, but please be assured...he was very convincing in his telling of the sins and of his regret. It seemed authentic, alright."

"Tell us again, to the best of your memory, of his reluctance to report himself and his insistence that you do so." Mwangi said. I went over those details again, and the canonist leaned forward in his chair, elbows on his knees, hands clasped, listening. At the end, a sense of failure draped over me, and without prompting I said, "I know I was wrong. I should have insisted he turn himself before granting absolution."

Both Wulfram and Mwangi shook their heads. "Absolution cannot be conditional on an action," Mwangi said. "It must be based solely on a penitent's remorse for his sins, a determination to avoid them, and a desire to be reconciled with God. Yes, you must urge him to take responsibility and go to the authorities. But there it ends.

"And," Mwangi fixed me with a stern face, "now you must forget."

"How? No," I flustered. "He's killed two women. It's obvious the compulsion is conquering his soul. If he doesn't turn himself in or give me the ability to do it for him…" I looked at them both in turn. "You know he's going to do it again. I'm no psychiatrist, but it seems obvious he's a psychopath, or becoming one. We have a responsibility…surely there's a way to inform the police of the danger without breaking the seal. They could do dragnets or stakeouts or whatever it is they do. They could tell the prostitutes there's a killer out there preying on them. They—"

"You must do nothing," Wulfram said. "The diocese has resources, you know that. We run shelters and have contacts in the social services and elsewhere. It's possible the bishop may use those outlets to inform these vulnerable women in a general way of a new, potential threat. Remember, Tom, we don't have proof yet—"

"With all respect," I broke in, perhaps a little louder and a little hotter than needed. "You weren't there. You didn't hear him. He was serious. He was genuine. There are two young women lying in graves somewhere. We have to do something to prevent more from joining them."

"I understand, Tom, and I sympathize. I absolutely do. That's why I'm saying the diocese, not an individual priest, should be the one…" He paused and stared as Mwangi shook his head, eyes closed. The canonist looked at Wulfram.

"First, the seal is inviolable. We may not act on anything heard in the confessional. You both know that, and your zeal to protect the innocent is laudable but misleading. In a rush to do good you risk committing great harm. There is another consideration, a crucially important one, we must face."

Mwangi turned to me. "This Penitent says he wishes to be stopped?"

I nodded.

"Yet when you offer him the means to do so, he refuses. You say he is repentant, so much so you granted him absolution. Yet he resists your entreaties to talk outside the sacrament, which would allow you to go the authorities for him. No, he does the opposite: he insists you go to the police with what you've been told in the confessional."

Wulfram squinted a little as he regarded Mwangi, a tic he was renowned for when pondering a problem. He seemed to follow the canonist's logic trail, but I didn't see it yet.

"There is the taint of the diabolical in this," Mwangi said, sliding one smooth palm against the other. "It is as though he sees reconciliation not as a way to erase his crimes, but his crimes as a way to erase the sacrament."

"To be clear," Wulfram ventured, his big arms sliding into skeptical hug. "You're not suggesting demonic possession?"

"Oh, of course not," the canonist dismissed with small shake of his head. "Nor even demonic oppression. But I am suggesting the potential for diabolic influence beyond ordinary temptations, due to the heightened circumstances." Mwangi looked from Wulfram, to me, then back to the scholar. "Generals, politicians, CEOs," he spread his hands. "Crime bosses, sports coaches, every human leader knows to strike faster and harder when the rewards are greater, no?" Wulfram gave a slow nod. I decided to stand pat.

"Why not then Satan?" Mwangi asked. "He sees across time as we see across a valley. He flits through human minds like a bird through trees. If he perceives a fine opportunity to damage God's kingdom on Earth, would he not draw deeply from the powers of hell to seize this advantage?

"Legislation is proposed to give the American government power over a church doctrine thousands of years old. If it becomes known that a killer of women conceals himself within the silence of the confessional, will not these politicians and their friends use that to insist the seal be torn away and thrown down?"

Mwangi leaned in. "Whether the Penitent's words were fact or fantasy, they present a trap. The devils place before this good priest a fateful choice – risk the lives of individuals, or the faith of millions." He turned to me, and his eyes were not hard but sad. "Say you take this information to the police, and they catch this killer. Surely news of it will travel far, here in this country and around the world, perhaps even to my home parish in Ngong. You will be excommunicated," Mwangi thought a moment with pursed lips, "and perhaps praised as a hero and martyr by the secular press. For years the sacrament of reconciliation has dwindled under constant assault. Do we not hear, over and over from intellectuals and celebrities that sin does not exist? Why seek forgiveness over nothing? Then there are many fellow Christians who teach that each person is his own pope, a libertine judge who rationalizes away or forgives everything. So many voices saying 'There is no sin' or if there is, God forgives all, so, do as you please.

"These enemies of Mother Church will use your breaking of the seal to say, 'Look at these liars. Look at the American priests. They reveal what is told to them in sacred secret. Away with these priests. Away with their church and away with their false sacrament.' And so, Satan laughs and claps his hands as more and more of God's lambs wander from the light and into the devouring darkness."

Mwangi pointed a slender finger at me. "Beware your kind heart, father, lest it betray you. You are a good man, but even a man's goodness can become a weapon in the claws of our sly foe. By trying to avert sorrow, you may bring about infinitely greater pain and suffering."

CHAPTER 13

I got on the scale Tuesday morning and saw I'd dropped eight pounds in about a week. That's crazy because past attempts to give up cigs always packed on the pounds. That oral fixation, I guess. But not this time. I was slimming down, which is not great if you're already a skinny guy.

Yesterday I threw in the towel and bought some Nicorette gum. Fruit Chill flavor. I wanted to maintain my fast through sheer will power, but sometimes you need a little help. And I was committed to this. Not only because it was already my longest success at kicking the habit, but because it felt like my way out. If my fasting helped the Penitent receive the grace he needed to turn himself in, or to call me to meet him somewhere, we could resolve this. The fast might help end the killing, save the Penitent's soul, and as a happy by-product, save me.

The meeting with Wulfram and Mwangi nearly tipped over my rowboat, if you know what I mean. I didn't get out of bed Monday morning when my alarm went off, and had just about decided I wasn't going to show up for the 7 a.m. Mass. The dozen or so parishioners would figure it out and eventually leave. There would be calls and concerns about Fr. Pastor's health, but I didn't really care. All I wanted to do was roll over, pull the blanket over me and block everything out.

The cursed RLD saved the day. Bongo started barking and baying in his crate. He probably needed to pee after a night's sleep, but I suspected he also was demanding breakfast. Let him wet himself, part of me said. Who cares. But that barking. If you've never owned a beagle, you have no idea how persistent they can be. I got up, finally, released him from his crate, and walked him to the fenced-in area. He did have to pee like the proverbial race horse, but then got the lingering scent of the lure and it was play time. By the time I'd finally gotten him in again, I was so fully awake I gave up on the bed, got dressed, and stumbled into my day.

I remained in this grey existence throughout the week, although two incidents introduced a little light. The first was the continuing success of the lure experiment. Bongo is stubborn but not dumb. He quickly associated the sound of Stan's riding mower with a new game of Where's the Rabbit, so much so that whenever Stan fired up the mower Bongo lost what little mind he possessed and barked and howled until we let him out. I gotta admit, it's kind of funny. And with falling leaves and conscientious Stan relentlessly tidying up the place, Bongo got lots of exercise. The beagle was so worn out, one day after lunch he came in and lay down next to my desk while I worked, rolled onto his back with forepaws dangling and went to sleep. That night he followed me into the living room, jumped up on the couch next to me and rested his head in my lap while I watched TV. I absentmindedly scratched behind his ears and let the day's angst leak out of me. OK, so there are some advantages to dog ownership.

The other event happened earlier today. I was on my way to pay a sick call when I decided to first say hello to my office staff, which is a grandiose term for one office manager and a college student. Patty Romano is short, chunky, and middle-aged, with dark-eyes, classic Italian features and your basic mom haircut. She also possesses a low-key, pleasant personality and the most organized mind I've ever encountered. Contrary to the "church lady" stereotype, Patty doesn't wear her faith on her sleeve, or around her neck for that matter. I've never noticed a crucifix or other religious bling on her. Patty's Catholicism appears as natural and integral to her identity as being a mom, a sister, or a wife. She and her husband are regulars at Mass and observe most church traditions, but it doesn't seem forced or for show.

The college kid is a different story. Bridget Mullins is statuesque, not in the way of a queen but of a martyr. Shy and quick to drop her eyes, she's tall and wears her long, Irish-brown hair parted in the middle. The kid shuns make-up, perhaps to render her pale face plain and unremarkable, and dresses in baggy sweaters and loose-fitting jeans. A delicate gold crucifix always hangs outside her shirt, and you get the sense it's not a fashion accessory. Unfortunately for her, Bashful Bridget possesses womanly curves that cause deliverymen to linger when she's in the office. They're probably wasting their time, because Bridget Mullins is the likeliest candidate for religious orders of any girl or woman I've met. An altar server from 4th grade through high school, Bridget avoided the cliquey youth ministry and choir. She prefers volunteer work like the food pantry and clothing drive that put her alongside adult parishioners and retirees. Bridget also seems drawn to the serenity and silence of an empty church. It is not uncommon to see her on breaks or before her shift kneeling or sitting in a pew in the back of the empty church. Last year during Advent we had perpetual Adoration of the Eucharist and I often stopped by during the wee hours to pray, or exchange a few words with whomever signed up for those lonely time slots. It was 3 a.m. one cold night when I found Bridget alone in the church. I approached her to say hello, but her countenance silenced me. There was an intensity on her face I'd not seen since my seminary experience, head bowed, eyes shut, brows nit as though in pain. It's been on my mind to sound her out and see if she's pondered a vocation, but the right opportunity hasn't popped up, and this wasn't it.

The three of us exchanged pleasantries, chatted for a minute or two, and I turned to go when Bridget said to Patty, "Remember – the umbrella."

"That's right," Patty responded. "Father, I forgot to mention your sister left her umbrella here."

"Which sister and when?" I asked, hand on the door knob.

"Terry," Patty said. "You didn't know she was here yesterday?"

I shook my head.

"Oh, I thought you did. She was here with some guy installing cameras in the church. I'm glad you put those in, Father." I caught Bridget shoot a sidelong look at Patty, who shrugged it off.

"I know God watches over us," Patty added, "but sometimes when we're here by ourselves it can get a little spooky. And with it getting dark earlier now…"

"I'm sure we're all perfectly safe," I said, noting Bridget giving a small nod.

"I know, I know," Patty quickly added. "Still, it's a nice thought. Makes us feel a bit more secure."

I nodded, smiled, and headed out. As soon as my car rolled onto Manchester Street, I told my phone to call Terry. And blessedly, she answered. Without much banter I cut to the chase.

"So what's with the security system?"

"We talked about that Saturday," she said. "I checked at work and you should get a reduction in your insurance premium. And Tommie, these things are stupid cheap. No wiring, no extra hardware. Just screw it into a fixture. It's like a doorbell camera. It's got motion sensors so it only comes on when there's activity. It sends the video to the church's server. The parish council guy, the IT geek, helped set it up. He created an archive folder for it on your system. It automatically deletes after two days to keep from filling up your data storage."

"What is this costing us?"

"The monthly billing is $8.50, and the cameras and installation were free."

"C'mon."

"Seriously, it's only two units, I got 'em at cost for like $10 total. And I'm telling you it's gonna knock about $15 off your premium each month. Consider it my donation."

Traffic picked up and I'm not fond of talking while I drive. Still, this didn't sit well with me.

"You should have said something to me first," I grumbled.

"Sorry," she said with that sing-song tone that gets under my skin. "Didn't mean to step on toes. Seriously,

Tommy, I had the units, I had the time, so I got it done."

"Who has access to the videos?"

"The front desk at your office can open a window on their screen to watch real-time, but the archive is available just to the IT guy."

"And who else?"

"Nobody. If you want, tell him to give you access, too. You can even get it through your phone."

"Can we turn it off? During Masses or confessions?"

There was a long silence, then Terry said, "I suppose so but I wouldn't advise that. Too easy to forget to turn it back on."

"OK," I said. "I'm getting into some serious traffic, so I'm gonna go. We'll talk about this later."

"Fine," I could hear the irritation in her voice. "You're welcome, Father Pastor."

"C'mon, T, I know what you're doing," I said. "I suppose you're gonna tell me you don't have access to the live feed and the archives."

"Gimme a break," Terry replied. "Why would I want that? Get off your phone and drive. Go heal the sick or raise the dead or whatever it is you're doing. Bye."

The dashboard beeped as she hung up. I checked my GPS, glanced at the St. Michael's pendant swaying from my rearview mirror, and said to the warrior archangel, "For an ex-Army cop, she's a pretty bad liar."

CHAPTER 14

Bongo had undergone a conversion of sorts, either from an intercession by St. Francis or the exercise with the lure. The beagle had become my constant companion, his nails clicking on the floor behind me as I moved about the rectory, and more often than not his head flopped onto my lap when I sat on the couch.

This cold Friday morning Bongo and I left twin trails of faint prints in the frosted lawn, but before our extra-long walk led us back to the rectory, the rising sun transformed the ice crystals to dew. I watched the news on Channel 8 while Bongo scarfed down his breakfast, and the weathergirl promised high 50s today and even warmer temperatures through the weekend. Next week, though, not so nice.

The dog must have expected siesta time, but perked up when I attached his collar and tucked his bed under my arm. Bongo sensed what was coming, trotting happily beside me on the way to the church, and nuzzling my pants pocket where I'd stashed a fresh chew stick. Once inside my confessional, Bongo settled into his bed, a paw pinning one end of the chewy while he quietly gnawed the other as penitents came and went. For most he was a welcome addition, making the confessional homier and more casual, though one poor fellow professed a phobia of dogs and retreated to offer his confession from the kneeler.

During a lull between penitents Bongo got up, did a yoga stretch, circled around and lay back down, right on top of his chew stick. He kicked his back leg as though he didn't understand what was pinching him, so I got up, leaned over, and pushed him aside enough to get the stick. Bongo thought I was initiating a play session and stood up, grinning that open-mouth, tongue-lolling beagle smile.

"No, no," I murmured. "Just lay back down. Here, here's your chew. See if you can't whittle it—"

"Bless me father for I have sinned."

I froze at the voice from the other side of the room. It felt like someone had poured a jug of cold water down my back. The hair on the nape of my neck actually stood up. The voice was now unmistakable, and I turned to the dark silhouette in the red circle.

"It has been one week since my last confession."

I was too stunned to say anything, and slowly lowered myself back into my chair.

"And this will be my last confession."

"Why?"

"There's no point," he said quietly. "I tried. I really have. I thought coming here would, I don't know, cure me of this. But it's not working. Nothing works."

"Yes, it does," I replied. "But you have to want it and put in the effort."

"I have made the effort," he interrupted. "What do you call this? What do you call my coming here?"

"I call it a start. Listen, I've counseled alcoholics, and even gone with them to AA meetings. And I've heard about people, men and women, who go to a meeting but stop just outside the door. They get that close, but won't take the few critical steps to enter healing. They stop and walk away.

"That's you," I said. "You've gotten to the door, but you've got to cross the threshold. No one can do it for you. Once you take the step, you'll get all kinds of help. But if you walk away, the path you're on will lead to your destruction."

He remained silent, then said softly, "I think you don't know what you're talking about. I don't mean you're stupid, I just think you're not equipped for this." His voice picked up a notch, like a teacher interrogating a dullard. "Or are you? Did you go to your spiritual advisor?"

"I did," I admitted.

"And?"

"He questions whether these sins have actually occurred," I said.

A sound like panting came through the red beads, and I realized he was laughing.

"Done my work too well, have I? Covered my tracks so completely, the posse says they were never there. Oh," he said in almost a sigh. "I assure you, Father Pastor, I assure you as certainly as there is blood in your veins and flesh on your bones, these sins have been committed."

I'm not sure which freaked me out more, the macabre metaphor or the sudden elevation of his diction. I had the Penitent pegged as a blue-collar guy, maybe somebody in the trades or construction. But this new, lyrical phrasing felt like the dropping of a mask. Which begs the question, why come masked to an anonymous confessional? Then I heard for the first time the creak of the kneeler and his silhouette disappeared. A panic set in and I half rose out of my chair.

"No, hey, don't leave. Don't go. We can–"

Motion at the doorway caught my eye, and there he stood.

Not at all what I expected. My first impression was of an old-fashioned baby doll. He had a round, smooth face, and the padded cheeks and chin of a chubby toddler. Light brown curly hair, gold wire-rim glasses, and incongruously thin lips.

He wore a short-sleeve, pale-blue dress shirt open at the throat, the white crescent of a t-shirt collar visible beneath. The shirt fit loose in the chest, but bulged out in a muffin-top over his belt. Grey Dockers flowed down to a pair of brown, lace-up walking shoes.

"Hey, you got a dog. Hi pooch," he said with the enthusiasm of a kid. "He's chill for a beagle, not a peep. That's a good boy," he said, easing himself down into the chair beside me. Bongo accepted the compliment with two swipes of his white-tipped tail, then closed his lids again and dropped his chin onto the bed. Some guard dog.

A faint smile crossed the Penitent's lips as he took in my astonishment. Words failed me, but not him.

"Have you read Steinbeck?"

My mind staggered from first one oddity then another, like being pelting with snowballs on a beach in July.

"Who?"

"Steinbeck. You know, *Grapes of Wrath* and all that."

"I guess. High school or college."

"Do you recall '*East of Eden*?'" I shook my head.

"There's a character named Cathy Ames. She's a sociopath – well, really a psychopath, there is a difference, but Steinbeck probably didn't know that. He must have met a real psychopath, or even been one himself, because he wrote the most–" the Penitent paused and nodded to emphasize the word, "– insightful description of a psychopath. He said they have a malformed soul. Like a birth defect. If an infant could arrive in a body missing arms, another might be born with a soul missing empathy. It's just not there. Monstrous, he wrote, but then nature produces physical monsters all the time. Why not a psychological one? A quirk of nature, not a fault or a decision. Simply an abnormality.

"I read *East of Eden* in junior high, and when I got to the description of Cathy Ames and what she did to people, I felt such vindication," he said, fixing hazel eyes on me. "I always knew I was different from other kids but now I understood why. I was born different. Frankly, I was born better."

He saw the look on my face and pressed on. "You know what I've noticed about the people standing in line for your confessional? They're all kinds; old, young, men, women. Yet they all do the same thing. You know what it is?"

I shook my head.

"They have this somber look on their faces," he said and demonstrated by lowering his eyelids and twisting his mouth in an exaggerated frown. "Oh, they'll give a polite smile to the person next to them, but then back to the hangdog expression." He shrugged and shook his head. "Why aren't they happy, ya know, jumping up and down?" He made his legs pump in the chair, toes tapping the floor. Bongo turned his head to watch. "They think they're about to get a free pass. They should be giddy. So, what's with the frowny faces?"

"Guilt," I said. "That's a healthy thing for us as sinners. Guilt is to a wounded soul what pain is to an injured body. It says, 'Hey, stop doing that. You're hurt and need to heal.' The folks in line look sad because they know they aren't the people they want to be. They feel guilt or shame, which leads to remorse, which can lead to resolve and improvement. Confession is like a doctor's office, or even an emergency room for the soul."

The Penitent threw a mocking smile. "That's so stupid. First of all, you can't change the past, so just forget it. Second, this whole thing," he looked up and raised his hands, "is ridiculous. What is a sin? Breaking a rule set by some goat-herder back in the bronze age? Third, for the sake of argument say there is a God. He made us, right? He's all powerful, all knowing. He's aware of what we've done, and what we will do. It's hypocritical for him to punish me for choking out a hooker when he created the circumstances, he created me the way I am, he put the two of us together in that time and place. If," he raised his hands in protest, "we're going to go down that road, you have to admit he's more responsible than me."

"Those are all ancient heresies and false arguments," I countered, waving my hand in front of me as though I could wipe them away. "We can debate free will later, but for now let's get back to—"

"My name is Will Freeman," he said, those flat

eyes holding my own. "I live in Springfield township, on 83 acres of land. I've got it all: fields, timber, there's even an old quarry pond stocked with crappie and perch. During deer season I take my crossbow or shotgun, walk out my back door, and hunt on my own land. It's wonderful. Google it, you'll see."

He reached down and gave Bongo's head a scritch behind the ear, and turned to look up at me. "That's where the bodies are. Come on over. Bring your spiritual advisor – no, wait, don't do that. It won't help your cause because you'll never find the bodies, which will support his theory this is all made up." He eased back into his chair, and folded his arms.

Freeman suddenly rushed a fist to his lips and barely blocked a deep belch that lifted his shoulders.

"Sorry," he said with a chuckle. "Too much sage in the breakfast sausage. And the ghost-pepper jerky I had on the way here. Not a smart combination." He grinned as he said it but his sly eyes studied me for a sign that I understood. He'd discarded his penance as casually as he'd dropped my rosary to the floor after his first confession. Yeah, I got it. And a slow burn warmed my innards.

"Where was I?" he continued. "Oh yeah, *East of Eden*. Afterwards, I really studied psychopathy. Not just the lame documentaries and podcasts. Genuine academic journals and monographs. There are a lot of us, psychopaths I mean, but the violent ones make up only a small percentage of the total, just like in the general population. Most psychos are law-abiding citizens. Lawyers, salesmen, cops, journalists, doctors," he held a hand out towards me, "clergy.

"Then I read a comment from a detective who said that even among violent psychopaths, there are smart ones and stupid ones. That really resonated with me. The ones who get caught are either stupid, or undisciplined. They're too dumb to realize that rules keep the game going. Toss them aside and you eventually get caught."

He raised a finger. "How many people in this country go missing every year? Take a guess."

I didn't want to play his game. I didn't want to listen to him anymore, but I didn't know how to end this.

"You're probably thinking a thousand. Maybe even ten thousand." He leaned forward in his chair. "Try half a million. Yeah, about 500,000 missing-person reports every year. Some years over 600,000."

He sat back and crossed his leg like a professor in a club chair. God, how he was enjoying himself. "Now, of course, nearly all turn up after a week or two. Somebody goes on a bender, or a teenager runs away from home to be with her stoner boyfriend. Those are cleared up quick. Then there are the ones who don't want to be a mommy or daddy anymore, or hate their shitty jobs or owe somebody money, so they run off. Those groups make up something like 90 percent of that half million. Of the remaining 10 percent, we'll say eight percent are sad sacks who off themselves in the ocean or the woods, or OD beside a dumpster, just die somewhere without any identity. Their bodies might never be found, or if they are no one knows them, no one cares.

"That leaves two percent of missing people unaccounted for. They disappear. Vanish. Probably..." he put both hands beneath his chin and grabbed his neck, thrusting out his tongue. He grinned at me. "How are you at math, Father? Two percent of half a million is what?"

I wouldn't give him the satisfaction, but he saw it in my face.

"Yeah. 10,000. Annually. *Annually.* You know what that says to me? There are plenty of us wolves out there culling the herd. Most don't get caught because they're smart. Like me."

"Why are you here?" I moaned. "Why me? Why not some other priest?"

Freeman stared intently through his glasses. "I was led to you by an entity. An entity named..." he raised his eyebrows with the dramatic pause, then crooned, "Goooooogle." He gave a harsh cackle and shook his head. "You should've seen your face. C'mon, how do ya think? I did a 50-mile search for 'priests near me' and your 'Pastor Pastor' thing caught my eye. I dug a little bit more and decided we could be simpatico.

"As for why I'm here, I just told you. Ya know, 'Bless me father for I have sinned.' I've come for absolution again, because," he smiled a reptilian grin. "Oops, I did it again," he sang softly, tilting his head back and forth to the Britney Spears lyrics. He looked at me with an imitation of concern. "You're not pissing your pants, are you?"

"This one was different. A guy this time." He saw the expression on my face and laughed. "No, no. C'mon. No sex this time. Yecchhh. This was a smelly, old, homeless guy I picked up and took to my house. I told him I had a tent and camping gear I wanted to give him. He couldn't get in my truck fast enough.

"See, I wanted to try a knife this time. Something

different," his voice was as casual as if discussing a new restaurant. "And at home I have a very controlled environment," he assured me. "I would never make that kind of mess in my truck."

Freeman uncrossed his leg. "Even then, it was a lot more work. So much more to clean up. I knew that going in. Gore doesn't faze me; I've gutted animals since I was a kid. Blood and entrails don't bother me," he shrugged, "but they don't do anything for me, either. Not like Albert Fish or Dahmer or that Russian, Chikatilo. I guess some guys are fans of the red wine, I like white. Doesn't mean you can't have a taste for the other every now and then. But I'll stick with choking, ya know. It's closer, more intimate. I read about a trucker who lured hookers into his cab at truck stops. He choked them but didn't kill them right away. He'd let 'em regain consciousness, then did it again, and again, and again, until they didn't wake up. Called it his Pass-Out Game. Now, I get that. It prolongs the experience."

He looked at me and seemed amused by what he saw, so he leaned forward, elbows on his knees.

"Like I said, psychopaths are a natural phenomenon. A birth defect. Which, in your philosophy is determined by God, right? So I am not responsible for this, because I did not have free will in the commission of this act, so I should qualify–"

"No, no, no, no, no," I sputtered, shaking my head. "Don't even. There is no absolution this time. You show no regret. You're reveling in this." My voice began to rise. "There is no rejection of the sin – you're spouting all kinds of justification and self-denial. And as for resolve to avoid the sin, you're looking forward – you're planning more. There's no conceivable way absolution is possible."

Freeman grinned again and comically struck his fist against his thigh. "Doggone it. I thought I'd made my case. Oh well." He thrust both wrists toward me to accept handcuffs. "You got me. My sins go unforgiven, so take me to jail and throw away the key." They hung there as I said nothing, then he dropped his hands and showed me a toothy grin.

"See, we both know you can't do that, right?" Freeman's smile did not extend to his eyes. "You can't tell anyone because the seal still applies. Even if absolution is refused, the seal must remain intact, right? I checked that out myself. Found multiple sources."

He stood up. "Like I said, I'm not coming back. But just so you know, I'm far from done. In fact, I have been planning, just like you guessed. And I've got something special in mind. Wifey is leaving Sunday for a work thing and she'll be out of town until Thursday. I'll have the place all to myself. I've already figured this out." He lifted his hand and raised two fingers. "I'm going to pick up two. Tell them I want to fulfill my big fantasy of a threesome. Flash a lot of cash, promise them booze or blow, say they'll be back in three hours. Maybe tell 'em I want to video it, if they need convincing. Once we get to my place it'll be easy to separate and subdue them. And then maybe I'll try the Pass-out Game." He raised his finger and now his eyes did become alive, but with an evil light. "Maybe each one watches as the other is choked out." He raised his eyebrows at me and nodded. "And you know who else will be watching?" He pointed at me.

"That's right. You're going to be there, in spirit. In fact, I'm planning for Monday night, so you think about that while you're praying on your beads or watching football. Think about what's going on in Springfield Township. You can stop it and save two lives. All you gotta do is make one phone call. One anonymous call to the cops.

"But ya know, Monday might be bad for me. Maybe Tuesday is better. Wednesday is…" he fluttered his hands, "too close to when wifey comes home. Probably. Maybe Sunday night. The day isn't important. What's important is that one of those nights, I'm going to do a double, and only you can stop me."

He turned to the wall, but didn't really look at it. He seemed focused on something else, then gave a short snort.

"They really think I'm making this up?" he asked. Freeman turned to me. "What about you? What do you think?"

I looked away and shook my head. "I'm not sure what to think anymore."

When I turned my eyes back to him, Freeman's face was tight with anger. For the first time I thought of my own safety, and a thrill of fear shot through me. If he wasn't lying, and I didn't think he was, that meant I was alone in a tiny room with a serial killer. Freeman seemed to sense my fear, because an ugly sneer grew in the corner of his mouth and his hand dug into his pants pocket. I stared in alarm and my breath caught in my throat. Was he reaching for a knife? A gun? His clenched hand re-emerged with no weapon. The fingers relaxed and the room jingled with the sound of keys. Freeman bent his head and dug a thumb into his keyring, his thick fingers moving with surprising dexterity. It took him only a moment before the keys were back in his pocket and he extended his fist to me.

I held out my palm and Freeman said, "These'll help." Two objects dropped into my hand, one heavy and the other barely there. The first looked like an old-fashioned cufflink, a thick mushroom of pale green glass ending in a short section that swiveled sideways to hold it fast. The other was a small, thin gold ring, too tiny for even a child's finger. Its outer edge held a shallow band of three pale-blue glass chips mounted in a narrow, scroll-worked crest like some Victorian bauble. I shook my head at them, mystified.

"The green one is a gauge," Freeman explained.

"Gauge?" I asked, staring at the smooth, almost luminous glass. What kind of gauge lacks numbers or letters or other markings for measurement?

Freeman smirked again and tugged at the bottom of his earlobe. "An ear gauge. You know, those big, stupid holes kids put in their ears, like natives. Usually gauges are hollow, but not that kind. It came from the Black hooker. She had all kinds of crap on her ear." He gestured with his chin. "The other is a nose ring I got from the junkie. Probably some cheap Chinese crap or she'd have sold it for drugs."

The horror of it dawned on me and I dropped them onto the table beside me.

"Trophies," I whispered, aghast at the thought.

"Nah," Freeman demurred. "More like mementos. But you can keep those two." I stared up at him, open-mouthed. He cocked his head and grinned. "I'll get more." He leaned slightly forward toward me. "Unless you man-up and turn me in."

He made as though he was going to leave, but instead walked over to the wall where a large crucifix hung. He raised his hand and for a moment I thought he was going to reach for it. Instead, he merely pointed at the figure on the cross.

"This fella. You guys believe this fella died for everybody, right? But you also believe he was God, and could have stopped it at any point. He said so himself. Didn't he tell Pilate he had a legion of angels at his beck and call? So really it was suicide – for the good of all mankind, of course.

"That's what you've got to do, Father. You've got to sacrifice yourself if you want to save others. You call the cops and you'll probably save some women's lives and put me in prison, where I can't hurt anybody again. Not only that, you and your fellow men of the cloth will have years, maybe decades to try to get me to see the error of my ways. And maybe you'll succeed." He placed his fingertips on his chest, "Maybe you'll save my soul."

Again, that finger wagged at me. "But you gotta have skin in the game. We both know if you do this, your conscience is not gonna let it go. Sooner or later, you'll tell your confessor you deliberately broke the seal. And they'll excommunicate you. Quietly. Can't let people know a priest broke the seal, that's real bad PR. But what if," he grinned his devil's grin again, "*I* tell somebody. Imagine what that'll be like, reporters tracking you down. Once they find out you've been excommunicated, they'll know you did something very naughty. And it'll all come out. But you will have saved two lives."

He stared at me a moment longer, then turned. "Well, I'll leave you be, you've got a lot to think about. And I have preparations to make." He walked to the doorway, stopped, and looked up at the sunlight flooding in through the stained-glass window. In the multicolored glow he looked almost cherubic.

"It's a really nice day," he said. "You should try to get out."

CHAPTER 15

It's astonishing how God works. When you think about it, and open your heart to it, it's fascinating how He moves under the cover of what cynics call coincidence.

I remembered hardly anything on Friday after my encounter with the Penitent or I guess I should call him by his name, Will Freeman. When I left the confessional, the church was empty save for Bridget Mullins kneeling in a pew off to one side. Maybe she was on a break from the parish office, or praying a penance but I didn't recall her making a confession. It's weird, I can't remember that yet I do recall pieces of the Knights of Columbus council meeting I attended to say benediction. The half-dozen or so greybeards spent most of the time quibbling over the sausage they'd buy for the next pancake-breakfast fundraiser. While they argued whether to buy regular sausage or the slightly more-expensive, maple-flavored links and charge a quarter more a plate, I imagined Freeman busy with his preparations, shoving yellow nylon rope into a backpack, or spraying black paint onto the windows of a shack. I saw him on a wooded hillside, hacking into the ground with a long-handle shovel, a hip-high mound of dirt beside him.

That night, as I laid in bed, I kept thinking of the two awful souvenirs Freeman had inflicted on me. They were in my desk drawer in a sandwich bag, in hopes they might someday be used as evidence. I prayed decades of the rosary until I finally fell asleep.

Saturday morning the black dogs had me by the throat. In fact, it felt like there was one on each limb, holding me down. I managed to take Bongo out for a quick potty, dumped some kibble in his bowl, then shuffled over to the church in my bathrobe. From the sacristy's doorway I announced to the handful assembled for 7 a.m. Mass that I had a stomach flu, apologized, and withdrew. Back in the rectory I put a protesting Bongo in his crate, muttered "Shut the hell up" and headed to the bedroom. I called Patty and told her to cancel or postpone anything on my calendar that morning, and repeated the lie I'd used with the parishioners a few minutes prior. She asked about 5 o'clock Mass, if she should call the diocese to get someone to fill in. I told her I'd handle it. The truth is, I didn't give it any thought at all. I turned off my phone and went back to bed. No breakfast or lunch, just me in the sheets that day. I fantasized about being in prison, curled up on a cot in the shadows of a cell, out of the light. It was comforting, the idea of being alone, nothing affecting me, me affecting nothing. Simple, blessed nothingness.

Around two in the afternoon somebody began banging on the front door, which set off Bongo. I had dozed off, and woke with a full bladder. The combination of the banging, the barking, and a painful need to urinate got me out of bed. I hit the bathroom first, then seriously thought of hitting that yapping dog next, but bypassed his crate and went to the front door. I pulled the door open and was about to launch into the stomach flu excuse when I recognized the figure on the other side of the screen door. Paul Kennedy, our deacon, stood with hands jammed into his jeans, staring off toward the school. This was perfect. He couldn't say Mass, but he could do a Communion service in place of the 5 o'clock. Which meant I could stay in bed the whole day.

"Hey, Paul," I said, faking more weakness than I actually felt. "You're just the man I wanted to see."

"Sorry to bother you, Father," he interrupted. "I tried calling but couldn't get through. Stan Schumacher's wife is in the ER, she had a massive stroke. He's asking if you could come give her Last Rites."

"Oh my," I muttered. Emmy Schumacher was one of those dynamic old ladies always on the go. Petite, wrinkled, looked like an elf. She had taught fourth grade at the school when it was still St. Al's Parochial, made the transition to Holy Spirit Academy, taught for a few more years then retired. She and Stan worked bingo on Thursday, helped with food distribution at Thanksgiving, and managed the church kitchen for the Oktoberfest. One of those types who jumped in wherever needed. And she made insanely good apple strudel. I can vouch for that.

"Which hospital?" I asked.

"Metro," Paul said. Dammit, I thought, downtown. It'll take 30 minutes to get there. "You want me to go?" Paul asked.

I considered it. The black dogs gave a tug, but the shock and surprise had weakened them. Stan was too good a guy to stiff.

"You know what," I said. "Can you stick around? Depending on what's happening at the hospital, I might need you to do a Communion service for the 5 o'clock. Maybe lead a prayer for Emmy. Can you do that?"

"Sure," he said.

No time for a shower. I dressed quickly and was on my way. Thanks to blessedly light traffic, I made it to Metro in under half an hour. The take-in nurse in the Critical Care Pavilion started outlining the directions needed to get me to the Comprehensive Stroke Center but an orderly volunteered to lead me there, which probably saved me from getting lost for 20 minutes. As I entered the specialized ICU, a dark-haired, female doctor in turquoise-blue scrubs near the nurses' station intercepted me.

"Are you here for Mrs. Schumacher?"

"Yeah, Father Pastor from St. Al's. I know the family, and they requested an anointing. Is she conscious?"

She shook her head. "Probably won't regain."

"Big one?" I asked. She nodded.

"The husband is with her, if you'd like to go in. It's Room Three, past the nurses' station."

I nodded and walked to the doorway. Emmy's small form in the huge hospital bed looked like a kid's doll pushed into the cushions of a couch. A blue and white ventilator tube taped to her cheek disappeared into her open mouth, and an IV monitor beeped placidly beside her. Multiple tubes and cords leashed her to the machines that kept her body alive, and not one but two white computer stands with open laptops crowded in on her right. To her left, on a small, wooden folding chair sat Stan Schumacher, head down and his back to me. He held his wife's motionless hand to his lips while he talked softly. The intimacy of the moment kept me from interrupting, so I stood and listened.

"Brian's wife said he got a flight out of Houston, and should be at Hopkins by 10. Ginny's on her way, but there's construction on 71 so it'll be 7 or so before she gets here. Just hang on, darlin. Hang on until the kids get here. That's all I ask. Just that."

His breath caught in a shudder as his shoulders rose and fell.

"I don't want ya to go. Not yet. If you stay, Emmy, I'll do everything. I'll take care of you at home. I'll set up the spare bedroom for ya, and I'll learn all about these machines. And we'll have nurses come so you can stay at home. And I'll read to ya, and tell you what the kids are doin'.

"But if He says ya gotta go, ya gotta go," he said, and a sob came out before he could continue. "I wanna tell ya first, I wanna thank you, darlin. Thank you for my life. I wouldn't have made it without you. Thank you for our kids, for our life together. It's been a good life, hasn't it?"

An electronic screech issued from one of monitors. Stan looked up in wonder at the bank of electronics and displays, trying to find the source of the commotion. A young nurse brushed by me at the door and deftly stepped into the room. She checked a panel of lights and told Stan she needed to "adjust something" and suggested he step out into the hallway. He wiped a sleeve against his eye and rose. Turning, he caught sight of me.

"Oh, hey, Father. I didn't see ya there," and quickly dashed a finger at his other eye. A bubble of snot was caught in his finely trimmed moustache, and I spotted a box of tissue and grabbed it.

"Hey, let's go grab a cup of coffee somewhere," I said. "And we'll let these folks do their thing."

"There's a Starbucks on the ground floor, and a Subway on the fourth," the nurse called to us.

Stan nodded, stopped, and glanced at my empty hands. "Did you bring what you need for Last Rites?" he asked.

"Anointing of the Sick," I corrected, and tapped the breast pocket of my jacket. "Got everything. C'mon, we'll have coffee then come back. They'll be done and I can give Emmy the sacrament."

I offered him the box of tissues, but first took one for myself.

CHAPTER 16

I promised to remain with Stan until his daughter arrived from Dayton. Emmy received the Anointing of the Sick, or what we used to call Last Rites. That seemed to comfort Stan. He held his wife's limp hand as we prayed a rosary aloud, our voices drifting into soft chant. Later I listened to the tale of their life together; how they met, had children and raised them to adulthood, their work careers, and the long-anticipated retirement years. And as I'd overheard when I entered the room, Stan told me his intention to bring his comatose wife home. Ever the pragmatist, he pondered what electrical upgrades might be needed to accommodate the monitoring equipment, if doorways should be widened, and how to marshal the social services to assist with her care.

"That's a lot to jump into so soon," I observed. "It may be best to wait a few days, until Emmy's condition stabilizes. You'll have your hands full enough with the kids arriving today, probably staying at your place."

He lowered his head and nodded silently.

"Have faith in God, Stan. Leave it in His hands for now and ask for His guidance. That's all He asks of us, to trust Him. We do what we can do." Stan's head jerked up and his greyish-blue eyes locked onto mine.

"What made you say that?" he demanded. I thought I

had somehow offended him and sputtered out an apology, but he held up his hand in a soothing gesture.

"My dad said that to me all the time, those exact words. 'Do what you can do, Stanley.' But," he raised a finger and shook it gently for emphasis. "He didn't mean it the way most folks say, like a limitation. Like you can only do so much. My old man meant it as a mandate. When something is wrong or goes bad, don't sit on your hands." A grin spread across his wrinkled face. "That was another of his sayings, 'God didn't put hands on the ends of your arms for you to sit on 'em. Do what you can do.' That's how he looked at things, and I guess I do, too. There's always a way to improve a situation, either by preparing, repairing, or replacing. That was another one of his lines. Ya know, for a bus mechanic he had a lot of sayings. Maybe he thought he was Ben Franklin."

*   *   *

Night had fallen by the time I left the hospital and drove toward St. Al's. Once off the expressway, I passed by retail and residential areas. Halloween was less than two weeks away, as witnessed by the displays on homes and businesses. The storefronts seemed uniformly restrained with their decorations, mostly vinyl clings of cartoon witches, Draculas and Frankensteins. Nothing intense, they don't want to scare away customers.

With private homes you can almost guess the occupants by the intensity of their displays. Tastefully arranged cornstalks, pumpkins, Indian corn and haybales meant DINKS, empty nesters or retirees. Cutesy jack o' lanterns and inflatable, goofy ghosts were reliable indicators of families with little kids and elementary school children. If you spot ghouls lurking in doorways, skeletons swaying from nooses, or zombie arms emerging from wilted flowerbeds, good chance there are teens in the house. The haunted-house wannabes are a bit tougher to guess, other than to proclaim the owners' passion for horror firms. Two blocks down from our church is a house with a dummy of LeatherFace, a blood-splattered butcher's smock over his shirt and tie, seated in a rocking chair with his signature chainsaw in his lap. A late-model white F150 sporting landscaping logos is usually parked in the drive, which one could argue is a useful, if accidental, addition to the macabre motif.

But then you've got the house I passed on my way back from the hospital. You can't miss it because a rotating amber light similar those used by city plows in the winter flashed in the yard and swept the road for hundreds of feet in both directions. As I rolled past, the rotating streaks illuminated a massacre. A body lay on the porch roof, arm drooping over a red-smeared gutter, an ax protruding from its head. More bodies of men and women lay contorted on the ground, each splashed with red. A wheelbarrow held a trash pile of human limbs, and a cluster of rusted chemical barrels appeared to be filled to the brim with gore, loops of intestines hanging over their sides.

In the daylight it looks cheap and clownish, but tonight as I passed my chest tightened, my hands clenched the wheel and I kept my eyes on the taillights ahead of me. Murder was no longer theoretical to me. We laugh at imaginary monsters, but don't try masquerading as the real killers among us. I knew a guy in college who attended a Halloween costume contest dressed as a cancer cell. He went home with a black eye. Something similar happened a few years later at a house party when some fool showed up as a junkie zombie, complete with hypodermic in his arm and track marks. In his defense, he didn't know the host's younger brother had ODed the year before, but that didn't save him from an ass-kicking.

I pulled into the rectory's garage, got out and went through the inside door to the kitchen where Bongo loudly demanded his dinner. Paul must have taken him out at least once, but by now he probably needed to go again. Off we went to the fenced-in area, where Bongo's nose banished any other bodily needs in a quest to find the rabbit. After a while he took care of business and happily trotted on the leash back to the rectory where his empty food dish waited. Like a guilty parent, I compensated for my neglect by pouring him a larger-than-usual portion of kibble.

So far I'd had only coffee and a vending-machine package of cheddar crackers with peanut butter, but didn't feel hungry yet. I'd promised Stan I would pray for him and Emmy, and I still had a rosary to say for Will Freeman. Grabbing my keys, I headed over to the church, let myself in, and found a pew in the soft shadows.

The prayers came easily, and I thanked God for the opportunity to serve Stan and his family, which had pushed my depression onto a backburner. When I had wrestled this demon as a seminarian, my therapist, Fr. Fiester, observed that I was one of those patients for whom serving others seemed to ease my own inner pain. "It takes you out of yourself, Tom," he'd said. "It breaks the feedback loop you're in." He had assured me that by helping others heal, I would find healing myself. Of course, it wasn't that simple but it helped. A lot. And in the relief I experienced through service, God's plan for me became clear. Mrs. Pastor's thick-headed boy finally understood, and my vocation proceeded.

I knelt in the pew, got out my beads and began the Sorrowful Mysteries. The challenge with the rosary is keeping your mind focused on the mystery, because thoughts stray in and out. Despite my efforts to focus on Christ's agony in the garden and his scourging at the pillar, my mind wandered. I recalled images of Freeman's babyish face bathed in reds, blues and green from the stained-glass window, as well as an image of Stan holding his unconscious wife's hand so tenderly to his lips.

I finished the rosary, got up from sore knees and sat in a pew in the dark for a while. Why, I silently asked Him. Why start the day with Freeman and end with the Schumachers? What are You trying to tell me?

I replayed the day in my head, and nothing seemed clear. Rest your mind, I decided. Just let it float. If horrors drift in, don't engage them by resisting, let them drift out. Whatever demon is assigned to torment me must have taken that as a challenge, because it wasn't long before my mind conjured images of Freeman's two victims. They illogically lay buried side by side, sisters in death, looking like exhausted sleepers sprinkled with damp soil and tree roots. The Black girl was missing an ear, and one side of the addict's nose was sliced open and the skin pulled back. I shuddered at the images and, engagement or not, I forced them from my mind.

Instead, I summoned up the memory of Emmy

Schumacher, and the medical machinery crowding in on all sides, softly humming and clicking. Stan reappeared, seated on the wooden folding chair, face down in sorrow. Suddenly his head jerked up, and he stared at me with grey-blue eyes sharp and intense. "What made you say that?" he demanded. His snowy eyebrows knit together over his narrowing eyes. He repeated the question, insistent to the point of anger.

Say what? What had I said? I groped for a recollection, then it hit me like a hammer.

Do what you can do.

CHAPTER 17

The forecast proved right for once and it stayed warm into Sunday. After the 11 a.m. Mass small kids romped out of the church, dragging jackets on the ground until caught by their scolding moms. The pleasant warmth made everyone a bit giddy after our recent taste of the coming cold. When I walked Bongo that afternoon kids rode bikes on the side streets, the pungent smell of lit charcoal wafted on the air, and a guy raking leaves out of his flowerbed listened to the Browns game on a radio. They missed an easy field goal. Again.

Later it was so summery I felt a twinge of doubt as I unpacked a plastic tub from the basement and hung my few flannel shirts and jeans in the bedroom closet. I decided to leave the heavy socks and sweatpants in the tub for now. This unpacking wasn't related to the weather. I picked out the lightest flannel shirt and laid it on the bed, then decided there was no point in waiting and tossed a pair of jeans beside it. A glance at the window showed the sun clipping the tops of the trees and turning the sky orange. Still too soon. I changed clothes anyway, closed the bedroom door and checked my reflection in the narrow, full-length mirror hung from a nail on the back. Add a sixpack of beer and bag of chips and the guy in the reflection could be any suburbanite headed to a backyard barbecue. Perfect. I went to the kitchen, grabbed a beer, and slipped out the backdoor while Bongo snoozed in the living room. There was time to go through everything one more time in my head. The cool, sweet beer helped steady my nerves, but I wished instead for a smoke. And for night to fall before second thoughts took root.

*   *   *

My Nissan's headlights remained on even though I'd turn the engine off and removed the key. The empty curb in front of me blazed in their harsh light, as did a telephone pole with a small, rusted bus stop sign a few yards away. I panicked for a moment, then seized the plastic stalk jutting out from the steering column and rotated the light switch from "auto" to "off."

I blew out a sigh, hands resting on the bottom of the steering wheel and asked myself what the hell was I doing here. I had parked in front of a single-story building with brickwork painted white many, many years ago. Its single, low rectangular window frame held graffiti-splattered plywood instead of glass. A rusting grey metal door topped a cement stoop sprinkled with the glittering brown shards of a malt liquor bottle. No sign, no address numbers betrayed an identity. I couldn't recall where Freeman had said he'd picked up the prostitutes he'd killed, so I did a Google search for "streetwalkers Cleveland." It yielded a two-year-old TV news report about a local merchant who videoed prostitutes on his street and posted their images on a Facebook page in a forlorn attempt to drive them out.

The location had been Lorain Avenue and West 150th, so I parked a few blocks away.

What I should have done was research the topic, talked to a few diocesan social workers, and wrapped my head around this thing. But there wasn't time for that. Freeman said his wife was leaving town today, and he planned to hunt new victims on Monday, which was tomorrow. I didn't have the luxury of a slow approach. Like Stan had said in the hospital, and what the Spirit led me to realize in the church last night, I had to do what I could do. Which at first seemed like nothing. The seal not only prohibited actions that might compromise Freeman's identity, but also demanded silence on anything said in the confessional. So no mentions of a killer roaming the streets. What was I to do, pace up and down the street with a sign reading, "Harlots, Get Ye Hence?" I decided if I couldn't tell the truth, I'd have to tell a lie.

Throughout my preparations I pondered and pondered what motivation would be most effective. I put myself in the prostitutes' high-heeled shoes and asked, 'What would get me off the street for the next few days or so?' What could supersede the all-important need to make money? If I couldn't pose the possible loss of life and limb, what about the loss of freedom? You can't turn tricks from a jail cell.

In retrospect, I got a little carried away as I polished the lie while driving. Tonight, I wouldn't be Pastor Pastor of St. Al's, I would be…Jack Somebody-Or-Other, a local community activist. I might hint at ties to BLM or even Antifa. I'd say our sources warned us the cops (maybe I should say "the heat," or "the man," or "the po-

po,") planned a sweep of sex workers in Cleveland over the next three days. They would target massage parlors, online escorts and the most visible presence, the streetwalkers. All part of the mayor's scheme to look tough on human trafficking for his re-election campaign. As Jack Whatsisname, I was outraged at another attempt by our misogynistic, xenophobic, homophobic, racist, fascist (maybe pick just two of those) government to oppress sex workers and not the real source of the pain: the privileged johns. So our activist cell planned to sabotage this oppression by spreading word all over the 216 for working girls to lay low, take a well-deserved vacation, or if they absolutely had to work, do it online or indoors for the next three days. What would the mayor boast about then?

It sounded good, right? I was particularly proud of the "216" reference, which I remembered LeBron James using at some point. A fake police sweep would be the perfect cover story.

Thus reassured, I took a deep breath and yanked the door latch. It was still unseasonably warm, but a few steps beyond the brick building I felt the blast of a stiff breeze from Lake Erie carrying the distant rumble of thunder.

Only later did I realize the rumble wasn't thunder. That was God, and He was chuckling.

CHAPTER 18

It's an unwelcome shock when we realize how many of our assumptions are based on things we've seen in movies and television and thus, are ridiculous.

Walking down Lorain Avenue, it dawned on me I hadn't the faintest idea of what a real prostitute looked like. I wasn't expecting Julia Roberts from *Pretty Woman*, but I presumed they would be readily identifiable by such clues as high heels, short skirts, skintight tops, and overdone make-up. Likely blonde, but not necessarily.

I'd forgotten Freeman said he avoided the fat, ugly, or older women. He'd chosen his first victim because he thought she was an addict, and in my mind's eye I envisioned an anorexic, drooling wraith swaying in a gale only she felt. I didn't see anybody like that. In fact, I didn't see anybody at all. A thin veil of light from street poles and building signs illuminated a deserted Lorain Avenue, but behind the store fronts darkness swallowed all else. An uneasy thought arose that prostitutes weren't the only ones prowling these night streets in search of quick money.

The impulse to return to my car strengthened, but at that moment I saw three women inside the plexiglass of a bus stop. All were Black and two looked to be teens in leggings and long, shapeless T-shirts that hung halfway down their thighs. Just typical kids. The third, however, was older and stout, her girth accented by a tightknit blue dress that bulged at her bust, belly and buttocks. This being a Sunday night, I supposed it possible she was heading home after a long day of worship, dinner and socializing with a congregation. I discarded the theory almost immediately. Form-fitting dresses ending only a few inches below the fanny and gleaming red pumps on the feet aren't exactly church clothes.

They spotted me, and Blue Dress had apparently been awarded the prize because she waddled/shuffled in a beeline toward me, thrashing a tiny, black purse back and forth as she moved.

"You lost, honey?" she called.

"No, not really," I stammered.

"Uh-huh. Well then you need a date if you gonna walk around here. Why don't I come with you. You lookin' to party?"

"I'm not. I have something specific in mind."

"Mmm-hmm. I bet you do. Where's your car, honey? Let's go there and do that thing you thinkin' bout."

This was not heading the way I intended.

"We don't need to go to my car. I just wanna talk with you."

"Talk?" she said, her voice spiking shrill as her liquid black eyes assessed my face.

"Yeah, I wanna," I suddenly remembered that I was Jack Somebody-Or-Other, street activist. Desperately I scrambled into character. "I wanna lay something on ya, while we're conversatin'." Inspired, I thought to myself. Absolutely inspired.

She closed her eyes and nodded. "I git it. Yeah, I git it.

Sure, honey. Whatever you want." A chuckled snort blasted out of her. "But not right here. Oh, no way. C'mon, I know a place where you can lay what you want on me." And she grabbed my hand and started toward the corner, nearly dragging me off my feet and I stumbled to keep up with her.

"My name's Jack," I announced as she led me around the corner into a side street.

"That's cool," she said, not breaking stride. "You havin' a good night, Jack?"

A dark house with no visible lights squatted at the end of an ancient gravel drive dotted with weeds. Blue Dress pulled me toward a tiny, rickety wooden garage with peeling yellow paint and a battered corner where someone had misjudged the entrance. Overgrown bushes gone thickety from neglect lined one side, and Blue Dress yanked me into the gap between the musty-smelling wall and scratchy branches.

"OK, look, look," I babbled, out-maneuvered by her aggression. "I just want to talk with you."

"I know, baby, I know. That's cool," she said, nodding her head. "Talk is cheap. Only cost you a dub."

"A what?"

"A dub," she said with a hard nod. "Twenty."

I held up my hands, "No, you don't get it. I just want–"

"Get that Jackson out, or we gone."

What could I do? I gave a frustrated sigh, produced my wallet and thumbed past several ones to find a lone twenty. She snatched the bill from my hand and disappeared it into her tiny purse with astonishing speed.

"Aw right," she said crisply. My face must have been quite the study, because she laid a hand on my shoulder. "Relax honey, this gon' be fun. You'll see, I'm good at this," she gave me a reassuring pat. "OK, go 'head and take out lil' billy an' start doin' your thing. And I'll tell you bout the time me and Tina, this little white girl, took on this big muther, I mean he make Shaquille look like a baby. But if you want me to finish you, it gonna cost another dub."

"No, no, no," I blurted, appalled and shaking my head.

"Oh, hell yeah," she shot back, her voice indignant. "What you think I am, Piggly Wiggly and this is BOGO night?"

The gravel crunched and I saw her gaze shift behind me. She flung an obscenity at whatever she saw and I spun in time to meet a white-hot sunburst. I mean, I stared into the heart of a nuclear detonation. A corona of magnesium white rays spiked out in all directions. My pupils dodged to avoid it, leading ringlets of that fierce light in a dance behind them. I raised my hand to block it and squeezed my eyes shut, but a fat larva of yellow-white dots drifted against the inside of my eyelids.

"Alright," said a bored male voice. "You guys know the drill. Come on over to the van. And I swear to God, Monique, if you make me run again I will tase your fat ass."

CHAPTER 19

I couldn't help but think of St. Paul in prison at Philippi. When midnight came it found me in prayer, just like the apostle, but there was no earthquake to shake the foundations of our jail and throw open the doors. Acts 16 says Paul and Silas also had been singing hymns, so maybe I should have tried that, but I don't think my companions in the holding tank would have been as appreciative as the Philippians. Definitely not the two who were sobbing.

They did all the things I'd seen on TV; fingerprints, photographs, ID taken and checked. When the young uniformed cop who booked me saw my driver's license photo with the roman collar and goofy grin, a frown crossed his face. He thumbed my diocesan ID from the wallet, got up and went into a back room. After a moment he emerged with another cop, older but big with hulking shoulders, thick neck, a nose like a toucan's bill. His brown hair had greyed at the temples, but he was as formidable as cops come. He looked at the ID, then at me with brown eyes as cold as a frozen mud puddle.

"You a priest? Active?"

I nodded.

"What parish?"

"St. Al's."

"Where's your black clothes and collar?" the younger cop asked. The older one shot him a glance packed with even more derision than what he'd given me. He swiveled back to me, and said two words so filled with resentment I knew there had to be a crucifix hanging from a chain under his shirt.

"Process him."

"I was not soliciting," I said. He reached down, shuffled through papers until he found what he wanted and read. With eyes still on the sheet, he declared "She says you paid her twenty to talk dirty while you masturbated in public."

"No. That's not what happened. Ask your officers if I was exposed or not."

His eyes came up and met mine. "Did money exchange hands?"

This was my out. This was an open cell door, a hallway to the exit and freedom into the night air. All I had to do was deny it. My word against hers. They aren't going to dust the money for fingerprints for something as minor as this. He stood waiting, his eyes never leaving mine.

"Yes, but it wasn't for that. I just wanted to tell her something. She wouldn't stay if I didn't give her money, so I had to."

He nodded. The big cop wanted to believe me, I could sense it, I really could. He wanted it to be true. The possibility produced the faintest thaw in those eyes. But he was a cop, too, and had to ask.

"What did you want to talk about?"

My mouth opened but nothing came out. The whole fake activist thing now sounded so absurd I couldn't

believe my own stupidity. I couldn't say I had fabricated
a story about a police prostitution sweep, when in fact
there *had been* a police prostitution sweep. And there was
no way I could even begin to approach the issue of Will
Freeman. So I stood there with my mouth open, and
watched his eyes frost over again.

"Go ahead," he muttered to the young cop, turned
and walked away.

*   *   *

No earthquake occurred at midnight, but apparently it
had not been cancelled only postponed. Around 1:30 a.m.
a cop came into the common area where me and the
dozen or so other men stood or sat on metal benches, and
announced we were being released on our recognizance.
Expect a court summons in the mail, declared the little
uniformed cop with a big voice and bad comb-over. We
got into line to collect our things and waited. A
commotion at the front rippled back and I learned from
the guy in front of me that our cars had been impounded,
so each of us needed to call someone for a ride. Christ in
heaven, I thought, how much will it cost get my car
back? Lucky for me, I've used Uber a few times, so it
saved me the humiliation of waking up someone to pick
me up at the jail. Thank God for small favors, because
there was plenty of humiliation ahead.

A few guys had hit the door as quick as they could,
but a thin, older man with expensive-looking wire-rim
glasses stopped just shy of them, staring at his cell
phone. His mouth drew down into an angry arch before
a torrent of obscenities burst out of it. He turned to the

rest of us still in line, and held up his cell phone.

"You see? You see what these bastards have done?! Sons of bitches," he barked. "They gave it to the news people. Just in time for news shows, with our photos and names." Several men moaned, others did not react at all, and a young guy, two up from me, began sobbing again. I stepped around the man in front of me and put my hand on his shoulder.

"Hey, it's gonna be OK," I said. "You'll get through this."

"My wife," he moaned. "Oh my god, my wife."

"C'mon," I said and pulled him from the line, if nothing else to avoid the angry glare from the guy I cut in front of. "C'mon, let's go sit down. It's gonna take a while to get through everybody."

We were the last two released, and I was alone when I finally got my wallet, cell phone, keys, loose change, and rosary. The first thing I did was to open the Uber app to get a ride. At 2 a.m. in Cleveland that's not a sure thing, but I got lucky and one would be here in about 35 minutes. Plenty of time to watch the video.

It wasn't hard to find. In fact, the 10 o'clock news had it first, so the cops must have really wanted to get this out quick. The headline for the link read, "Trafficking Sweep Nets Clinic Doctor, Catholic Priest." The report used our booking shots, not our IDs, thank God. My flannel shirt allowed me to blend in with the other schmoes, but the cops had taken the trouble to put "Fr." in front of my name under the photo. And the TV station had pulled my image up to full screen. No goofy grin on my face this time.

The only other person to get the full-screen treatment

was the doctor, a surgeon from the Cleveland Clinic. Turns out he was the skinny old guy who ranted about the news coverage as we got our possessions back. And he was our unlikely savior. A friend of his had seen the news report and contacted his attorney, who in turn contacted the police. The cops had released the information – publicized it would be more accurate – even before anyone was charged and apparently that is a big legal no-no. As a result, we were released on our own recognizance to wreak our lust-crazed mayhem upon a helpless, sleeping city.

The cops let me sit on a bench in a lobby while I waited for my Uber. With great reluctance, I punched the Gmail icon on my phone. There's a small red bubble in its corner showing the number of unopened emails. I'm a bit anal about that, and it's rare for the number to be more than four or five. The little red circle held the numerals "17."

The first three were from people I didn't know, and I felt so awful I went to the men's room because I thought I might throw up. After splashing water on my face, I dried off and realized I'd better wait in the lobby unless I wanted to miss my ride. I went back and sat down with my phone.

I noticed three items in my Messages app, so I checked those before returning to the email. God bless 'em, they were from the Tulips, a message of support each from Auggie, Mike and Jim. I read and reread their messages, which felt like a flicker of dawn in this nightmare. This lifted my spirits to the point I could face the emails again. Most of the names I didn't recognize, and it wasn't hard to tell the tone from the six or so words that showed under each name. One name, however, stood out from all the rest. I opened it and read the concise text.

My brain needed a few moments to digest the message and react. If the Uber guy or gal wasn't delayed, I should be able to get home with time enough to bathe Bongo and clean his by-now soiled crate, then take a shower, maybe grab a Pop Tart, and arrive at Cathedral Square in time for a 6:30 a.m. meeting. The email had not come from IBS, who wouldn't dirty his hands with this mess, but his vicar general, Auxiliary Bishop Timothy Flannery. And for some reason Flannery had copied Wulfram and told him to be there, too.

I was planning out the logistics when I saw headlights park outside on the street and figured it was my ride. It was just past 3 a.m., the hour of the devil. I trotted down the steps toward the Kia Sportage with the correct license plate for my Uber request when the thought hit me.

How was I going to get to the bishop's office by 6:30 a.m.?

I didn't have a car.

CHAPTER 20

Auxiliary Bishop Timothy Patrick Flannery is Irish. I
don't mean his family came from the Old Sod; *he* came
from the Old Sod. We Tulips guessed his age at
somewhere between 65 and 186. The only certainty was
that his boyhood had occurred at a time and place where
supreme authority in a Celtic village rested with the
parish priest, not the mayor or chairman. Flannery
grudgingly accepted the realities of the 21st Century, but
it wasn't hard to miss his longing for "the grand old
days." And it was impossible to accurately guess his age
because morbid obesity ballooned his face smooth. The
man's weight was legendary and it was said his belt
stretched taller than he. He often wore a biretta, the
small, square, black cleric's hat with four vertical fins and
a pom-pom in the middle. It was an unfortunate choice
for a man whose profile was already somewhat
pyramidal. On his sloping torso rested a grandiose
pectoral cross and silver chain that would excite envy in
the heart of any A-list rapper. Flannery would be pitiable
or comical if only he didn't scare the hell out of us.

Mike's parish was the closest to St. Al's, but he's on
his own for the 7 a.m. Mass. Auggie was at St. Luke's in
Lakewood, almost an hour from me, but he shared his
rectory with a retired priest, so I called him at 3:30 a.m. to

bum a ride into the city. Auggie also is the most athletic Tulip in our little bouquet, infamous for waking before 5 a.m. to go jogging. Nonetheless, he sounded groggy when he answered his phone. I promised him an overpriced coffee at Starbucks and a keto breakfast of meat, meat, and a side of meat if he'd stick around and take me to an ATM, then to the impound lot. Auggie said of course, and would pick me up at 5:45. I don't deserve such good friends.

Cathedral Square in downtown Cleveland includes the cathedral, rectory, chancery building and parking deck. The diocesan offices are not located in beautiful St. John's Cathedral, as one might expect, but in the eight-story glass and concrete chancery on East 9th. Sounds imposing, but it was fairly understated. In fact, the CVS Pharmacy that used to be next door had a sign three times the size of the blue-and-white diocesan shield and lettering over the door.

The sun wouldn't rise for another hour, and while the pre-dawn twilight evaporated some of the dark from the sky, it was still night on the floor of the city's concrete canyons. Twin streams of yellow headlights and red taillights flowed up and down E. 9th. On the ride in I had told Auggie as much as I could about this mess. He had listened and said simply, "It's all damage control now." I nodded glumly and we rode in silence the last mile or so. When we got to the chancery, Auggie found a spot right at the door. I wasn't sure how to interpret that omen.

He parked, I unbuckled, and Auggie stuck out his hand and said, "Good luck, man." I gave him a sick grin as we shook. "Don't park under any of these windows," I told him. "I'd feel awful if I saw it was your car beneath me on the way down."

"Though I should walk in the midst of the shadow of death," Auggie said, quoting the old Douay-Rheims bible.

"I will fear no evils, for thou art with me," I replied. It was a call-and-response thing we Tulips used in the seminary to remind one another we had each other's back. It helped take the edge off the heebie-jeebies and I got out, shut the door, and waved.

No lights shone in the offices facing the street and I half wondered if the entrance was locked. It was not, and as I slipped in, I caught a glimpse of Auggie's taillights merging into the traffic. I took an elevator up to the eighth floor, where I knew Flannery's office stood down the hall from IBS. The lift gave a too-loud ding as the doors swept open, and I walked as quietly as I could down the carpeted hallway. About 30 feet from the end, I saw an open door and entered the suite, surprised to see the admin's computer and desk lamp up and running. The chair behind her cluttered desk was empty, but a few tentative steps brought me within range of Flannery's voice.

"Marjory dear, I'm sure you sent in the correct order, but as you can see the buffoons put bacon on the sandwich instead of sausage. My guests have declined it, so please take this for yourself, and call the deli again and ask them to send up the proper order."

A small, nimble woman in a demure pantsuit scuttled out of the office, clutching a partially unwrapped bundle in both hands. She stopped short when she saw me, and her eyes filled nearly every centimeter of her glasses. She backpedaled a few steps and turned to announce,

"Excuse me, Your Excellency. Father Pastor is here." Oh boy, I thought, even the admin knows who I am. Wonder if she recognized me from the news.

She turned to me with a smile though, and stepping back to her desk briskly laid the greasy wrapper on the lone bare spot on her desk and said in a kind, professional voice, "Go on in, Father, they're waiting for you."

I'll bet they are, I thought. Flannery's probably looking forward to something more toothsome than a sausage-egg-and-cheese bagel to sink his dentures into. Whatever courage I possessed melted away as I did the deadman-walking shuffle into the auxiliary bishop's office.

"Close the door, if ya please," he groused when he caught sight of me. This was my first visit to Flannery's office, which appeared pretty much as expected. Lots of dark oak and nail-studded green leather furniture, lawyers' bookcases with glass fronts, a little side bar with two ornate decanters and what I'm sure were Waterford crystal tumblers. A small collection of standing crucifixes, some looking very old indeed, adorned a marble-topped side table.

To my right, I saw Flannery seated like a magistrate behind his broad wooden desk. Above and behind him hung a magnificent framed print of Heinrich Hoffman's *Christ in the Garden of Gethsemane*. It had to be at least three feet tall, and an overhead light revealed brush strokes on the gleaming surface, so maybe it wasn't a print but an actual reproduction. Probably every Catholic has seen this image on holy cards, in prayerbooks or online. A very Caucasian Jesus kneels against a stone outcropping, surrounded by darkness and illuminated only by a single shaft of moonlight beaming down from a distant break in the clouds. His cloak has slid off his shoulder, a foreshadowing of the literal stripping to come. The savior's face has been interpreted as displaying obedience, divine serenity, and/or devotion. I always thought Christ's expression seems to ask his Father, "So we're really gonna do this, huh?"

"It's quite a sack of shite you've brought us, Father Pastor," Flannery declared. "Come in, come in, don't stand there like a frightened rabbit." As I walked into the center of the room, I saw two wingback guest chairs, and the guests occupying them. Wulfram had the good sense to exchange his scholar's grunge for clerical neatness when summoned by a bishop. And in the other chair, leg crossed and serene as ever, sat my own personal inquisitor, Fr. Mwangi. I guessed Wulfram would reluctantly play the role of defense attorney, Mwangi would stand in for prosecutor, and Flannery, of course, sat as Hizzoner the Judge. I noticed there wasn't a third chair for me. The accused must stand in the dock. Yup, my butt was as good as gone. Adios, goldilocks parish.

"Before this goes any further," Flannery intoned with much of his brogue still intact, "nothing said here leaves this room unless I say otherwise. Understood?" Wulfram nodded emphatically and Mwangi with more reserve, but both reactions were unnecessary because Flannery's words clearly were intended for me.

"Next, you are to speak to no one about this misadventure, save only to our Lord (with his accent it came out, "Lard") and even that in silent prayer," he commanded. "If you say one word, even one word, to the press or any reporters, I will see you laicized. Am I understood?" I nodded obediently. The Church calls it laicized, everyone else calls it defrocking but it comes to the same thing. You are stripped of the rights, duties, and privileges of the priesthood.

"Alright then," Flannery paused himself, and leaned his bulk toward his desk phone with its array of buttons. He punched one and the admin's voice chirped, "Yes, your Excellency?"

"Marjory, when they deliver the order this time, check it first, would ya please? If they got it right this time, put it in the microwave. We can warm it after this meeting."

"Certainly, your Excellency."

He punched the button again, settled into his chair and blinked his piggy eyes at me.

"Let's have it," he said.

I don't think I said three syllables before Flannery cut me off to explain that Wulfram and Mwangi had filled him in on our prior meeting. He added, somewhat presumptuously I thought, that the Penitent's permission to discuss his case with my confessor extended to himself as well. That was a relief because it dispensed with tiptoeing around Will Freeman's first two confessions, but they didn't know about the third. All three priests listened raptly as I described the meeting, especially when I told them of the third murder.

"So, the reason I was on the street last night was because the Penitent indicated his intention to escalate his crimes–"

"Sins," Flannery corrected.

"Both," Wulfram murmured.

"And, and," I flustered at the interruption, "and that

would put a vulnerable population at an even greater risk."

"Was he under the sacrament at the time he told you this?" Wulfram cut in.

"He was," I acknowledged, and gave as good a description as memory allowed of Freeman's discourse on psychopathy, his culpability, and dubious request for absolution.

"From Fr. Pastor's account, it seems unlikely this was an authentic confession," Wulfram said to Mwangi, and offered a rationale. Midway through I had to shake my head.

"I respectfully disagree, Fr. Wulfram," I said. "The Penitent followed the form of confession and his denunciation of the sacrament may come from a place of despair rather than disdain. He tried to justify his actions. Doesn't that indicate guilt, however small? He told me he had come to confession because he thought it might 'cure him.'"

"Did he give any evidence of his claims?" Mwangi asked. "Any proof they have actually taken place?"

I stared at the brown carpeting between my shoes and recalled Freeman's creepy, panting laughter at the news his crimes were doubted. I relayed his gothic response about the murders as real as 'the blood in my veins and the flesh on my bones.' And to put an end to this line of evasion, I dug into my pocket.

"It angered him to hear that his crimes were questioned," I said, "so he gave me this." I drew out the sandwich bag with its two objects. Wulfram took it and began to peel it open, but stopped when I said, "Don't. Those might be evidence." The Wolfman stared at me and I explained to all what they were looking at. "There may be traces of the women's DNA on those. Maybe the police can use these to identify them."

Wulfram frowned, but left the seal closed. "Tom, he could have picked these up at a store."

I shook my head. "Why would he do that? He didn't know his claims would be questioned. When I told the Penitent there were doubts, he was insulted. And think about it," I said, pointing at the baggie. "These were on his keyring. What do you put on a keyring besides keys?" I let that hang for a moment. "Only something of personal value or interest." Wulfram blinked, and the other two men sat in silence, probably recalling their own keyrings and how they validated my argument.

"We can't wish this away," I said gently. "He's the real deal. A bona fide serial killer. And he will keep taking lives until he is stopped."

Mwangi caught my eye as he passed the baggie back to me. "How do you know those items were on his keyring?"

"I watched him take them off," I replied. I scanned all three faces and nodded at their unasked question. "He revealed himself to me. He came around the wall and sat down beside me. He told me his name, where he lived, and that the bodies were there." Mwangi stared but said nothing.

"He released you from the seal?" Wulfram asked.

I shook my head. "No. In fact he was very specific about that. He said he did not release me. He used those very words." I looked from one face to the next. "He wants me to break the seal. Like it was a bargain. He would accept prison only if I broke the seal to inform the police. Otherwise, he will keep killing. He said he would start tonight." I told them how Freeman interpreted Christ's sacrifice on the cross as suicide, and how he urged me to sacrifice myself as well.

Mwangi's head nodded shallowly. "That is why you were on the street last night," he said softly. "You were trying to warn the sex workers."

I nodded. I told them my foolhardy plan, but Wulfram interrupted.

"I don't understand. If you knew of a police sweep of prostitutes and their customers, why—"

"I didn't know there would be a real one," I protested, perhaps a bit too loudly. "I made it up, as a story to scare them off the street long enough to thwart Fr—" I caught myself in time. "To thwart the Penitent. He said he had only a few days to commit more killings, so I thought if I could convince this woman and maybe others to spread the word, it would get them off the streets during that window of time."

Mwangi looked down into his hands. "You understand, do you not Fr. Pastor, that in doing so, you already have broken the seal. You have taken actions based on words spoken to you in the sacrament."

Flannery and Wulfram said nothing, and I didn't know how to interpret their silence. Were they agreeing with Mwangi?

"I understood that was a possibility," I replied. "I am uncertain of how much latitude we have in such extreme—"

"None," Mwangi said sadly. "You have no latitude. No freedom to act."

"But," Wulfram broke in. He shifted in his seat,

fingers combing his beard in thought. "By enticing his confessor to break the seal, by intentionally leveraging the sacrament in order to lure another into mortal sin, the sincerity and intent of his confession is obviously questionable, and thus its validity." He turned to Mwangi. "Isaac, do you remember the Italian media scandal a dozen years ago?"

The canonist stared for a second then nodded. "When the reporters made false confessions to see what individual priests would say about birth control. They then did a story about the inconsistencies."

"Right," Wulfram replied. "The Vatican denounced those false confessions, and the priests were not bound by the seal because the bogus penitents' intentions were not for forgiveness but to gain information for a news story. And to take a swipe at the Church." Wulfram looked back and forth between Mwangi and Flannery.

"This penitent is far worse. He's confessing his sins, his crimes, not with the hope of forgiveness, but to drive his confessor into the mortal sin of breaking the seal. There is no way that's a valid confession."

"Begging your pardon, Ken, but I think you're wrong," I said. "I do think the Penitent, at least some little part of him, wants to extinguish this darkness within him. I think he wants absolution. He even offered, maybe as an enticement to break the seal, the possibility he could eventually be brought to remorse and genuinely seek forgiveness. In which case," I said slowly. "Fr. Mwangi is correct. I broke the seal."

Wulfram shook his head no, but said nothing. I glanced at Mwangi, but his eyes were on his hands.

"It's not for you to decide," Flannery declared. "And

you're wasting my time with this moral theology debate. One scandal at a time. Among the many prayers you'll be saying today, Fr. Pastor, is one of gratitude for that supercilious surgeon who shared a jail cell with ya last night. He's raising a holy stink about the police releasing your identities before formal charges, probably to keep the clinic from firing him for his dalliances. The morning news on Channel 5 focused on him, and God be praised, they left out the part about one of my priests in the clinker.

"Don't be such a fool as to think this will last. There will be calls for your head, Pastor, and I'm inclined to provide it on a charcuterie board. But this other matter about the seal," he pursed his lips and rubbed a finger under his nose. "A mine field is what it is. No, it's worse. With mines you're safe if you don't move, but in this case inaction itself could be a wrong step." He sucked at his lower lip, then glowered at me as though I were the source of this migraine. Which, arguably, I was.

"Your monkeyshines last night have earned you an administrative leave. Take no comfort in that, Pastor, it's only a formality until I can tee you up a formal suspension. In fact, you'd best think of it in those terms. You'll go on a silent retreat at the Jesuit facility in Summit County. That'll take you out of the press's face." Flannery glanced at his watch. "I have another meeting to prepare for, so here's what's to be done. Nothing more from you, Fr. Mwangi, and thank you for joining us and offering your insights. Wulfram, you give me a paper tonight, with citations and summary, on the question of the seal in this case. Do I need to say what level of confidentiality is required here?"

Wulfram shook his head.

"Good. And you, Fr. Pastor. Go home. You will hear from me presently as to what happens next. In the meantime, I strongly suggest you sequester yourself in your room with your rosary and breviary, and say not one word to anyone, about anything. There is just and reasonable cause for you to say the Mass *sine populo*, and I order you to do so in your private room in the rectory. Someone else will handle Masses at your parish. Be off now."

I nodded and thanked him for his kindness. To my horror, he extended his pudgy, pasty right hand to me, knuckles forward. The tradition of kissing a bishop's ring died out in this country long before the Wright Brothers got famous. But like I said, Flannery was more Irish than American, and I was not about to incite him further. Without hesitation I stepped forward, puckered up and bussed his episcopal ring. And then I fled. Out the office and past the admin, who looked up at my haste and got up herself. I was halfway to the elevator when I heard the distant, electronic pings of a microwave being programmed.

CHAPTER 21

The bad news was the impound lot did not open for another hour and when it did, I'd have to fork over $200 to retrieve my Nissan. The good news? They would graciously accept plastic as well as cash.

The sight of a panhandler smoking a cigarette nearly tempted me to beg Auggie to pull into the first convenience store we spotted. Instead, he drove to St. Claire Avenue and found a parking spot about a block away from a Starbucks. I got a dark roast straight up, Auggie said he was coffee'd out, and got a chai tea instead. A single open table stood like an island among the crowd of business types and college students. A Canadian cold front had arrived and the temperature outside was in the 40s, maybe upper 30s in the shade, but the outdoors offered privacy so we found a bench and watched the commuters scamper to their hustles.

"Who do you think will replace me when I'm suspended?" I asked with genuine nonchalance.

"You're catastrophizing again," Auggie said.

"Nah, if I was catastrophizing, I'd be at the pier on E. 9th holding a cinder block tied to my ankle."

"I get that you were trying to give some kind of warning last night," Auggie began, "and I know you can't tell me what about, but…is it something I should worry about for my parishioners?" he asked.

I inhaled a sip from the plastic lid of my cup and let the hot fluid scald my tongue. "First of all, Flannery slapped a gag order on me. If the Holy Mother appeared next to us, I'm not allowed to say good morning to her." The coffee's slightly bitter bite seemed a fine accompaniment to my mood. "Mwangi is arguing I've broken the seal, but I think Flannery sees a political advantage in declaring the confession inauthentic. He told the Wolfman to supply him with academic citations to support that view." Telling Auggie all this was the exact opposite of what Flannery demanded, but I figured I was doomed anyway, so what the hell.

"Mwangi is your inquisitor, not Flannery?"

I shook my head. "No, Flannery plans to tack my hide to his wall. But right now, he'll do anything to avoid news of a priest breaking the seal. And Mwangi…" I stared at the morning's orange sunlight reflecting off the very top windows of an office tower. "The guy is kind of unreadable, other than being a by-the-book type."

I considered what Auggie had asked a moment ago. St. Luke's is in an old part of Lakewood, and surrounding neighborhoods ranged from gentrified to worn but well-kept. "Your people don't have anything to worry about," I said. "If you ask the Wolfman, he'd probably tell you nobody's in danger. In fact, he may think the Penitent is a figment of my imagination."

Auggie sipped at his cup. "You OK?"

A young business woman stalked past us in high heels, furiously tapping on her phone. I watched her go and said, "No, not really. The black dogs are back."

"You reach out to anybody?"

"Not yet. Like I said, Flannery wants me to disappear for a while."

"That may not be such a bad thing," Auggie said. I noticed for the first time he had zipped his jacket over his roman collar. Hiding the flag, eh, Auggie? I don't blame ya, buddy. Thanks to me, this will not be a good day to be a priest in Cleveland.

"It's pretty chilly," I declared. "You wanna go sit in your car?" As we hoofed it back, I felt my cell vibrate in my pocket for what seemed the 800th time that morning. More out of a sense of duty than real curiosity I took out the phone, thumbed it awake and glanced at the email; 28 and it was only 7:45 a.m. Just wait until people started reading Cleveland.com online, or chat with coworkers about what they'd seen on the morning news shows. The real fun would start when the Boomers spread the news on Facebook and NextDoor: Did you hear about the priest at St. Al's?

In the car we listened to sports radio and debated if the Browns leaky secondary would prevent them from making the play-offs yet again. Auggie thought so, and though I don't follow sports very closely, I argued the point for the sake of conversation. We plugged the impound lot address into the GPS and drove there in less than 15 minutes, getting in line behind six other cars waiting for the gate to open. Auggie tapped the screen on his car stereo and another station came up. An ad for a radiator shop played as Auggie and I speculated as to why the guy in a tricked-out Jeep in front of us was in this line. I hadn't been paying attention when the shock jocks came back on, but the words "human trafficking sweep last night" punched through my consciousness.

"Yeah, it says they got a priest in the sweep," a snide voice said." Some guy named Father Pastor."

"Wait, what? Is that his title? Father Pastor?"

"No dummy, that's his name. It says here Father Thomas Pastor."

"I looked him up," said a female voice. "He's the pastor at St. Alphonsus Liguori Church."

"So he's Pastor Pastor?"

"Yeah, geez what a name. They nailed him for soliciting hookers."

"Sure, ya gotta give the altar boys a night off once in a while."

Auggie jabbed a finger to cut off the sarcastic laughter booming from the car speakers. "Sorry man," he grumbled.

"It's alright," I said staring at the Jeep's back tire. "I gotta get used to it."

And then He did it to me again. Undeserved, unexpected, God gave me one of His little love pats. It's like I've told parishioners in homilies, look for these in your lives. They often aren't a big deal, just a small expression of love when you need it. Non-believers dismiss them as coincidence, but if you open your heart, you'll recognize them. Usually it's a small thing, like a bit of song on the radio, a phrase on a TV show, or a line in the day's scripture reading that fits perfectly in your particular circumstances at that moment. I compared it to squeezing a little kid's hand to reassure them you're right there beside them, and they'll be fine. Sometimes, though, these heaven-sent reassurances are not so subtle. Like this one.

My phone vibrated in a different cadence, which

meant it wasn't an email. I got it out and saw a "1" next to the Messages icon. I didn't recognize the phone number, but the text below said only "Isaiah 50:7."

"What's in Isaiah chapter 50, verse 7?" I asked Auggie.

He shrugged. "Go ask a Baptist."

"What about area code 202?"

Auggie thought a second. "That's DC."

"I don't know anybody there," I muttered.

"Could be a phone solicitor. You donate to any political groups or politicians? Probably somebody asking for money."

Frowning, I googled the verse and read it. Then I read it again. By the third reading a lump had formed in my throat. I turned my face to the passenger window.

"What it is?" Auggie asked. I couldn't speak, so I handed him my phone.

"The Lord God is my help," he read aloud. "therefore I have not been disgraced. I shall set my face like flint, knowing that I shall not be put to shame."

CHAPTER 22

By the time I skulked my car into the garage at St. Al's, the church parking lot was empty. Any parishioners who'd shown up for the 7 a.m. Mass must have realized it wasn't going to happen. Again. Maybe no one at all had shown up, thanks to the 24/7 news cycle and social media.

At least Bongo was happy to see me, and as a reward I took him to the fenced area to run. The Starbucks coffee had held exhaustion at bay, but I hadn't slept in over 24 hours and needed more caffeine if I was going to function. I avoided my bedroom because that's where the black dogs lay in wait. Sunlight now lit the windows, so I made a pot of French roast and sat at the little table in the bright kitchen, thinking I needed to get my head around this thing before laying down.

Sophie should have been here by now, so I checked the rectory's ancient answering machine and sure enough, she'd left a message saying she wasn't feeling well and wouldn't be in today, and maybe not tomorrow. Since I'd used the same dodge on Friday, I couldn't really blame her. Out in the yard Bongo barked enough to let me and the rest of the neighborhood know he was ready to come in. I fetched him, poured some kibble in his bowl, and got my coffee mug. While the beagle crunched and gulped his way through breakfast, I sat down in the sunlight and decided it was finally time to face the music. I got out my phone.

Whatever else you might say about the Internet and social media, it is efficient. A member of our parish council who worked for a computer software company had volunteered his time to help with the parish's digital needs, and so became Gary the IT Guy. He had warned me not to put my personal cell number on the parish website, but I had insisted. As St. Al's only priest, I had to be available if people needed to contact me in the wee hours of the night. It didn't occur often, but it did happen.

Gary could now claim vindication. The app showed 133 new emails, and seven new texts. I slumped back into my chair, slurped more go-juice, and decided to check the messages first.

Five of the new texts were from Terry. They began as brief requests to call her but by the fifth had degenerated into a panicked declaration that she would come over if she didn't hear back from me soon. I twitched my thumbs on the screen and sent her a message that I was OK, was maintaining radio-silence until the diocese said otherwise, and that I'd call her as soon as I could.

The other two texts were from Mike and Jim on our Tulips group contact. They thanked Auggie for updating them, promised to provide any support they could, and Jim suggested we gather at his parish tonight. I texted the group back and let them know I appreciated everything, but had to lay low until Flannery removed his chubby foot from the back of my neck.

Then I began reading the emails. The first four were

positive, which I found touching. All promised to pray for me, although the one from a Knights of Columbus member seemed to add it as an afterthought, following an unhinged rant about the lying media, Hollywood, and the Democratic National Committee.

The rest were pretty much what I expected. A handful came from Catholics denouncing me for bringing shame on the faith. The majority appeared to be a stew of lapsed Catholics, folks who don't like organized religion, and garden-variety trolls. Tons of obscenities and altar-boy references. Three emails from the same person threatened to rally the digital mob to protest at the church. Those I would forward to the diocese as an FYI, but not today. Someone claiming to represent an advocacy group for sex workers named Protect Women Now! sent an email laden with F-bombs to inform me I've been added to their Predator A-List and "would never know a moment's peace for the rest of my life."

At the very bottom was the oldest email, sent even before this whole "misadventure" as Flannery so accurately described it, had begun. I didn't recognize the email address, but my heart leapt into my throat at the first words, "Sorry to bother you so late but Dad wanted you to know." It was Stan Schumacher's daughter. Emmy had died last night. While I was off playing hero, this sweet, good family entered the chasms of grief without benefit of clergy to console them.

My gut twisted, my shoulders sagged and the black dogs bayed hungrily from the bedroom.

CHAPTER 23

Do what you can do. I mentally stuffed my self-pity into a bag and sat on it, then called Stan. He answered on the second ring. Either he hadn't heard the news or he didn't care because he was genuinely, blessedly glad to hear my voice. I apologized that I hadn't been there and he apologized to me that no one in his family had thought to call me. We talked for a short while until a commotion erupted on his end – an infant wailed, a TV blared and what sounded like a drill or a mixer whined in the background.

"Father, we'd like to have the funeral Mass this Wednesday," he shouted over the racket. "Is that too soon? My son has to get back to Texas, and we aren't expecting many out-of-towners to attend."

"Wednesday is fine, Stan," I said. Normally we'd check the calendars but I wasn't going to do that to him.

"And you'll say a Mass, right? Nothing against Deacon Paul, but we want a requiem Mass for Emmy, not just a service," he shouted.

"Um..." Damn it, he hadn't heard the news, I thought. "I'll plan to, Stan, but I have to check into something first."

There was a pause, and I could almost feel the hurt coming through the phone against my ear, but he added,

"OK, yeah. Hey, I gotta go. Thanks for calling, Father."
We said good-bye and he hung up.

Do what you can do. I'd messed up so much, let
circumstances blow me around like a leaf against a brick
wall, but this I could do. I ventured into my bedroom
long enough to get my laptop, and sat at the kitchen table
with more coffee and typed. It was an email to His
Awesomeness, Auxiliary Bishop Flannery, and I copied
Wulfram. I didn't have Mwangi's email and wouldn't
have included him if I did.

I kept it short, after a deliberately obsequious
salutation. I informed Flannery that a key parishioner
had passed away and the family specifically requested I
do a Mass of Christian Burial on Wednesday. I said I was
sequestered in the rectory as directed, but thought it
might be in the diocese's best interest if I honored this
family's wishes. Since it was not a scheduled Mass, the
media would not know about it. The Schumacher family
was well-liked and very active in our parish, but not
politically or financially prominent, so again, not very
newsworthy. On the other hand, if it became known in
the parish that I was in residence but unwilling to say
this funeral Mass, it may inflame some who might take to
social media to complain, which in turn might interest
reporters. In short, it might be better to let me out of my
hole for an hour or two rather than attract attention.

I hit send before I could chicken out, then decided I
didn't know what to do next. If I read, I'd fall asleep, and
I wanted to avoid the black dogs' turf as long as I could. I
had already said the Divine Office as well as multiple
rosaries, including ones for my accuser Monique, and
yes, one for Will Freeman. But prayer can put you to

sleep just like reading. I had to do something active, which can be tough when you're under house arrest. Bongo would go for a walk, but not until later, when it was dark.

So, I connected my phone to a Google speaker and selected "dog music" on Spotify to mollify Bongo. Down the basement steps I went and headed to my little shooting range. I keep a Beeman P3 and a tin of Meisterkulgen target pellets in an old camera bag lined with foam rubber. It's a single shot, polymer gun that looks like a toy. But it's German-made and at 10 meters the P3 will produce a 5-shot group you can cover with a dime, provided you do your part. It's so good I've considered trying to replicate my old candle-shooting stunt, albeit at a shorter distance. But I always dismissed the thought because of older eyes, flabbier muscle tone, and almost no time to practice.

The Beeman was my sole air gun purchase, made several years ago. On a nearby shelf rested the grey case containing the .22 Smith & Wesson Victory that Terry loaned me, but I ignored it. I didn't have any ammo, and even if I did, shooting a firearm in the basement would have been deafening, hazardous to our homeowner's insurance, and probably illegal.

But there was that tubful of BB and pellet guns I'd inherited from Dad. He had boasted that nearly all his air guns could pass for the real thing. I had rarely opened the tub, practicing instead with my Beeman, but with time on my hands now it seemed a good idea.

It took some effort to excavate the long, grey plastic tub from under other boxes, and I'd forgotten its heft. My initial reaction on opening it was disappointment. Dad never saved the packaging for his airguns, so after he died my brother, John, had wrapped each piece in a blue shop towel soaked with Balistol, secured it with rubber bands, and packed it away. The tub breathed a solvent halitosis, and the contents looked like the kind of oily rags featured in 1950s fire-hazard brochures. But then I started unwrapping.

First, I hefted a Colt M1911, the iconic handgun of US troops from World War I through Vietnam. Next, in a genuine leather case I found a gleaming German Luger so realistic I had to pop the magazine to make sure it was an air gun. Dad had collected replica handguns from every major nation that fought in WWII. His collection also boasted four different cowboy six-shooters, with realistic cartridges visible in each cylinder. The tub also held a few replicas of rifles and modern handguns, including the huge Smith & Wesson M29 made famous by Clint Eastwood in the Dirty Harry movies. Yes, I admit it, I aimed the massive revolver at a chipped figurine of St. Jude and recited Eastwood's famous line, "This is a .44 magnum, the most powerful handgun in the world, and it can blow your head clean off." St. Jude appeared unimpressed, perhaps due to the chips.

In the bottom of the trunk was a shoe box filled with tins of lead pellets and BBs, and a 40-count box of Crosman CO_2 capsules. And thank goodness, a thick manila envelope bulging with manuals, without which I'd have no idea how these things worked. These were among my last links to the old man. Even today, in my mind's eye I can still see him in his basement, sitting at his hobby bench that smelled faintly of mildew, Balistol and pipe smoke, his air guns displayed on a pegboard behind him, explaining his plan to replace the furnace himself, all the while rubbing his pant leg where a compression sock bit into his swollen calf.

I set the Dirty Harry gun aside, and began riffling through the envelope for its manual when the doorbell rang and Bongo got to barking.

"Range day is done," I said to no one, set the envelope down, and headed up the stairs. I was almost at the top when it occurred to me maybe I didn't want to know who was at my front door. I imagined a TV camera man staring back at me through his lens, hovering over the shoulder of a primped and perky brunette with a microphone. But Bongo would not stop barking or scratching the wood door until I least peeked out the glass. I did and saw no reporter or camera man on my front stoop. I would have preferred them to the visitor waiting there.

I let go a sigh, made a useless attempt to hush Bongo and hooking my forefinger into his collar, dragged him back and opened the door for Fr. Mwangi.

CHAPTER 24

"We have the rectory to ourselves," I said to the canonist as we walked into the formal dining room, but he followed me into the kitchen where I'd gone to get us something to drink. "Coffee?" I asked.

"Tea, if it isn't too much trouble," he replied. "A little milk and sugar, please."

"Sure," I chirped and swirled the kettle on the stove to see if it held water (how long has that been stagnating in there), and decided to be nice and get fresh from the tap. I put it on the stove and set the blue flames so high they licked the kettle's bottom. Meanwhile Bongo had replaced his semi-threatening bark with tail-whipping enthusiasm and sniffed at my guest's ankles. Mwangi clearly was uncomfortable, but did his best St. Francis and gave Bongo a tentative scratch behind the ear. As every dog owner knows, canines can tell when people don't like them so they become extra friendly in a vain attempt to change hearts and minds.

"Perhaps he needs to relieve himself," Mwangi suggested. I took the hint and led Bongo by his collar out the door. "Good boy," I whispered as I frog-marched him to the fenced-in run. At least one of us could get the better of a canon lawyer. The beagle gave me a panting smile, which broadened when I produced the rawhide stick he knew I had in my pocket. I handed him the reward and he trotted away with it, head held high, as though it was a blue ribbon from the Westminster Kennel Club.

When I returned, Mwangi gave me an appreciative nod. "Americans are so invested with their pets," he observed.

"I'm afraid we are," I admitted and waited for the lecture on shamefully spoiling dogs and cats while children starved around the world.

"It is an endearing quality in your countrymen," he offered. Ohh-kaay, I thought, not quite sure where he's going with that, but I'll smile as though it's a compliment.

"It's very kind of you to stop by, Father."

He slid two hands together as though shining something.

"Bishop Flannery sent me," he said. The black eyes cooly assessed me as he spoke. Which would it be, I wondered: defrocking or an excommunication trial? Well, Flannery sent a lawyer, so what does that tell you? I suddenly felt incredibly, overwhelmingly, tired.

"He shared with me your email from earlier today, in which you asked to say a funeral Mass." I nodded weakly, but said nothing. I felt myself sinking, and what was worse, I didn't care. The black dogs are gonna eat well tonight, I thought.

"Bishop Flannery did not accept the logic of your arguments," he said, and the tea kettle interrupted him with its shrill whistle. I began to rise when Mwangi continued. "Not until I explained them to him." I stepped over to the stove, clicked off the burner and turned back to him.

"I'm sorry I haven't had much sleep. I'm not following you."

Mwangi nodded and said gently, "You will say the funeral Mass for your parishioner. Bishop Flannery has agreed."

I felt so relieved I slumped a bit against the kitchen countertop.

"That's wonderful news," I said.

"Is it?" he replied, a touch of school teacher in his voice. I found the Lipton tea bags, and drowned one in boiling water from the kettle.

"Are you monitoring the news?" Mwangi asked. I shook my head.

"It is not as bad as the auxiliary bishop thinks, but you should prepare yourself for unkindness."

I nodded and told him about the emails I'd seen so far. That reminded me that I hadn't checked my phone for a while and I took it out of my pocket. I couldn't believe my eyes.

"Eighty-three new ones," I mumbled. "That's just in the last couple of hours."

He nodded. "The first days will be the worst, but something new will seize their attention. Not all of them, of course. There may be those who see in you a chance to push their agenda. I think the tea has steeped long enough."

This guy probably had experienced high tea at the Vatican, but here in the 'burbs you get 2% milk and Splenda. He thanked me, nonetheless. I filled my mug with lukewarm coffee and sat down. "What agendas?"

Mwangi shook his head. "You know your local

politics better than a traveler such as I. It could be women's rights, or anti-Church groups." He shrugged. "It may go the other way, arch-conservatives saying you are proof of the ruin brought by the Second Vatical Council."

I nodded. The first batch of hate mail had given me an inkling, and now Mwangi confirmed it.

"If either of these learn you will say the funeral Mass, they may try to use it. Bring signs and bullhorns to protest. And they will call the TV people first, promise them good video."

I shook my head. "I don't want to inflict that on the Schumachers. They're kind, decent folks. I'll call Stan today and explain the situation, tell him we'll get another priest—"

Mwangi shook his head emphatically. "No. Do not do that, Thomas. Leave this in God's hands, and do as you planned. He will not desert you. This is part of your formation. In this furnace you are being forged into the priest He needs."

It was my turn to shake my head. Mwangi had no idea what he was talking about. I was already a cracked, hollow clay vessel. Much more heat and the Big Guy was going to have a pile of shards in His hands.

Almost as though he read my mind, Mwangi added. "Is this not why you were subjected to a painful time in the seminary? From which you emerged stronger. You do not see it but those who know you well do. In fact, one said he thinks of you and a quote from the American writer, Hemingway: 'The world breaks everyone, and afterword many are strong at the broken places.' God is tempering you like steel, Thomas. He is shaping you. All

He asks is your trust. He will never desert you. Take courage from that. Set your face like flint and be at peace."

I looked up at that last line and my jaw dropped. No way, I thought. Then an idea popped into my head.

"Did you get a new phone when you came to America?" I asked.

For the first time since I had met him, Mwangi's studied coolness melted with a wide smile. He pointed a finger at me.

"Very good. You see, Thomas, even though you are exhausted your mind is still quick. Yes, the embassy in Washington arranged one for me."

We were silent until I asked, "Why that verse?"

He spread his hands. "I thought it would help."

"It did. It truly did," I said. "Thank you."

Mwangi nodded and smiled again, but it slowly slid from his face.

"I have given much thought and prayed earnestly for clarity about your dilemma. Thomas, it may be this misunderstanding with the prostitute came from the Holy Spirit, not from the Enemy."

I shook my head in disbelief. "I don't see how that could be."

"You are a good priest," Mwangi said slowly, staring at his mug and running his thumb against its rim. "I know this from what others have said about you, from your own words in our meetings ...and from your well-intentioned, if not fully thought-out, actions. With the blessings of the Holy Spirit, Thomas, perhaps you will be a great priest in your little corner of the world. I am sure you will lead many souls to our Lord. And I think, perhaps, you will inspire others to vocations."

Before I could voice the protest that formed on my lips, Mwangi raised his eyes to me and they were no longer smiling.

"And that makes you a worthy target for the Enemy."

CHAPTER 25

The sun shone cheerfully through the kitchen window, lending a delightful autumn light to the room, but I got a cold chill staring at the African priest.

"I hope you will remember the Isaiah verse and find comfort in it in the days ahead," Mwangi said. "But more important is another verse. Take this one to heart, Thomas, and pray and meditate on it every day. Luke 22:33," he intoned, his musical accent lending an almost biblical air to the words, "'Simon, Simon, behold, Satan has asked to sift all of you like wheat.'"

Mwangi cocked his head at me. "This business with the woman last night. I believe the Holy Spirit permitted it to occur to open your eyes. Yes, the devils will cause you pain because of it, and will shake the faith of some. Both are serious matters, but perhaps a necessary burden to prevent a much greater calamity."

He shifted in his seat and leaned in toward me, and the priest's voice dropped slightly. "I disagree with Fr. Wulfram's hope that the Penitent is lying. This has the feel of a powerful evil at work. A man is murdering others for sport. Why then would he reveal himself to a priest in the confessional? What good does it do him?"

I replied, "I believe he genuinely sought absolution as a way to bring this to an end."

"Yes, and he could do so if he followed your instructions to speak outside the sacrament. Yet he insists you break the seal of the confessional Why?"

I didn't have an answer. The same question pricked me over and over, but I had not arrived at a satisfactory answer. Mwangi, however, appeared to believe he had.

"I grew up in Nairobi, my country's capitol, but we often visited my grandfather in the countryside. I loved to listen to my *babu's* stories of the old days. He was born in a small village in the 1930s and as a boy worked on a coffee plantation. He and his brothers walked through the bush to get there and to return home.

"One night a leopard stole a goat from a herdsman in their village. The beast saw how easy goats are to catch, so it came back again and again. The herdsman could not have this, so he and his kinsmen waited for it one night and drove it away with fire and spears. The leopard departed for a time, but returned and stole another kid goat."

Mwangi tapped a finger against the table top. "When a leopard takes an animal, it kills it swiftly. Then it carries the carcass into the tree branches where hyenas or lions cannot steal it, and eats its meal in peace.

"But this night, the leopard did not kill the kid. It carried it into a tree, where you could hear the poor animal cry in pain and terror. The herdsman saw this as an opportunity to find the leopard and kill it, but none of his kinsmen would go into the bush at night. Finally, one young fellow who wished to prove himself a man volunteered. He carried a torch, and the herdsman took a spear and machete, because the British did not allow our people to have guns.

"His kinsmen built a large fire and waited for the men to come back. After a while, they heard screams from the darkness, and the two did not return. The next morning a party of men with spears and blades went to find them. They found the youth's body close to the village. A bite had pierced the back of his skull and he had fallen dead. A tracker followed the beast's paw prints to the herdsman's body, or what was left of it, under a thorn bush. The leopard lurked nearby, they could even hear its growls, but in daylight the cat dared not challenge so many spears. The kinsmen got the herder's remains and returned them to the village, with the boy's body as well."

Mwangi looked at the window. "My *babu* said the tracker was very good, and could read the ground. He said the leopard had not been in the tree when the herdsman arrived, but had lain in ambush and leapt upon him when he arrived to rescue the kid goat. The boy must have fled and the leopard ran him down.

"That very night, the leopard returned and rampaged through the goat herd. It killed several and scattered the rest. No one dared go into the night to stop this, because the cat was now a *mla watu*, a man-eater, and would have no fear of humans."

Mwangi's grandfather would have been proud of his grandson's ability to spin a yarn. As the priest told his tale I could picture the scene, smell the stink of rotting vegetation from the jungle, feel the humid heat. I stood shoulder to shoulder with a kinsman, staring out at the wall of shadows while a fire crackled behind us, and took an involuntary step back when the first scream erupted from the dark.

"No workers went to the plantation that morning," Mwangi continued, "nor would they go when the British sent an open truck for them. For two days no one left the village. Finally, the British sent a hunter and men with guns. It took two more days, but they found and killed the leopard. My *babu* said he watched them carry it into the village, hanging from a pole. They loaded it into a truck and took it away."

He finished his story and took a long sip from his mug. When he was done, Mwangi stared at me with eyes like black marbles set into white stone.

"Thomas, do not be that herdsman. Beware the darkness, where the predator waits."

I shook my head and looked away. "He's a man, not a leopard," I mumbled.

"He is neither," Mwangi insisted. "He is the lamb astray, crying from the jungle, calling its shepherd. The Evil One lured him into the darkness to draw you there.

"This Penitent has surrendered his will to Satan, who works through him now. The Enemy wants you to break the seal, and so be destroyed yourself. Then with the shepherd down, he will rampage among the faithful. Yet if we do nothing, more of our sisters and brothers may die at his hands."

"Well," I said, trying for a jolly tone though my voice was dry. "I guess the devil didn't count on me being put on administrative leave…if I haven't been suspended already."

Mwangi shook his head, uncomprehending. "What are you talking about?"

"Flannery. You were there, you heard him say he was going to suspend me."

The priest slowly shook his head. "No, Thomas. Flannery has the–," he flipped a hand, "the PR people working on a statement. The bishop will stand beside you, and deny any wrong-doing. It would be counter-productive to suspend you now."

"The bishop believes me?!" I was stunned.

Mwangi gave a slow smile. "It is still in Flannery's hands and he was persuaded to belief," he said slowly. "The official view is you engaged in street ministry on your own time, and your actions were misinterpreted. Once that is officially released this afternoon, your administrative leave is revoked and you will resume your ecclesiastic duties."

I breathed a sigh, and allowed myself a smile. But then a thought came in like a November cloudbank and my relief faded.

"What about breaking the seal?" I asked. "Is that still in question?"

The canon lawyer's face lost some of its warmth. "Wulfram is preparing an argument in opposition to that." He gave me a stern look. "At first, I would have said yes. By acting on something told to you in the secrecy of the confessional, even though you did not reveal the Penitent, you violated the seal. But knowing now what he told you on his third visit..." Mwangi stared away into space. "I am no longer certain."

"No longer certain that the seal was broken?" I asked.

His eyes returned to mine. "No longer certain it was a confession. I believe now it was an attack."

*   *   *

171

Hours later, long after Fr. Mwangi had left and the buzzing of my cell had diminished to once or twice an hour, I watched the 6 p.m. news. To my astonishment I saw that the prostitution-sweep story had nearly fallen off the news budget. It lasted maybe 10 seconds, far behind stories about a protest at a school board meeting, an approaching blast of early winter weather, trade talks for a fan-favorite Guardians player, and a teaser about two pet monkeys that escaped from a house on the West Side and were still on the loose. Even I stuck around to the end of the broadcast for that one. Who doesn't love a good monkey story?

Around 7:30 p.m. my cell dinged and I saw that Cleveland.com had updated its story about the sweep. Nearly all the text focused on the Cleveland Clinic surgeon and a civil suit he was bringing against the police. One paragraph near the bottom was a short squib about me.

"The sweep also involved a priest of the Cleveland Catholic Diocese. Church officials say their preliminary investigation supports Fr. Thomas Pastor's claims he was not soliciting, but conducting a street ministry. The prosecutor's office did not respond to our questions if charges against the priest have been dropped."

I whistled while I slid a frozen pizza into the oven, called Terry and referred her to the Cleveland.com story to share with the family. My new email total had risen to 112, but that was a definite slow-down. I traded texts with my fellow Tulips, ate half the pizza, and took Bongo for a long, satisfying walk in the cool night air. Afterwards, I had the church to myself and spent two hours in prayer, overwhelmed by a sense of gratitude. It felt like a thousand pounds had been lifted from my back.

When I climbed into bed I felt better than I had in days and even taunted the black dogs with a cry of "back to the kennels, boys." But it didn't last. I woke in the night with my heart thumping and hair slicked with sweat. Panicked, I swept the darkness with my eyes and saw the green digital numerals of my clock reading 3:10 a.m. The realization I was in my own bedroom did not erase my fear because I could have sworn, I mean I was absolutely certain, I had heard a low, rumbling growl in the night.

Mwangi's story must have revisited my dreams, but I could grasp no lingering shred of nightmare. I lay still in my bed, listening and hoping it was merely Bongo in his crate wrestling with his own sleep-borne anxieties. But I'd heard that dingbat growl before and this was not the same. This had that big-cat, continuous throaty bubbling, like a slow-idling Harley-Davidson parked beside my bed. Logic works wonders in the light of day but loses its mojo in the dark. A leopard in a suburban bedroom outside of Cleveland was highly unlikely, but there are other kinds of predators, not of the mortal world, that can enter any home, any room, any mind. Closing my eyes, I blessed myself and began a rosary in my head. I hadn't prayed one this evening, and realized I had not yet said my daily prayers for Will Freeman as I had promised to do.

That's when it hit me, and I opened my eyes to stare at the shadowy outlines of my bedroom furnishings. The growl must have come from my subconscious – or my guardian angel, take your pick – trying to rouse me to the fact Freeman was still out there. And this was Monday, the night he'd said he would go hunting. All the satisfaction and relief I'd felt leaked away.

Yeah, it had been a whirlwind of a day, but in the end what had I accomplished? Not a thing. A killer still haunted the streets, I still could not report him, and my only option to stop his predations was spiritual immolation and vandalizing the faith I loved.

CHAPTER 26

After my morning shower and shave, I didn't bother with the hate email on my phone or scan the news. My mind kept revolving around the conundrum of what to do about Freeman, which overrode my depression and enabled me to function.

The 7 a.m. Mass typically attracts a dozen or so worshipers, but this morning there were only the small handful of regulars: two old couples, a guy I called Bob the Businessman because he dressed in a suit and always left right after communion, and Mrs. Santos, a sweet little Filipino lady who wore a white-lace mantilla to Mass. Afterwards I stopped by the parish office where Patty and Bridget practically jumped out of their skins when I gave my usual, "How's everyone today?" The two had been talking in low tones, Patty with head slightly cocked upward to look into the tall girl's face. If I didn't know better, I might have thought my office manager was giving our student receptionist a dressing-down. The kid looked unhappy, and Patty seemed unusually peevish. I went to the chest-high counter and reached into a wire tray holding yesterday's share of junk mail and bills.

"You heard about Emmy Schumacher?" I asked without looking up.

"Yes, terrible," Patty replied. "She's on the schedule for Wednesday. So sad for Stan, I hope he's holding up."

"He sounded OK on the phone," I said. "His kids got in quick. I was there Saturday and gave her the anointing, but she never regained consciousness."

"Oh good," Patty said, then touched her fingertips to her throat in shock at what she'd said. "I mean, good that she got the sacrament." I nodded and asked "Can you check with Mark to see if Marie is available to sing at the funeral Mass? I'd like to have our best for the Schumachers. Is Fletcher's funeral home handling the arrangements?"

Patty sat down at her computer, keyed in, and after a moment confirmed the fact.

"OK, could you call Dave and tell him there will be a graveside blessing, too, so I'll need a ride with his people."

"Um, father?" Bridget ventured in a soft voice. "There're some messages on the church voicemail that are, well, awful—"

"You know what," I interrupted. "Leave 'em. I'll go through them tonight to see if there are any I really need to respond to. The ones who are just blowing off steam, I'll hear 'em out then dump 'em."

"What about the emails?" Patty added. "There's not as many as I was afraid there would be…" she stopped at my nodding.

"Yeah," I said and tapped my hip pocket where I kept my phone. "Most of those folks went right to the source. Same thing, Patty. Forward them to my email and I'll handle them." She relaxed her shoulders in obvious relief, and with more than a little guilt I realized the ripple effect of my actions.

"Look, I apologize for the extra work and stress I've created for you guys." Both women shook their heads, but their downcast eyes acknowledged the fact. "It was a stupid thing for me to do. It's not like I don't have enough work around here, but I go off to try to save the world, too. I'm sorry to put you through this. You really are the best.

"I'll probably hear from the bishop's office again today," I added, "and if not, I'll check with them." A shadow of concern crossed Patty's face, so I hurried on. "The diocese is going to issue a statement supporting me." Boy, that felt great to say.

"Bridget, maybe you should put the statement on our website," I said, then reconsidered before she could utter a reply. "You know what? Forget that. The bishop will probably tell me to keep my big, fat mouth shut for once and take whatever lumps come my way. We'll play it by ear but be ready in case we can make that addition."

I headed to my office and mentally listed the calls I needed to make, starting with Wulfram. If he recommended to the bishop that Freeman's confession was invalid, I saw no reason why I couldn't go straight to the police. On the other hand, if he concluded that the confessions were covered by the seal…what did that mean for me? Normally I would sit on my hands like a good boy and wait to hear from Wulfram, Flannery or even IBS, but I couldn't do that this time.

Wulfram's phone goes through Dolores, whose response to my greeting wasn't hostile or even frosty, but formal enough to convey disapproval. She put me through to the Wolfman anyway.

"How ya doin', kid?" Wulfram asked with enough bounce in his voice to raise my hopes. I told him about Mwangi's visit and how delighted I was to be released from house arrest.

"I haven't seen the statement the diocese sent out." I said. "Think I should ask?"

"That might not be a great idea. Let me see if I can get it, and I'll send it to you. Unless I'm told otherwise."

"Thanks Ken," I said. "Hey I appreciate everything you've done for me, but I'm dyin' to know what we're going to do about the Penitent."

He said nothing and for a moment I wondered if one of our phones had dropped the call. Then I heard him clear his voice.

"It's not certain yet," he said at last, drawing out the words. "From a theological perspective it's difficult to definitively say if the confessions were genuine or invalid. There are arguments for both sides. But I think politics will shove the theology aside. It's this damned legislation in Congress. The bishop doesn't want to give the bill's supporters any ammunition to use against us."

Wulfram cleared his throat and lowered his voice. I could picture him alone in his office, hunched over in his chair behind his desk, cell phone pressed to his face. "Tom, you can't share this with anybody, OK? None of the Tulips, nobody. Don't even tell your dog."

"Ken, you got it. Not a word."

"This is blowing up," he whispered. "Flannery took it to Sanchez, who got cold feet and kicked it upstairs. It's under review by the papal nuncio in Washington."

"Get out!" I blurted. "The Vatican is looking at this?"

"Well, right now just its representative, but if he

decides it's worth their attention, yeah, Rome will know about it."

I was too stunned to speak, and felt a steel band tightened around my chest

"It's that damned legislation," Wulfram said again, his voice rising with agitation. "It's got the bishops absolutely freaked out. Some are calling it the camel's nose. The conservatives are painting an apocalypse over it. They're claiming if this gets through, the Left will come after our schools and hospitals, get rid of the tax exemption, and bleed the Church white. They're talking like it's the French Revolution all over again." When I heard that, my chest loosened slightly. The one thing guaranteed to get the Wolfman worked up and off-track was Left/Right politics. This had that feel to it, so maybe the situation wasn't as dire as he painted it.

"What do you think will happen? With our problem, I mean, not the Congress thing."

Wulfram's breathing settled down over the phone. "Well," he said pensively. "I dunno, Tom. My perspective is the circumstances point conclusively toward inauthenticity, but without questioning the Penitent as to his motives, it's tough to get a declaration of invalidity. It's kind of a push."

"So, what then?" I asked.

"Stasis," he muttered. "No movement either way. You can't go to the police, but your activities Sunday night do not constitute an actionable offense against doctrine. And frankly that's the scenario we should pray for."

"What do you mean?"

Wulfram sighed. "I don't have a good feeling about this, Tom. I see this going the other way. If the nuncio leaves it in Sanchez's lap, my guess is the bishop will let politics sway him. He'll declare the confessions valid, that the seal must be maintained, and we are unable to confirm or deny anything about this man's activities. That means your actions on Sunday were a deliberate and punishable violation of the seal."

"Punishable how?" I managed to get out. "Excommunication?"

Wulfram was silent for a very long time before finally saying, "Possibly. But even if it goes that far, remember, there are two kinds of excommunication."

"Wait, what?"

"What is it with you guys," the Wolfman fumed. "Why do we bother trying to teach you anything? *Latae sententiae* versus *ferendae sententiae*. Remember?"

"No, obviously, I don't," I shot back. "Ken, I'm sorry, this is really intense. Could you just give me the Sparknotes version?"

He harrumphed. "I hate that you guys use those. OK, here's the skinny: *latae sententiae* is automatic, it happens when the breach takes place. But it remains in the forum of conscience, meaning it's not public and you quietly seek absolution. And circumstances are considered, such as your mental state, if alcohol or drugs clouded your judgment, the degree of identification, that kind of stuff. The penalties can be as light as a temporary suspension from hearing confessions. But that's the minimum and least likely. It ramps up from there. You could lose the faculty to hear confessions for good. You could be stripped of your pastorship. The bishop could keep you from ever serving at a parish again."

That steel band around my chest constricted a little

more at this news. "What about the other one?"

"*Ferendae*. That's the big enchilada, Tom," the Wolfman said softly. "It's applied when the facts are in dispute, like your case. That means a public judicial or administrative process."

"How public is public?" I asked.

"Very," Wulfram said and sighed. "Look, I'm not gonna mislead you, Tom. Even if found innocent, nine times out of ten – actually more like 9.9 times out of ten – the priest's reputation is destroyed. To the point that their bishop can't assign them anywhere. They usually encourage the priest to seek a dispensation from Rome from the obligations of the priesthood."

"What?" I gasped.

"You'll be laicized. Back to being a member of the flock, not a shepherd. And that's if you're found innocent. If the decision is guilty of intentionally breaking the seal, you're automatically laicized and barred from the sacraments. You'll remain in a state of grave mortal sin."

"No chance for absolution?" I whispered. The Wolfman must have heard the dread in my voice.

"Oh sure," he said, his voice brightening a bit. "The Apostolic See in Rome will consider remittance of excommunication if there is true remorse and repentance by the guilty. And like I said, extenuating circumstances are factored in. But just like in criminal law, Tom, appeals are a longshot. What does it tell you that the department responsible for judging remittance is called the Apostolic Penitentiary?"

"You're kiddin' me," I groaned. "So there's no way to have the excommunication lifted other than through this penitentiary thing in Rome?"

I could hear his breathing as he pondered it. "I believe there is a circumstance under which your confessor can lift the excommunication and grant absolution."

"You mean like you?" I snatched at this hope.

"Yeah, yeah in theory, I could. If I determine you are clearly and absolutely remorseful and repent breaking the seal, I could grant absolution. Under this one, particular circumstance."

"Which is?"

He paused a long time.

"You'd have to be on your deathbed."

CHAPTER 27

As is almost always the case in Northeast Ohio, the mercurial weather pranked the local TV forecasters. Wednesday morning brought none of the predicted snow squalls or even flurries, but it did bring wind. Gusts tore the past-peak leaves from branches and flung them in brown cyclones against walls. Sometimes the wind spat a splatter of cold rain while the leaden sky guaranteed a cheerless day. In other words, perfect weather for a funeral.

The dozens of cars in the church's parking lot that morning gave testimony to Emmy Schumacher's fine character and quality of life lived. Few things are sadder than a funeral Mass with only two or three people seated in the first two pews. The church was almost half-full, which is very good for a weekday funeral. Grey hair and wrinkled faces predominated but younger generations were represented, too. Guys and gals in jeans, as well as men in dark suits and women in black pantsuits. Even a handful of small kids attended, including one boy wearing a clip-on tie and his sister in what was probably her Easter dress.

Emmy's casket rested on a bier in the back of the church when I got there with the three retirees in cassocks and surpluses who volunteered as altar servers for funeral masses. The processional down the main aisle had to wait for Stan to emerge from the bathroom. During the delay I chatted briefly with his son and daughter who smiled and maintained that weird, semi-cheerful bravado we seem to expect from the immediate family at a funeral. Then Stan appeared, neat as a pin in his charcoal grey suit, though his eyes were rimmed red. He held it together as I gave him a hug and whispered, "We're gonna give Emmy the good-bye she deserves." He nodded, wiped his eyes, and joined his family.

It was as good a funeral Mass as ever I officiated. Marie was in fine voice as cantor and when she sang "Amazing Grace" the whole congregation joined in, with a few coughs and sobs audible amid the music. Emmy had earned renown for her bountiful vegetable gardens, which made for an easy homily using a theme of seeding, fruitful harvest, and rebirth.

So many vehicles joined the funeral process to the cemetery that once there, two mourners in suits took it upon themselves to direct parking on the narrow winding road. We waited as the crowd swelled and eventually encircled us. The cemetery crew had erected a canopy large enough for the coffin, immediate family, and about a third of the crowd. Lumpy green astroturf spared our shoes from the grave dirt gone muddy with last night's rain, but nothing shielded us from the wind gusts buffeting faces, defeating hairspray, and tugging at the heap of long-stemmed flowers piled on the ground in front of the coffin. At least the rain held off.

Dave Fletcher, the funeral director, gave me a thumbs-up from the back to indicate the crowd was in place. I raised my hand and thanked everyone for coming to the graveside.

"Let us pray," I began.

"Not with you, whoremonger!" a female voice shrieked. The crowd gasped and people twisted and turned to see who shouted. I stood there, mouth agape until I caught Stan's stricken face and regained my composure.

"In the name of the Father, and of–"

"Shut your filthy mouth," the voice screeched again. To my left, a thin, older woman stepped out from the wall of dark jackets and coats. The wind whipped her medium-length, coal black hair to reveal almost an inch of grey roots. Her dark-blue coat with a faux leopard collar fluttered unbuttoned, displaying a burgundy pantsuit beneath. Gold flashed around her turkey neck in links too large to be anything but costume jewelry. Despite the thick eye-shadow and penciled-in eyebrows, her eyes were little more than slits. Her mouth, however, had plenty of room.

"Get out of here, pervert," she shrieked. "Go back to your hookers downtown." She jabbed a knobby finger at me. "The bishop covered for you, but he's not foolin' nobody. You're a false priest and don't belong here."

It took my astonished brain a moment, but a name clicked: Lena Lacagna. I'd heard stories of how years ago she and her late husband had been a power couple at St. Al's. They ruled parish council, chaired committees, and led fundraisers. I'd also heard how Lena terrorized teachers and administrators when her kids were enrolled at the school, and was once escorted out of the stands at a CYO basketball game. The old-timers in the Knights council shook their heads at the mention of her name.

But her day had passed, and to me she was merely another older face in the pews, part of a gaggle of grannies who stood on the sidewalk after the 9 o'clock Mass, gossiping and debating where to go for breakfast. In fact, I'd never spoken a word with her.

But she was talking to me now. Bent forward at the waist, she stalked toward me and jabbed the air with her finger as she spoke.

"You're an embarrassment. You made us a laughing stock on the news, you pervert! That's what they should call you, Pervert Pastor. You're no priest," she shouted and with a flexibility borne of fury, bent down and thrust her hand under the edge of the astroturf. She came up with a handful of mud and flung it at me. I twisted and dodged, most of the spray hitting the back of my shoulder, but a gooey gob slid past my chest, leaving a brown trail across my black shirt. For a second time, I heard a gasp rise from the mourners.

"Look at him. Now he's as filthy outside as he is inside. Get him out of here. Bring us a real priest to lead the prayers!" she roared.

A jostling in the crowd nearby made me think someone finally was moving forward to contain Lena. Instead, I saw another old woman, shorter and stouter than Lena, push through the crowd while tugging on an elbow, and she succeeded in extracting a white-haired man in a long black coat. It was none other than Fr. Scarpelli.

Pink scalp was visible beneath thin, disheveled hair, and thick, black-framed glasses with broad lenses gave him an owlish look. A broad expanse of even, white dentures lit up his face in a smile. He waved with both hands like a politician at a campaign rally, and limped over to me. The rotund older matron helped him along, glancing at Lena and shooting an evil look at me as Scarpelli stepped alongside.

"This is not good, not good," Scarpelli said to me confidentially, almost consolingly. "This family, they should have a serene funeral for their father."

"Mother," I said. "It's the mother."

He smiled and nodded like he was soothing an idiot. Scarpelli raised both hands and touched them lightly on my shoulder. "You can go, my son. I'll take over here and do the blessing. It'll be alright." Before I could reply, the stout woman beside him picked up the holy water vessel with its sprinkler, and pressed it into the old man's hands. He beamed at the touch of the metal and nodded vigorously at her, then at me.

I looked past him at the family. The daughter was bawling into her hands, and Stan had an arm around her. The son, a slightly taller, prematurely bald man with a brown beard, glared in our direction but I couldn't tell at who.

"Throw him out! Throw the pervert out," Lena shouted.

"Lena, Lena," Scarpelli hushed, patting the air with his free hand. "It's OK now. Everything is OK now."

"Go home, pervert," came another shout. "Go back to your whores." It was a woman's voice, but not Lena's. It came from the other side of the crowd. Scarpelli turned toward me and I saw he had looped around his neck a purple stole, the thin strip of fabric that symbolized priestly authority. His accomplice again held the holy water bucket, and the old priest pulled from his coat pocket a brown booklet titled "The Rite of Christian Burial," which he flipped at me in a shooing motion. "Maybe you stand in the back, eh. It won't be long. Go ahead, I'll take care of this."

He turned and with a grand gesture, slowly crossed himself as he shouted in Latin, "*In nomine patris, et filii, et spiritus sancti...*" The mourners had no idea what was going on but when it comes to ritual, you can count on Catholics to follow a priest's lead every time. The crowd crossed themselves and most lowered their heads.

I might have done something. I might have pushed the old buzzard aside, grabbed the holy water pot and crowned Lena Lacagna with it. But that second voice, another person in the crowd, had picked up the taunt. In that moment it wasn't only Lena, it was all of them. That's what they all thought of me. Pervert Pastor. And I looked at Stan, still comforting his daughter while his son whispered to him. Emmy's funeral had turned into a circus, and the only way to end this farce was for one of the clowns to exit, stage left. Sidling backwards, I edged past a few shoulders and stepped through an overlap in the canopy. Then it was just me beneath the grey sky, isolated from everyone by the shiny green plastic wall. I listened as Scarpelli read the blessing, repeatedly referring to the deceased as "Ellie" instead of Emmy.

I would have sunk straight into the ground then, if I could. But I would have liked a cigarette first.

CHAPTER 28

For most of the ride back the funeral director and I allowed an awkward silence to fill his polished Cadillac, its interior intoxicating with the faint, warm scent of leather shampoo. Finally Dave broke the spell as we waited at one of the last stoplights before St. Al's.

"Sorry about that BS back there."

"Why are you apologizing?" I replied. "If anything, I should apologize to you. And to the Schumachers."

"You? No. Lena's always been a piece of work. We did her husband's funeral and it was a nightmare. Her kids are as bad as her. You know, my wife's family is Italian and her parents speak it pretty well. Guess what lacagna means in Italian." I shrugged, not really caring but thinking it sounded like lasagna.

"It literally translates to 'the bitch.' Honest to Pete, I googled it. That's what her name means in Italian."

"Lena the bitch," I murmured, and could not suppress a grin.

"No, you gotta do it right," Dave said, and I turned to see him take his right hand from the wheel, press the back of it under his chin and flicked it at the windshield. "*Ehhhh, Lacagna,*" he spat with an exaggerated Italian accent. "*Lena é una stupida stronza.*"

I shook my head and gave a hearty chuckle. Dave

deserved it for that bit of kindness but inside I was dying. I wanted nothing so badly as to go to my bedroom, shut the door and drapes, and dissolve. Dave's decades in the service industry made him an expert at reading people and he saw through my fake mirth.

"Hey, I've got to go to the social hall to manage things but I can drop you off at the rectory," he suggested.

"That would be great, thanks."

He parked his beautiful ride at my front door and I walked around to his window and held out my hand. When he accepted it, I asked, "What do you think, Dave? About this whole thing." We both knew I was talking about Sunday night.

He gave my hand a shake and released it. "In my business, I meet a lot of priests, ministers, even a rabbi once. I know a good one when I see one. That's you." What a balm his words would have been, if only he had stopped there.

"And since you asked, I'll tell you. I wish the pope and those bigshots in Rome would allow you guys to get married. We'd have more priests, better priests, and a whole lot less problems."

I smiled and nodded. So the answer was no, he didn't believe me. I thanked him anyway and gave the Caddy a tap as it pulled away.

The rectory was empty and I suspected I'd not see Sophie again. Couldn't blame her, who wants to risk guilt by association? I let Bongo out for a potty break, and headed for the high kitchen cabinet where I kept the bourbon. The digital clock on the microwave read a.m., but I was in a p.m. state of mind. When I clanked the bottle of Woodford Reserve on the countertop, the sound triggered a memory: Fr. Feister, my old therapist, sitting in his office chair with one, thin leg folded over the other, saying, "Alcohol offers us a Faustian bargain; a momentary escape from pain in exchange for a doubling of it later." It didn't sound like a bad deal at the moment, but somehow my better angel won out and I put the booze back. I am capable, from time to time, of making a good decision.

Bongo's barking reminded me he hadn't had breakfast, so I brought him in and while he gobbled kibble, I told him about the morning's fiasco. Some words were used that would need confessing later, but since it was only me, a beagle, and the Holy Spirit – Whom I'm sure has heard much worse – I didn't dwell on it. It was time to pray anyway, so I got my beads, knelt beside my bed, and got busy.

I still prayed a rosary for Freeman in addition to my others, and had made it a habit to say consecutive rosaries. Each one takes only about 20 minutes, but for whatever reason, my concentration crumbled by the second decade of the second rosary. Somewhere in the third Glorious Mystery my prayers got jumbled, I kept losing my place on the beads, and my head drooped. Twice I caught myself drifting off, and as they say, three strikes and you're out.

The combined clatter of my phone vibrating on the dresser while chirping the "phone call" alert woke me. I had crumpled into a half-kneel, half-sit on the floor and my cramped thigh muscles complained bitterly when I clambered to my feet. How long the phone had been ringing could be anyone's guess, but whomever it was had no intention of hanging up. When I looked at the screen, I didn't recognize the name at first, but then remembered it as the parish's IT guy.

"Hey Gary," I said, putting the phone to my ear. "What's up?"

"Hi father, I hope I didn't interrupt anything."

"Nah, not at all," I looked at the clock by my bed and couldn't believe my eyes. I had been out for four hours.

"Have you been…uh…are you checking your phone?" he asked.

"No, I haven't. I cleared most of the junk last night. There were a couple this morning. Has it picked up again?"

"Um, way worse. The kid who updates the parish website called me. She spotted it."

"What happened, did we get hacked?"

"No, no, nothing that sophisticated. Somebody's accessing the parish chat board to post a link on all the subgroups. The kid and I were able to scrub it, but the same person keeps reposting. I'm calling for your OK to block her throughout our site."

The cobwebs from my impromptu nap vanished. "That seems drastic. Who is it?"

"The email address is 'mammachichi13@aol.com.' We know who that is because it's listed in the parish directory. I mean c'mon, how dumb can you get? Chiarra DeVito. You've probably seen her, Father. Heavyset, older lady, dyes her hair jet black, dresses to the nines. Calls herself Chi-Chi. We see her at bingo almost every Thursday. She's in a group of three or four others who sit at the same table. She usually isn't a problem, it's the other one who complains all the time."

I knew without asking, but asked anyway. "Who is

that?"

"Maybe a sister or cousin, they look and dress alike. Pretty sure her name is Lena or Lisa, or something like that."

I sighed. What had I ever done to this woman? "Yeah, block her and erase whatever rants she put up."

He was silent for a moment. "It's not a rant, Father. It's a YouTube link. Somebody took video at the funeral this morning. They're trying to drive traffic to it, but like I said, they're not sophisticated. However," he let the tension hang for a split second, "all it takes is one savvy grandkid to help her, and this could go viral."

I stared at the wall across from me, too stunned to reply. Viral?

"Send me the link, Gary. No, never mind, I'm sure some kind soul already has," I added with more snark than was necessary.

"Sure, and Father, how about we take down your contact info from the web? Just for a few days. This'll be over by the weekend, you'll see. But for now–"

"Yeah, absolutely. Gary, you were right from the start. And you know what, I trust your instincts. If something comes up, use your professional judgement. Just keep me in the loop."

We ended the call and I looked at the email icon. I had cleaned it out last night and frankly, I was surprised and relieved to see only 17 new ones. Imagine my shock that only six of those had to do with the video, the others were spam and one late-comer to the Sunday news. But somebody had included the link and I opened it up.

The subject line read, "Pervert Priest Thrown Out of Funeral." The opening screenshot displayed the crowd of mourners. I clicked the start triangle and instantly the view wobbled, as if the camera-person had been jostled or struggled with something. The view panned over the crowd and past Stan and his kids seated morosely on folding chairs near the coffin. My black-clad figure was visible only for a second, the view swinging away rapidly as though to avoid contamination. It continued searching, then stopped. In the center of the frame stood Lena, staring right back at the camera. She might even have nodded, but it could have been the unsteadiness of the videographer. The focus stayed on Lena as I heard my own voice thanking the mourners for coming. At my words Lena transformed. Her eyes narrowed and a blood-red upper lip pulled up like a snarl. I watched, fascinated, as her shoulders rolled back to let her lungs fill to capacity, her fists balled against her blue coat, and then her body jerked forward to launch her insult.

From there the video stayed almost exclusively with Lena. It swung too late to document the mud splatter, but did catch me in semi-cringe (way to cover yourself in glory, Pastor). When the pudgy woman towed Scarpelli into view, the camera person tried to focus on him, but the image blurred out and jerked down at the crowd's feet. And then the view jerked again as a new voice, very loud, screeched, "Go home, pervert. Go back to your whores." I stopped the video there, scrubbed the progress bar back several seconds and played it again. I repeated this over and over until I was certain. Whoever recorded this also had shouted the insult. Her words were much louder than the ambient sounds, so the shouting had to come from very close to the camera. And why did the camera – well cell phone, it had to be a cell –

jerk just then? Almost certainly because whoever held the phone had flung the abuse.

I let the rest of the video play out. It focused mostly on Scarpelli, and thank God Almighty, did not pick up my craven exit. It stayed on him, picking up his mistakes with Emmy's name, then roamed the crowd perhaps in search for a missing pervert priest. After the crowd murmured "Amen" in unison, the picture jiggled again and went black.

I watched the whole thing a few times, then looked at the counter box below. To my utter shock, there were 12 thumbs up and 65 thumbs down. I scrolled through the comments section and slowly grinned. I'd love to see Lena's face when she read them. Only a small handful applauded her performance, and most of those were trolls with names marxxyman115 or vudubeotch12. The rest blasted Lena with comments like "There's no excuse for disrespecting a family's funeral," and "Jeez mee-maw, take your Xanax," and my favorite, "What a low-class thing to do. Why do white trash act like this?"

Lena's ambush had backfired, making her the object of scorn and derision instead of me. The Internet mob had spoken, and who was I to contradict them? I went to the kitchen, searched the fridge, and found a scotch ale. The sweet, strong liquid tickled my palate, and the tiny buzz it set off in my brain was fine, too. It had been a heck of a day, and a man is entitled to a little relaxation.

My phone buzzed, and I saw Terry's name. I emptied the bottle with a mighty chug and wondered if another scotch ale might be hiding in the fridge. But the cell phone chirred again, so I hit accept instead.

"Hey," I said brightly.

"Tommy are you OK?" anxiety pushed Terry's words into high octave.

"I'm fine," I said, drawing the words out. "How's you?"

"T, I'm serious. I just saw what happened at the funeral. What the hell is the matter with that old bitch?"

"Easy, easy," I said. So protective, my older sister.

"How can you be laid back about this?" she shouted.

"You obviously didn't look at the comments, Terry. Take another look, beneath the video. They're running like five to one in my favor, or at least critical of Lena. This has blown up on her."

"I didn't see it online. I saw it on the Channel 5 News."

"What?"

"Yeah. They had it on their 5 o'clock show and will probably run it again at 6. They're calling it 'Fracas at the Funeral.' Who is this woman they talked to?"

The happy little buzz in my brain evaporated. "They interviewed somebody?"

"Of course they did. The old bat who hit you with the mud. And some old priest, looked like he was half blind. Tommy, he threw you under the bus."

"Crap," I muttered. I walked into the living room with the phone still against my ear, and began hitting buttons on remotes because it takes three of them to get a picture to pop up on our old system. It opened onto ESPN, and I jumped to Channel 5, but they were interviewing a cop about a car chase.

"Tommy," Terry's voice came through tight but under control. "Have you talked with Fr. Feister lately? Maybe it's worth giving him a call. I looked him up online and he's still doing counseling."

"No, I haven't and what the hell, Terry. Why are *you* calling *my* therapist?"

"Because I figured you aren't. And anyway, I didn't call him," she said in a slow, irritated voice. "I said I looked him up. Do you still have his number? I can text it to you."

"No, thank you, I don't need him. This thing was looking like it was going to work out until this."

"Tommy, what's going on? What were you doing out there on Sunday? I know it wasn't a street mission like they say, I know you better than that. And I know you sure weren't out there looking for…ya know."

I had to quash an impulse to tease her with, "As a matter of fact, I was looking for hookers." Instead I said, "Terry, I still can't talk about anything – oh, wait, it's coming on. I'll call you back," I said and hit the red button ending the call before she could object.

The TV lit up with a still image of Lena in mid throw, with a chyron that did indeed say "Fracas at the Funeral." But it was only a promo, followed by a fat man with a jack-o-lantern on his head shouting about scary deals at his Honda dealership. I sat down in a recliner and checked my cell while I waited. The email icon now read 48. There were six new text messages, too. I scrolled through and saw that three were from Terry. One was from Mike, and two I didn't recognize. But before I could open any, the news intro music welled up and I set the phone down.

"A Catholic priest involved in a human trafficking controversy found himself facing an angry crowd at a funeral this morning," the anchor man gravely intoned.

"It wasn't a crowd!" I bellowed at the screen. "It was a couple of old yentas and a senile retiree. That's not a crowd!" Bongo trotted up beside me and gave two of his big, booming woofs. "You tell him," I said to Bongo and gave an appreciative scritch under his chin.

Lena's scowling face filled the screen, and even as a man of God I gotta say, the camera is not kind to her. Her make-up lost the struggle with the wrinkles, and in her righteous anger her eyes again narrowed to slits with a hard, mean glitter at their center. "If the diocese won't get rid of these perverts, then us people in the pews have to do it. We threw that pervert out of the funeral, and we'll throw him out of any other place he shows up. Until he's gone for good."

Her harpy image was replaced by a dazed Scarpelli, Polydent-white smile glowing and eyes all but lost behind Coke-bottle lenses. He held up both hands in front of him as though cradling an imaginary bowl of cherries, and his words came out hesitant and lost.

"You can't…ah…you know…so many good priests out there…we just, you know…we need to pray more…even for these lost ones whose sins give us all a bad name."

"Son of a bitch," I roared. I shouted a few other choice words over the anchorman's report, then had to back up the video when I heard him say "bishop's office." It turned out to be merely a no-comment from the diocese.

My phone-call signal chirped again and this time it was Mike.

"Hey, Tom," he said.

"I just saw it on the news," I shot back. "What is with Scarpelli? What'd I ever do to him, other than throw him a party every year on his anniversary?"

"The guy is senile, you know that," Mike soothed. "Did you see him at the Chrism Mass last year? He walked around with his fly down the whole time, even after people told him about it. I thought he was totally decommissioned."

"I thought so, too," I said. "You know what I think? I think he was a prop used by this clique of old ladies." Mike listened as I shared my observations from the video.

"Yeah, sometimes those tiny, hard-core groups will cut your legs out anyway they can," he said. "Geez, the TV guys made it sound like everybody at the funeral turned on you."

"That would be better TV, wouldn't it? It was three, Mike. Three. OK, four if you count Scarpelli. That's four out of more than a hundred. You know Dave Fletcher, the funeral director? He handled the arrangements and was there. Call him and ask."

"Hey, hey, easy. I'm not doubting you, Tom."

"Did you see the YouTube video?" I demanded. "Read the comments. I was–"

My phone alert chirped and I looked at the notification. My rage deflated, my shoulders dropped and I put the phone back to my ear.

"I gotta let you go. Flannery's calling."

CHAPTER 29

The alarm woke me at 5:45 a.m., and to my own amazement, I got up. Took a shower, shaved, put Bongo outside to potty, even made some coffee. The whole time I felt like a zombie, just going through the motions, but hey I was getting it done.

Morning twilight had not yet lightened the sky when I left my backdoor and walked to the church at 6:50 a.m. It was cold, had to be in the high 30s, and I could see my breath on the air in the yellow glow of a light post. I've always enjoyed the return of cold weather, and on the first frosty night or morning I'd blow a big blast of breath, marvel at the small, grey cloud and sometimes say, "Welcome back, old friend." Today I hardly noticed it.

The church held only three people: one old couple and Mrs. Santos. Bob the Businessman and the other elderly husband and wife must have departed for holier climes. After genuflecting at the altar, I stepped down into the aisle and rested a hand on Mrs. Santos' pew. I thanked them for coming, told them how God appreciated their devotion, but there would be no 7 a.m. Mass. In fact, I added, it was suspended until further notice. "Check with the parish office in a day or so, and they'll let you know when morning masses will resume."

Before I could turn, Mrs. Santos lightly tapped my hand with her fingertips. "You are a good priest, father. I will pray for you."

"Us, too," said the old husband from the other side of the aisle. "Every day."

I had expected frowns of frustration or irritation, but instead they showed me kindness and support. I could only manage a weak smile, thanked them, and scuffed my way back to the rectory.

With Sophie permanently AWOL, I'd need to find another housekeeper. Dirty dishes, mostly cups and glasses, crowded the kitchen countertop so I made soapy water and began washing. Anything to stay out of the black dogs' lair. With time on my hands now, that would be a challenge. After the dishes I found the vacuum. It took a minute to figure out how to release the handle, but to Bongo's alarm I began sweeping. In the living room I noticed a light film of dust on the furniture but decided it could wait.

Then it was time to say Mass. I attached Bongo's leash to his collar, took the bouncing beagle out to his run and let him go. As he snuffed his way across the lawn, I entered the church through a side door. I collected what was needed but halfway to the door set everything down, turned and went to the altar. I knelt beneath the big suspended crucifix, slumped back on my heels, and let a dark wave wash over me. Tears rolled down my cheeks and splashed onto my chest. I didn't pray, I didn't speak, I just let the shame and despair and self-pity pour out. When all that gunk finally emptied, I wiped my eyes with my sleeves, and looked up at His face. I really needed to see Him, the God-man who suffered torture and death for sinners like me, but His face wasn't there. This modern corpus was all smooth angles and artful shadows, as impersonal as a robot.

Back in my room, I cleared my dresser top and placed there the rectory's portable altar. The beautiful box of carved mahogany wood unfolds into a narrow platform for a small ciborium and chalice. I completed my preparations, lowered my bedroom window shade, and was about to close the door when Bongo wandered in, head down like a tardy parishioner skulking to a pew midway through the first reading. The dog curled up next to my bed, and I silently thanked God for overruling Flannery and sending me one attendee. Then I opened my Roman missal, the heavy, leather-bound book containing all forms of the liturgy throughout the year, and began the lonely business of celebrating Mass by myself.

CHAPTER 30

It was late morning, almost noon, when I heard the banging upstairs. After saying Mass, I had fed Bongo and took him outside again for some free time. Not feeling particularly productive, I went to the basement to fling pellets. I chose a Dan Wesson revolver, a gleaming chrome replica of the real thing, and lost myself in the cycle of breathing, holding, sighting, and firing. I even tried some two-handed, tactical-style holds and though I'd never admit it to Terry, produced a few six-shot groups the size of a quarter. Normally such a performance would have me whistling and feeling quite good, but now I examined the groups with an almost mechanical detachment. I got only one emotional rush at my indoor range, and it wasn't a good one.

When I loaded a fresh CO_2 cylinder and clicked the plastic grip back in place, it occurred to me only someone who really knew firearms would recognize this as a pellet gun. At five feet, even they might not be able to tell. Staring at the silver handgun, the thought popped into my head it would be an ideal tool to commit suicide by cop. No chance of actually hurting anyone, but if you point this thing at a blue uniform and thumb back the hammer, the last thing you'd see on this Earth is his or her muzzle flash. I shook my head and said aloud, "Where the hell did that come from?" I kept practicing, but my concentration was gone and the shots scattered across the paper.

Then banging began on the front door and would not stop. Almost gratefully I set the gun down, went upstairs and when I swept the door open, my stomach dropped into my shoes. On the other side of the storm door stood Stan Schumacher. He wore work boots, blue jeans and an ancient Carhart jacket, with yard gloves sticking out of the pockets. A grease-smudged John Deere hat sat on his grey head.

"Mornin' Father," he said as I swung wide the door. "Sorry to bug ya, but could you put the dog in the house for a while? I'm gonna clean up out back. Maybe run a lure for him to chase later."

"No, Stan, the leaves can wait. Go home, go to your kids."

"They're gone," he said. "Brian flew out last night, and Ginny left this morning. She was gonna stay, but I told her there's no point. Her kids had school, and I'll be fine," he lifted a corner of his mouth in a grimace. "As long as I keep busy. So I came here."

"I get it," I said, and reached for the hook beside the door and grabbed Bongo's leash. "Time for that knothead to come in anyway."

We walked to the fence and I looked at him. "Stan, I'm so sorry about yesterday. I almost got another priest to do the funeral, and now I wish I had. The last thing in the world I wanted was to bring any more pain to you and your family."

He shook his head. "Ya know, it's the darnedest thing.

The people who do good in this world are always apologizing, and the ones who do bad couldn't care less. The Mass was beautiful, Father, you did fine. The only person who did better than you yesterday was my boy, Brian. Did you hear about it?" I shook my head as Bongo trotted up at the sight of his leash. I clicked it on him and turned to Stan.

"Scarpelli and his crew tried to come to the lunch," he said, his face gone hard. "Can you believe the nerve of those people? I didn't see them, I was inside, but Brian was outside talking to somebody when he spotted them coming down the walk. God bless him, he laid into them. Lena started running her mouth and Bo Zipke told me he thought Brian was going to deck her. Big Jim showed up in his security jacket and escorted them back to their cars. Too bad nobody took a video of that."

He saw the look on my face and gave a hard shake of his head. "Don't take this on yourself, Father. Don't let them do that to you. Everything's gonna be OK. You'll see on Sunday. The church will be full like usual."

I sighed. "Stan, you can't tell anybody this, not yet. I won't be at Mass this weekend. The bishop put me on administrative leave. I'm waiting for the formal letter, then I pack my bags and go."

He shook his head, lips working but no words issuing from them. Then he blurted, "Goddamn it." His cheeks flushed red and an electric intensity lit his blue eyes. "I really mean that. I do. I hope and pray that God damns each and every one of them to hell. Starting with Scarpelli."

"No, no, you don't mean that," I said. Bongo tugged on the leash, but I couldn't leave Stan stewing in this poison. "And Scarpelli, I think he was a pawn in this, certainly not the ringleader. He's so feeble he can't remember to zip up his fly."

Stan glared at me, and turned his head to the side. He could have set a tree on fire with the anger flashing from his eyes. The more he suppressed his rage, the more explosive it became.

"Lena," he seethed. "Alright then, I'll fix her," he said, his words low and menacing.

"No, let it go," I said, and he snorted in reply. "C'mon, Stan. Leave it in God's hands, walk away from it."

"Easy for you to say," he mumbled.

"Ya think? Really, Stan?" I shot back. "I'm suspended, or the next thing to it, thanks to her. And that video they posted on YouTube will never go away. It'll always be there. So wherever I go, I'll always be the pervert priest with mud thrown on me. You think it's easy for me to let it go?"

Sometimes it takes fire to extinguish a fire. The unholy light in Stan's blue eyes faltered and dimmed. He gave a sideways nod.

"I'm not saying we can forgive them right now, but we'll get there," I added. "We'll work at it. We have to. It's what Jesus expects of us. It's what He does for each of us, every day."

Stan blew out his cheeks and frowned. "You know that part," he began, "where He says, 'Take up my yoke because it is easy and my burden is light.' I'm having trouble agreeing with that right now."

"You and me both, brother," I said and clapped a hand on his shoulder. "Go on, go suck up some leaves.

And Bongo's lure is in the garage. Do that thing where you pick it up so he loses the trail. It drives him crazy and should keep him out of my hair for a while."

Stan grunted and strode away, and I let Bongo drag me back to the rectory. Once inside I went to my office, turned on the laptop and tried to review the parish finance committee's third-quarter report. Numbers aren't exactly my thing but if I apply myself, they eventually make sense. Today, though, I almost gave in to a cynical impulse to ignore them because this was not my concern anymore. But you know how it is, when you start something it's hard not to see it through.

Thoughts about Freeman intruded on my concentration, too. This was Thursday, and didn't he say his wife would be back from her business trip by now? Had he done more killings these past three days? How many acres did he say he had, 80 something? Plenty of space to bury bodies.

The doorbell rang, Bongo raised his usual racket and I got up slowly. It might be Stan again, but somehow I knew this was Flannery's formal letter to back my bags. A morbid curiosity made me look out the window to see if they used FedEx or UPS. I didn't see either vehicle in the parking lot. Maybe it was Stan again, since the riding mower hadn't yet roared itself awake.

When I opened the door there stood Mwangi, a small, blue plastic grocery bag dangling from one hand. As he stepped inside, the canonist held the bag out to me. "Baraka Chai," he said. "Very good Kenyan tea. A parcel from my family caught up with me today, and I thought it a sign to instruct you on how to make a proper cuppa." I smiled at his kindness, and pushed back the snarky thought that as a condemned man, I'd rather have the traditional last cigarette before my execution.

Mwangi again preferred the coziness of the kitchen to the formality of the dining room, and Bongo followed us in. The African reached into his jacket pocket and produced a baggie holding a single dog biscuit. He took it out, but before Bongo could seize the treat, Mwangi closed his fist around it and backed the beagle into a sitting position. "That's a good dog," he said as Bongo gently took the biscuit, lay down and crunched it in half. Then the little beast suddenly snapped up his head, let loose with a long, yodeling howl erupted and leaped up. Bongo brushed past my legs and clawed at the back door. The drone of the mower filtered through the dog's commotion.

"I'm sorry," I told Mwangi. "He's too smart for his own good. He knows the mower usually means fun and games later, and that winds him up." I explained the lure process and Mwangi nodded reluctant approval. It took a few shouts to get Bongo to quiet down, then his nose recalled the Milkbone pieces and he returned to the priest's feet. Mwangi wagged a finger at the beagle. "You are very rude to ignore a gift from a guest," he said sternly. "Maybe I was wrong and you are not a good dog." Bongo ignored the rebuke, crunched up the treat, then trotted off to stand on his back legs at a window in hopes of catching sight of the mower.

Mwangi walked me through the process of making tea the Kenyan way and when we sat down to our mugs, I had to admit that Baraka Chai is to Lipton as Starbucks Sumatra is to Folger's Instant.

"Well, father, what brings you here?" I asked with the

slow delivery that indicated I knew very well what.

He said nothing but slipped a hand inside his jacket pocket and withdrew a white envelope. He placed it on the table and slid it to me without a word.

I left it where it lay and looked at the man. "I'm trying to understand why a cleric of your status is delivering mail for the diocese." A bitter thought bloomed in my head and flew out of my mouth before I could crush it. "Oh, I get it. Someday you'll be a bishop in Kenya, and this is a great chance to observe the disciplinary process up close."

He simply stared back at me, and I felt like a middle-school brat. A well of darkness opened inside me, but I managed a shred of dignity. "I'm sorry," I said with a head shake. "You don't deserve that. You've been nothing but kind to me."

The canonist said nothing and looked down at the table top. With a sigh I picked up my doom. They hadn't even bothered to seal the envelope, just tucked the flap inside. I pulled out a single sheet, flipped it open and stared at it for a long time. Finally, I looked up at the man seated across from me.

"This is an insurance bill," I said.

Mwangi picked up his tea, took an appreciative sip, and looked at me as a grin spread across his face.

"Oops."

"Oops?" I repeated.

He nodded. "In my haste, I must have picked up the wrong envelope." He tapped a fingertip on the table top. "I am leaving from here for a dinner appointment in Youngstown, so I am afraid the delivery of the proper envelope must wait until tomorrow. You should know the auxiliary bishop was incorrect in his instructions. By canon law, your administrative leave does not begin until you receive a written notice."

Mwangi leaned forward, and wrapped his long fingers around his mug. "Your bishop and his auxiliary have many responsibilities and concerns. They weigh what will produce the greatest good, or prevent the greatest evil. Therein lies an opportunity for the Enemy. He tempts our leaders with the sin of pride, to rely on their own judgment rather than humbly seek divine guidance. To place political considerations above theology. This is an affront to the Holy Spirit, a denial of our trust and faith in Him. Though it may seem imprudent in the moment, we must trust God over our own clever calculations. The foolishness of God–"

"–is wiser than the wisdom of men," I said to complete the verse. "What are you telling me, Isaac?"

"We have much greater concerns than factional strife within your parish. Your Penitent," he said. "He has been on my mind."

"On mine as well," I mumbled. "He may have killed again. That was his plan."

"I have an idea," Mwangi said, and unlaced his fingers from around the mug and spread them, "which no doubt occupied my mind and caused me to pick up the wrong envelope today." His lips held the faintest memory of that grin.

"The Penitent told you he would not come again, but I think he will. He cannot resist tormenting you, Thomas. Like those unfortunates whom he strangles and revives then strangles again to prolong their suffering, he wishes to extend your suffering as well."

His words held an undeniable ring of truth. An uneasy feeling crept up my spine, but a tiny flame of hope flickered inside my heart.

"So, what do we do?"

"My carelessness with the letter has bought you another day as an acting priest," Mwangi said, his eyes bright, "so let us put it to use. You hear confessions every Friday? I think you should do so tomorrow. By then I will have secured the proper letter and returned here to deliver it to you. But first I will join you in hearing confessions. Your parishioners may appreciate the option of two confessors."

Mwangi's slight smile became a large one. It occurred to me if he hadn't chosen to wear the black, he'd probably be wearing a general's uniform.

"Then perhaps we may trap a man-eater."

DAVID NYPAVER

CHAPTER 31

I initially felt enthusiasm for Mwangi's plan, perhaps because I was so desperate for any action to stop the killer. But then the flaws in his strategy began flashing like little red warning lights. The whole thing rested on Mwangi using my confessional while I took up residence in the "visiting priest" confessional. That was the cleric's brilliant master stroke. I judged our chances of success at slim to none.

First, Freeman would have to contradict himself and show up. Second, we had no idea how the killer would react at finding a different priest in my confessional. Would he be rattled and leave, or stay calm and give an innocuous confession? Afterall, he could rightly assume Mwangi didn't know his identity (we had argued over this point, but the canonist refused to allow me to describe Freeman to him). Or would Freeman relish a new toy to inflict his gruesome tales upon?

Mwangi was more optimistic of our chances, probably because it was his idea. I tried to warn him of Freeman's cleverness and cool demeanor. He might show surprise or even shock at Mwangi's presence, but so would every other penitent who came in expecting good ol' Fr. Pastor. Freeman would likely recover his poise immediately, maybe rattle off a litany of ordinary sins and slip back

212

into the shadows. The whole plan hinged rather tenuously on Freeman's arrogance and mania driving him to repeat his performance with Mwangi.

The cleric listened to my concerns, nodding at some. He explained he had researched the topic since first hearing my tale. Mwangi leveraged his Vatican credentials to get Zoom meetings with the Canadian researcher who literally wrote the checklist for psychopathy, and with a Brazilian who studied such maniacs in that country's hellhole prisons. Those conversations convinced him the Penitent would return because the same dark impulse that produced his crimes also would lead him back to me.

"These experts say you have become a bonus," Mwangi explained. "At first you were merely a safe outlet for him to boast. He wanted an audience, not absolution, they said. But in you he found an additional source of amusement. A psychopath craves dominance and control, often to the point of destroying his object. They agree he is doing so with you. It amuses him to twist and twist the handle of the vise he has placed you in. He doesn't care if you break faith with God, or watch in helpless distress as others die, as long as he can make you writhe.

"These researchers filter their observations through the lens of science," Mwangi said. "But you and I are God's servants, and we must also look for the Enemy's presence in the Penitent's actions. Look what he has achieved so far. He used your good heart to almost break the seal when you tried to warn the women. In doing so, you fell into his trap. You inadvertently created an example of a hypocritical, lustful priest." At those words

I recalled the older cop glaring at me with the eyes of one betrayed. "This in turn gave Satan and his dark angels the opportunity to whisper lies into the hearts of the old priest and the angry woman at the funeral, to stir up factions and strife within your parish." Mwangi made a rolling motion with his two hands. "It cascades, Thomas. Yet another, larger door opens for the Enemy. He now tempts the auxiliary bishop to place politics above faith and to unjustly punish you, under the rationale that doing so would silence you and deprive the Washington politicians of a useful tool. But politics is the Enemy's territory, not God's. This error in judgment might draw the bishop and Church into another hidden snare more damaging to the faithful than the others."

I felt absolutely miserable. It must have showed because he placed a hand on mine and said, "Thomas, you intended none of these things, and are blameless and without sin in their regard. I tell you this to open your eyes and see how the Enemy encircles us with his snares and traps. This is why we must try to lure your man-eater back, with you as bait."

The man's eyes were kind but unyielding. "If the Penitent returns, his actions may give us the definitive evidence we need to declare his confessions inauthentic." Mwangi nodded his head encouragingly. "Then the bishop may go to the authorities and give them the information needed to stop this man."

"He won't do it," I said. "IBS is too focused on the legislation. He'll sit on this while watching what happens in Congress."

"Then you and I will go to the civil authorities," Mwangi said matter-of-factly.

I gave a harsh laugh. "And provoke IBS? Maybe the Conference of Bishops? Not a smart career move for somebody with a bright future like yours."

"Thomas," he said with a warm, toothy smile, and shook a finger at me. "You are well-named, you doubter. How often must I remind you to do God's will and leave it in His hands."

CHAPTER 32

The next morning, I sat in the visiting priest confessional, listening to graupel pelt the window above me. Bongo snoozed at my feet, the only familiar feature in this small musty-smelling room. It felt chilly here, enough that I double-checked the window to make sure it was closed. A thick layer of dust on a nearby table betrayed the church mice's neglect of this confessional. But they weren't the only ones who'd been inattentive to detail.

Mwangi and I had overlooked a simple, significant factor in our calculations. A pervert priest may be not the first choice of respectable folk seeking to cleanse their souls. More than one little old lady had come to my confessional and frowned in disappointment when she saw I was the "visiting priest." I didn't want to jeopardize our trap by peeking out to see if Mwangi had any takers, but the church sounded awfully quiet this Friday. I made good use of my time, though, by praying for the sick of the parish.

The confessional's door hinges announced a new arrival with a low squeak. I closed my breviary and rested it in my lap, waiting to see if this would be an anonymous confession or face-to-face.

Freeman came around the corner, a black puffer jacket

making him look even pudgier than before. A huge grin split his face, and he pointed a finger at me triumphantly.

"I knew it," he said. "I knew you'd be here. Don't ask me how, I just did. You threw me for a second, when I came in and saw the lights on for two confessionals." Freeman unzipped his jacket and plopped down on the chair near mine. He reached down and gave Bongo a scritch on the head. "Hey pooch, ya miss me?"

"I thought you weren't coming back," I muttered.

He looked at me. "I lied," he said and laughed. "Hey, that's a confession, right? Does it count?"

"You're not even going through the motions anymore."

"Well," he scratched the fleshy underside of his chin. "I don't have much to confess, it's only been a week."

I could see the anticipation in his face, the desire for me to ask about his murderous activity, but I denied him the satisfaction. "Congratulations. You are regaining control over the temptations afflicting your soul."

"Nah, nothing like that," he said. "They postponed my wife's conference because of a labor dispute at the host hospital. So..." he threw his hands up in frustration. "She stayed home. No hunting season. And of course, that hospital and the union reached a new contract the night before the strike, so the conference was postponed for nothing. They rescheduled it for next week. She leaves Sunday morning, so I've gotta be patient." I saw his eyes go down to Bongo. "I did kill a dog, though."

"What?!"

Freeman raised his hands in defense. "Hey, purely an act of mercy. One of my wife's Frenchies is like 700 years old. She's got four of them, and this thing was ancient.

He had arthritis, diabetes, his thyroid was shot. Cost a fortune in lab work and meds, and the damned thing still whined all the time. He stank, too. She came home Tuesday and found him dragging himself around by his front paws, figured he'd had a stroke. She wanted me to take him to an animal ER. I told her no, we had a big fight, but in the end, I convinced her it was time. She insisted I take him to the vet to be euthanized. Ya know, that's so stupid. That would cost like $150 or $200 for something I could fix for 10 cents with a .22 bullet." He touched the back of his head, "Right there, flip the ol' off-switch."

"Is that what you did?"

He smiled at me and shook his head. "I found an even cheaper way."

Freeman watched for a reaction and despite my best efforts to deny him again, I could not stop a faint shake of my head.

"You know, enough about me," he continued. "I really came because I'm concerned about you."

The gall of this guy infuriated me. "This is a sacrament," I snarled. "And you're profaning it with your flippancy. If you want a social visit come see me at the rectory."

"No, no," he replied. "This seems right. This is where it all began. And I can't help but feel responsible. When I saw the news story about you getting picked up for soliciting," Freeman frowned. "You're not the hooker type. And definitely not the kind you find on Lorain Avenue. So I thought, if he's not scratching an itch, what's he doing out there?" He lifted an eyebrow like a disappointed TV dad. "You were trying to warn them, weren't you?"

Before I could think of a clever reply, he went on.

"That's against the rules, Fr. Pastor. If you didn't break the seal, you sure as hell bent it. You tried to scare off the hookers when you thought I'd be on the prowl. Like those pathetic bitches from PETA, out in the woods blowing air horns and ringing bells on the first day of deer season. C'mon, man, you're smarter than that.

"But what blowback, holy cow," Freeman shook his head. "Ya know, I really started to feel bad. I've got this awesome rootkit I created and installed it on your parish's server and in the diocese' system. Wow, the trolls were out in force Monday, huh? Then that whole deal with the funeral on Wednesday. What was that all about? I must have watched the video 20 times. Did you see it?"

"Yeah."

"Man, I watched your face, over and over. That was freakin' awful what they did." Honest to God, Freeman looked at me through his wire-rimmed glasses like he really did care. "Ya know, I saw something in your face that worried me and, sorry for being a snoop, I got your records from the diocese."

"You're lying," I closed my eyes and shook my head. "That's not possible."

He hung his head and his shoulders shook with a chuckle. "You haven't figured it out. I'm an IT engineer. Like wizard-level. I kick down security systems just to poke around. Most companies are easy, and non-profits like you guys," he snorted. "Your security is about as tough as cotton candy."

Freeman looked at me with something like sadness.

"I'm telling you this, Tom, because I know. I know all about you, man. The nervous breakdown when you were a student, the clinical depression. I know your therapist, Fr. Feister, I know you were on Fluoxetine and Sertraline, Xanax, and the rest. I know the whole story.

"Tom," he said with a gentleness that touched me. "I know that guy Flannery put you on administrative leave." He drew in a deep breath. "And I know something you don't." He paused and place a hand on my knee. "They're gonna do some weird-sounding thing. Laicize? I saw it in an email Flannery sent to the bishop."

Just as I thought. They were gonna pitch me under the bus, and I probably deserved it. The high-pitched whine of tinnitus suddenly shrilled in my right ear just like it did back in the seminary when things got bad. I closed my eyes and covered them with my hand. To my dismay, I felt the dampness of tears on my fingers.

"Tom, I put you in an impossible place," Freeman was saying. "If you break the seal, you'll be excommunicated. Doomed. But if you don't, more people will die. Because I can't stop this thing."

I looked at him, probably with red-rimmed eyes, and said in a choking voice, "You can. You can stop. You can save us both." And for a moment, just a millisecond, I thought I glimpsed in his eyes a flicker of humanity. Like a trapped figure in the window of a burning house before smoke overwhelmed and obliterated it.

"No," he said softly with a small shake of his head. "Not me, not anymore. But you, I can save you, Tom."

"How?"

He looked up for something, but didn't find what he sought. He got out of his chair and stepped over to the cardboard boxes piled against a wall. He peered into the top one, moved it to investigate a second, and did the same with a third. "Ah," he said, and reaching into it yanked out an old church bulletin from Holy Week. The cover featured a full-sized color reproduction of Christ on the cross. Freeman sat down and pointed to the picture, tapping it with his finger.

"Remember what we talked about last time? This," tap, tap, "the most famous suicide in history. He chose to die, Tom. He sacrificed himself. He could have avoided it. He could have come off that cross, or had legions of angels rescue Him. But to serve a greater purpose, He allowed Himself to die."

Freeman laid the bulletin across my lap, and reached into his jacket. He pulled out a pint bottle of Crown Royal and set it on the table, then reached into his pocket and withdrew a prescription bottle. He gently set it beside the whiskey.

"I brought you a way out, Tom. Yes, yes," he said to my shaking head. "Hear me out. You can't break the seal, it will do too much damage. You'll destroy the trust of so many. They'll reject the sacrament, and before long, will lose their faith entirely.

"But if you don't break the seal, other deaths will come. And pain and suffering will radiate out to their families and friends. And all because you weren't strong enough to stop it when you had the chance.

"But this way," he motioned to the bottles on the table, "this way you'll do good. I swear to you by everything you keep holy, if you do this, I will turn myself in. You will be the last. It will bring this all to an end. This will spare your family, too, Tom. Think of the humiliation, the shame you'll bring down on them if you're thrown out of the Church. This avoids all that. And even more important, you'll prevent thousands, maybe millions from losing their faith.

"It'll be like falling asleep. I'll stay here with you until you're out, then I'll take the bottles with me. It'll look like a heart attack or a stroke. And you know that's what the bishop's office will say. That's what your family will want to hear and what they'll tell people. And how understandable, after all the stress and pain you've been under."

Freeman leaned forward and tapped the image of the crucified savior in my lap. "And He'll understand. If anybody would, He will. He'll understand and He'll welcome you. He'll put his arm around you and say, "Thank you, Thomas. Thank you for your courage and your trust in my mercy."

I smelled the warm, sour scent of whiskey. Freeman had opened the bottle and set the ornate, plastic cap down, and now had the pill bottle in his hands, pushing and twisting on the top. I just watched. I didn't object. It's like I was outside myself, a spectator.

The silence shattered and Freeman jumped and dropped the pill bottle onto the table as Bongo leapt away from my feet with big, booming barks. I twisted around, and saw him up on his back legs, scratching insanely at the door to the outside, yapping, yipping, and barking. Beneath Bongo's uproar I heard the distant motor of the riding mower.

In the enclosed room Freeman couldn't make himself heard over Bongo's barking. I jumped to my feet, the spell broken. Seizing Bongo's leash from the floor, I threw my shoulder into the door and pushed the horizontal release bar.

"My dog has to go out," I stammered and slid the loop of the leash over my hand as the door opened. Bongo dragged me into the freezing wind, kicking up wads of semi-frozen mulch in his eagerness to chase the rabbit lure. The little beagle weighs only 26 pounds, but he's all muscle and had me onto the grass and yards away from the door in only seconds. Freeman followed me out, his baby face scrunched together in fury.

"Get back here," he demanded.

"No," I shouted back. "No, I'm not doing that."

"Then the next ones are on your head," he bellowed, pointing a finger at me. "I'm gonna kill two more bitches this week. Maybe I'll slice up another bum, too. That'll be how many, Tom? Five, six? All because of you."

The wind whipped around me, and the thin purple strip of my stole flew up and slapped my face. With one arm fully extended at the end of Bongo's leash, I raised the other and pointed at him.

"Look where you are, Freeman," I said. He stared back, uncomprehending.

"Look where you are," I repeated, my voice rising. "You're not in the confessional anymore. You never began the sacrament, you never asked for absolution. This was no confession. The seal does not apply."

I wish I could say that stunned him. It didn't. He hesitated only a moment, then stepped off the landing from the room and let the door swing shut behind him. He dug a hand into his jeans' pocket and came out with a Buck knife that unfolded with a snick into a five-inch blade. All I could think to do was to strip Bongo's leash from my wrist and drop it to let him run clear.

But that dog, Saint Bongo of the Blessed Canines, did not run away. He didn't launch himself at Freeman, either. Instead, Bongo very sensibly circled to our right, well out of anyone's reach, yodel-barking encouragement to me, threats at Freeman, and general cries for help in Beaglese.

And it worked. On the wind I heard a high, female voice keening, "Tomm-eeee. Tommmeeeee." Freeman heard it, too. He spat out a curse and took off in a decidedly unathletic run to the parking lot, closing the knife with both hands as he went. Bongo took a few tentative steps toward him but seemed relieved when I called him back. He meekly waited as I picked up the leash.

Freeman climbed into a grey pick-up truck and gunned it across the parking lot. He climbed the drive and rolled out of sight before Terry came panting around the corner of the church building. She saw me standing there, alone with Bongo. Terry stopped, bent over, and put hands on her knees to catch her breath. Her red cheeks blew out big clouds of condensation, then she stood up, shoulders heaving. The Sig Sauer 9mm was in her right hand.

"What…the hell…is goin' on?" she gasped.

I stared at her, opened mouth. "What are you doing here?"

She shook her head, still gulping air. "You go first."

"No," I said firmly. "You go first."

"Don't be an asshole, Tommy," she said, the words leaving her mouth just as Mwangi trotted around the corner. He stopped short when he saw Terry. Bongo laid into another barking fit at the new arrival.

"Who the hell are you?" Terry asked in her best cop voice.

"I would ask the same," Mwangi shot back, not the least intimated.

"Terry, this is Fr. Mwangi, an esteemed guest and a friend," I said over Bongo's racket.

She was still sucking air, so she nodded and flipped a hand in greeting toward him. Unfortunately, it was the one holding the Sig.

"Fr. Mwangi, this is my sister, Terry."

"Your sister?" he said, staring at the pistol with eyebrows raised so high they wrinkled the skin on his forehead.

"Yes, my older sister," I replied. Mwangi looked at me, at the barking hound and back at Terry, who was tucking the Sig into a carry holster inside her waistband.

"Americans," he muttered.

CHAPTER 33

It turns out I'd been surveilled by my own sister.

We all agreed to talk things over at the rectory, but Terry (rather graciously, I thought) offered to stow the gun in her car first. While she did, Mwangi and I walked to the rectory and I explained my sister's military and police background. He replied with a grunt, which I chose to take as acceptance. Given the cold and our jangled nerves, I checked and discovered nearly a full pot of coffee. When Terry joined us, there wasn't room for all three at the tiny kitchen table, so we took our mugs to the dining room. Terry demanded an explanation even before we'd pulled our chairs from the table, but Mwangi and I outvoted her so she grudgingly shared her story first.

"It wasn't hard to figure out that whatever's eating you has to do with confession," she said to me. "When I set up the camera system in the church–" Mwangi sat back in indignant surprise, "–for theft-protection purposes," Terry continued defensively. "I realized the angles also happened to allow me to see who lines up outside Tommy's confessional." She looked from me to Mwangi. "I had no idea you two were playing True Detective on your own and swapped confessionals. So I had no eyes on the one you were in," she said with a nod to me.

"This is wrong. Very wrong," Mwangi declared, his eyes stern. "Spying on penitents is an outrage. Even the Chinese do not do this."

Terry rolled her eyes. "I was not spying on penitents, I was spying on him," she hooked a thumb at me, "Mr. Turn the Other Cheek. Somebody has to watch his six." She flipped a shrug at my offended expression. "I was in my car on the other side of the building and had the feed on my phone when I heard Bongo. I thought maybe he'd slipped his collar, so I got out and started walking. But as I got closer, I heard his barking become defensive, so I came running."

"And you happened to have a gun on you?" Mwangi interjected.

"Yes," Terry said, then tilted her head and gave as fake a smile as you'll ever see. "Americans."

Mwangi rolled his eyes and Terry took the advantage.

"So now it's your turn. Tell me what's going on."

I looked at the canonist and saw him watching me. "I can't–"

Terry slammed her open palm on the table hard enough to make us jump. "Dammit, Tommy," she spat. Mwangi gave her a look as though horns had sprouted from her forehead.

"I can't right now, Terry," I continued, "but very soon. Maybe even tonight." Mwangi looked to me and I said to him, "There's been a very sizeable development. I think the leopard's days are numbered."

"Oh my God, they're using code words," Terry groaned. "I really hope this is not serious because you two…" She snorted, pushed back her chair, and grabbed her jacket. "Give me a call as soon as you can, T." She put her plastic smile back on and turned to Mwangi. "Such a pleasure to meet you, Father."

Give the man credit, he got up, made a slight bow, and extended his hand. "God be with you," he said as she shook it. As soon as we heard the front door close behind her, he turned to me and said, "Sister?"

"Yep."

"And you grew up in the same house, same parents?" I nodded.

"Remarkable," he said. "Well, let's not waste time. What is this development you spoke of?"

He got the whole story, although I did not describe Freeman in case he disagreed with my conclusion. And I left out how seductive his dark urgings had been. "I should probably go get those pills and liquor out of the confessional before someone else goes in. I've got enough scandals on my hands." Mwangi nodded, "Good, good. I will use the time to think."

Only shadows and the Holy Spirit occupied the church when I returned. I genuflected toward the altar and hustled to the visiting priest confessional. The Crown Royal and pills remained where Freeman had left them, and the sight of them drove home the fact that he really intended to kill me. Was the knife in case persuasion failed? He would have needed it, I assured myself, because I wouldn't have taken his way out. My conscience, however, isn't such a sap. It pointed out that although I hadn't succumbed to Freeman's temptation of self-murder, I hadn't said no, either.

That was enough to make me want to throw the booze and pills in a small wastebasket, but I stopped my hand in mid reach. His fingerprints would be on those containers. I found a big manilla envelope filled with children's Sunday School homework, emptied it and gingerly placed the "evidence" inside.

Back in the rectory I found Mwangi perusing the titles in the bookcase. I handed him the envelope and as he peered inside, I cautioned him about fingerprints. He nodded slowly and gave me a glance.

"I agree with you, Thomas. The evidence strongly points toward an inauthentic confession."

"Yeah, him trying to kill me should move the needle in that direction," I growled. Mwangi pursed his lips and appeared to stew it over, then gave a shrug and nod of acquiescence.

"Yes, it does."

"So the seal is lifted," I said. "I know his name, I know what he looks like, I'm pretty sure I can find where he lives. When we're done here, I'm heading downtown to give the police the information."

Call me crazy, but I expected at least a little approval from the man. Instead, Mwangi's expression dropped and his eyes went to the floor. I turned my back to place the evidence bag on the table, and when I faced him again my friend held an expensive-looking, cream-colored envelope. He handed it to me and I flipped it over. The back was sealed with a blob of navy-blue wax with the bishop's crest pressed into it.

"I am so sorry, Thomas, but you cannot," Mwangi said, regret heavy on his face. "You may not speak to the police, to your parishioners, to anyone at all. Flannery has launched the suspension process and placed you on restricted leave."

I swallowed, felt the rage boil up inside and flung my words at Mwangi. "Well, if Flannery is relieving me of my duties, I take that to mean I can damn well do as I please."

As always, Mwangi was a rock. He let my fury flame over him with no attempt to deflect or defend against it. All he did was lower his eyes as I spoke, then raised them again when I was done.

"Thomas," he said as gently as a brother, "you and I both know it means exactly the opposite."

CHAPTER 34

I read my suspension letter aloud as Mwangi sat silent at the table. A priest from Hudson would handle Masses and sacramental duties, while another from Twinsburg would serve as administrator. I was to report to the Jesuit retreat house by the Portage Lakes as soon as an availability opened, probably in a day or two, within a week for certain.

"In light of this new evidence," Mwangi said, gesturing to the envelope with the pills and whiskey, "how can the suspension process proceed? Indeed, your leave should be reversed."

"Should be?" I asked, unable to keep the sarcasm from my voice. "A leave is the least of my troubles, isn't it?" Mwangi looked startled and shook his head.

"Freeman told me," I said simply.

"Who is Freeman?"

"The killer. The guy we incorrectly labeled a penitent," I said. "His name is William Freeman —"

"This is premature," Mwangi interrupted, holding up a hand. "The bishop must formally decide on the invalidity of his confession and until then –"

"…and he's an IT guy," I went on. "A very sophisticated one, apparently. He's a hacker. In fact, he's hacked into the diocese computer system." The other man's jaw dropped, and I nodded. "I thought he was bluffing, too, but he told me things about myself that no one could know unless they accessed my records. And he said he saw an email to Sanchez from Flannery about plans to laicize me. Excommunication will probably follow."

Mwangi's head wagged slowly side to side. "Thomas, there has been no discussion of excommunication. In fact, all advice to Flannery, my own included, was against even a suspension. I think the killer fabricated this lie to push you further toward the crime of Judas."

Mwangi's eyes seemed to search the room as he thought. "But if evidence exists that he has broken into the diocese computer," he looked at me and a smile split his face. "That is undeniable proof his deceitful confession is merely a tactic in a larger attack on the Church and," he raised a finger, "it implies diabolic direction. The bishop must rule on this. Thomas, you must write out a full report, as will I. We will submit these this afternoon and I will do all in my power to ensure they go directly to the bishop."

I shook my head with frustration. "That'll take too long. Freeman is planning more killings, possibly as early as Sunday night. We need to go to the police now."

The other man bit his lower lip. "I am sorry, Thomas, but we must wait until the bishop rules on the man's confession." He raised his hands at my reaction. "This should not take long, who knows, perhaps even by sundown today. I know, I know, Bishop Sanchez wrestles with broader considerations, but he will understand the danger and act to prevent further tragedy."

My face must have given away my skepticism, because Mwangi glanced at a crucifix on the wall and back at me. "You must have faith, Thomas. Pray for patience. Pray for guidance. And be assured, the authorities will learn of this man's crimes and his evil intentions.

"Very soon this maneater will face the hunters."

*   *   *

Mwangi wasn't gone an hour when I finished my "report" and hit send. He probably hadn't even arrived at the diocese offices yet. Writing a narrative of Freeman's murderous visit proved weirdly cathartic. The tension of the past few hours flowed out as my fingers tapped out keystrokes. I kept my tone professional and objective, as much as a person can after being threatened with a knife. Two happy results followed: I got it done while all details remained fresh in my mind, and my heel stopped its involuntary tapping against the floor.

I went to the kitchen and considered settling my nerves with a bit of Kentucky's finest. But by now word had probably gotten out, albeit quietly, that other priests were handling duties at St. Al's. This could prompt phone calls or even unannounced visits. Whether visitors might be Lena's geriatric goons or bona fide friends, bourbon-breath would not be helpful. I emptied the coffee pot into my mug, indulged in a splash of French vanilla creamer, then headed to the living room. It was about time for Nones, the midafternoon prayer for the Liturgy of the Hours, but before I started, I had one more thing to do. No point in putting it off. And I was beyond caring what Mwangi would say.

Through the window I saw hedges swaying with the wind, and a world so darkened by overcast skies it seemed much later in the day. I set my coffee down on the end table next to my recliner, and sat down with an "oof." Bongo clicked his way down the hall, came in, and flopped down in front of my feet. All I needed was a cracklin' fire, but that would necessitate a fireplace, which we did not have. For a moment I considered casting a YouTube video of a fireplace from my iPhone to the TV, but discarded it as depressing.

Stop stalling, I told myself, and get it done. Then you can pray. I pulled out my cellphone and made the call.

"Hey Terry, how's it goin?" I asked. Before she could answer that stupid question, I plowed ahead. "Look, I'm sorry about earlier. I'm not thrilled about the cameras in the church, but I am very grateful for what you did today. God knows what might have happened if the guy had not heard you coming." She managed to squeeze in, "What guy?" but I kept going.

"Terry, this thing is almost over. I'm close, really close, to being able to tell you everything. But I've got to get permission first, and that'll probably come tonight. As soon as I can, I will call you and give you the whole story." I took a deep breath and let it out. "But until then, there's bad news. I wanted to tell you myself, and maybe you can let John and the others know.

"The bishop has kicked me out of St. Al's."

CHAPTER 35

I waited all Friday afternoon and early evening for Mwangi to call or text. As the minutes ticked away, so did my confidence. Surely when the bishop saw our proof, the administrative leave would be lifted. Yes, I was being disciplined for my arrest Sunday night and Lena's public insurrection on Wednesday, but Freeman was indirectly responsible for all. And now that his confessions were proven bogus, we could go to the authorities.

When Mwangi failed to respond to several texts, the last of my hope drained away to be replaced with a black, oozy dread. I began doomscrolling "excommunication" when something bumped into my calf and I met the urgent gaze of a beagle with a full bladder.

"Oh yeah, you didn't go out after dinner, did you?" I asked and hooked him onto a leash. He practically pulled me out the door, where the sharp, cold air came as a welcome slap in the face. I let Bongo drag me to the fence gate, and foolishly indulged him by letting him off the leash once inside. The graupel and cold rain certainly washed away the lure scent, but old Voodoo Nose might still pick up a trace. Not a smart move. I had forgotten that while the fake scent might be gone, the genuine article usually comes out at night to feed and frolic. Bongo's gut-punched "AAARROOOO" bounced off every hard surface in a one-block radius. I at least retained the good sense to secure the gate behind me before charging after my fast-trotting dog.

The good thing about beagles' obsessive sniffing is it obliterates everything else in their peanut-sized brains, even when they're playing Catch Me If You Can. Once locked onto a scent, its black nose huffing, snuffling, long ears brushing the tips of grass blades, a beagle is easy to catch. Just walk up and snap on the leash. Or you can theoretically grab it by the tail and swing it around your head, an impulse that's crossed my mind more than once. I was two or three yards away from my quarry when my left leg shot out from underneath me and down went Fr. Pastor. Putting my hand beneath me to push myself up, my palm contacted something cold and slimy. The stench arose in the next instant. I'd hit a Bongo bomb. I said more things I had to confess later. The dog must have spotted the flash of a fluffy white tail across the lawn because he was off again. It took some time to corral the laughing, panting, little beast, get him back in the house and into his crate with his bedtime treat, and clean the dog feces from my hand, jacket sleeve and shoe. When it was all done, I pulled out my iPhone to see if I could still catch any of the 11 pm news when I saw a notification I'd missed a call.

Sure enough, Mwangi had called at 11:12. My eyes went to the voicemail icon and spotted his message. It was nearly two minutes long, which meant it contained much more than simply 'Call me back.' A nicotine craving came from out of nowhere, but I had annihilated my stash and needed an alternative sedative. I retrieved the Woodford Reserve. Ain't nobody comin' to call at midnight, I reasoned, and a little Irish courage would come in handy listening to Mwangi's message.

It turned out I was right.

"Hello Thomas," he said, his melodic accent intact even on a recording. "I am sorry to call so late and apparently at an inopportune time. And I further apologize for the poor sound quality. You see, I am traveling."

My eyes stared at a potted palm plant on the floor beside an old piano. I sipped from my tulip glass and the bourbon felt sour on my tongue.

"I am a passenger of Mr. Gorshank, who very kindly agreed to drive me to Washington for a meeting with the papal nuncio. Thank you again, Mr. Gorshank." The driver mumbled a reply I couldn't make out, and Mwangi made it a point to repeat the man's name a third time. I found that curious and at first thought it a courtesy unique to Kenyan culture. The guy came from a wealthy family by African standards, so, Third-World *noblesse oblige*, perhaps? Then it dawned on me that Mwangi was letting me know he could not speak openly, and I needed to listen close to discern what he was really saying.

"Thomas, I personally delivered the package you gave me into the hands of Bishop Sanchez this afternoon. I explained the unique value of the enclosed items and he seemed quite enthralled by the tale of how they came into your possession.

"He also said to thank you for your information, and he would have the diocesan computer system inspected immediately.

"On the theological question we've debated, I'm afraid the bishop is...uh..." I could almost hear the gears grinding as the priest searched for words both opaque and meaningful, "...he does not share our interpretation of the facts." I think I groaned aloud and perhaps swore once or twice, because I missed what Mwangi said next and had to rewind. "That was his initial reaction, and perhaps his thinking will evolve to align with ours. But until Bishop Sanchez finds time to ponder the matter again, we are obliged to adhere to the known constraints."

I let out a deep sigh.

"Be patient, Thomas. The nuncio may bring additional perspectives to these important matters. In the meantime, I will hold you in my prayers, and ask that you be granted strength and grace and peace of heart.

"You have my envy and best wishes, my friend, on your retreat. Your silent retreat. I understand that you cannot reply." He said the last three words so deliberately that even Mr. Gorshank had to have noticed the emphasis.

"Go with God, Fr. Pastor. Let us both pray to St. Hubert to intercede on our behalf so we may successfully complete the task laid upon us."

I listened to the message three times while I sipped the Woodford. So, the seal was still maddeningly in effect. I knew in my bones Freeman's confessions were bogus and not protected by the seal, and Mwangi agreed. But apparently the bishop hadn't, and his vote mattered most. If Mwangi told Sanchez I revealed Freeman's name, it wouldn't be a suspension. It would be excommunication.

I shook my head. Mwangi would not rat out a friend. In fact, I suspected he was up to just the opposite. English may have been Mwangi's second, or third, or eleventh language, but he wielded it with precision. I listened again and again to the recording. He never said he was summoned or sent to Washington. So what was he doing? I tried not to let myself get too carried away, but his veiled reference to the papal nuncio bringing "additional perspectives" meant IBS might end up with footprints on his head.

And that last line, why pray to a saint as obscure as Hubert? I googled the old boy and when his Wikipedia page opened, I was gob-smacked by a symbol I'd not seen since my undergraduate days in college: a stag's head with a glowing cross between its antlers, better known these days as the Jägermeister logo.

"Hubert," I muttered as I read, "patron saint of metallurgists, woodsmen…and hunters."

CHAPTER 36

The cold snap had broken during the night and Saturday dawned warm enough for an unzipped jacket when I took Bongo out for his morning constitutional. By 10 a.m. the window in the kitchen was open to catch the lovely autumn air. I made my Divine Office, said three rosaries, and thought wistfully of taking Bongo to the park for a long, long hike. But as I was once again under the Church's equivalent of house-arrest, it seemed prudent to stay inside and compile a list of contacts and critical information for the priest from Hudson and the administrator from Twinsburg. We also needed to switch the after-hours call-forwarding to the new priest instead of me, so any anguished summons at 1 a.m. for Last Rites would not end in voicemail. As I puzzled over this, the first of the day's two visitors arrived.

I had no idea who stood on my stoop when the doorbell, then Bongo went off. To avoid an interruption with this mystery guest, I shut the dog in my bedroom and went to the front door. Boy, was I glad I had. My visitor looked like Wild Bill Cody had come back from the grave and received Holy Orders. The old priest wore a wide-brimmed black hat, from which flowed a curtain of thick, straight white hair down and beyond his collar. His wrinkled, ruddy complexion set off a snowy van dyke beard worthy of the Wild West showman, but the cowboy vibe took a hard left turn into hipster territory with a pair of tortoiseshell horn-rim glasses.

He introduced himself as Fr. Gannon and we had coffee in the dining room. He explained that the Hudson pastor had miraculously convinced the diocese he could not possibly handle two parishes, so the bishop's office had dug up this retired Navy chaplain to temporarily replace me. I found myself liking Gannon. He didn't ask why I was leaving, complimented me on the financial condition of the parish (these military types do their homework), and asked the right questions about how to drive this particular bus. Between us we completed my list of contacts and information. Gannon said he would say Masses beginning tonight, but couldn't move into the rectory until late next week. I think the guy was giving me space for a graceful departure. We walked over to the church and I showed him around. Within 30 minutes was he was waving his black hat to me in goodbye, not from the back of a magnificent stallion, but from the driver's window of a Volvo. My flock would be in competent hands, and that left me with a good feeling. I wish I could say the same about my second visitor.

Around 3 p.m. the doorbell rang for the second time, and Bongo again was incarcerated in the bedroom. At least I tossed him a chewy stick as compensation. I knew it couldn't be Mwangi, unlikely that he could get back from DC so soon. Not likely to be one of the Tulips this close to 5 o'clock Mass. When I opened the door, my jaw and heart dropped to the floor.

He was still as gaunt as I remembered, but grey had spread from his temples to salt the rest of his black hair.

His glasses looked thicker and more smudged, and the lines on his face had deepened. But when he broke into his lopsided grin and breathed out, "Thomas, how are you?" it was like he'd stepped right out of my past.

"Father Feister," I greeted my old therapist. "What a complete surprise."

He made a too-familiar nasally chuckle that pulled up his lip to reveal a few dingy teeth. "Oh, I hope not an unpleasant one," he said.

"Of course not," I lied. So this is how the diocese is going to play it, I thought. Smart move. Word would quietly spread about Fr. Pastor, a well-meaning but flawed vessel who cracked under the strain of his duties. Bishop Sanchez, always the wise and thoughtful shepherd, provided the same professional help that this poor man had needed back when...well, let's not gossip about Fr. Pastor's sad past.

"Come in, please," I said and held the door open.

He cocked his head apologetically, "Thank you, but uh, I understand you have a dog. I love the animals but I'm quite allergic. Could we go somewhere else?"

The choir would be practicing at the church now, and unlocking the school required deactivating the security code and other hassles. I looked at the red and gold trees made brilliant by the afternoon sun.

"Why don't we take advantage of this warm day?" I suggested. "There won't be many more. We have very comfortable benches over by the grotto. It's a good place for conversation if no one's there praying or meditating."

"That's right," Fiester said, with a nod. "You've always had a special devotion to the Blessed Mother."

I never considered my devotion more special than any

other priest, but the grotto was my favorite spot on our church campus. Peaceful and usually private, it attracted only occasional visitors to seek Mary's intercession on some personal matter. And the grotto was outdoors, of course, which meant Fiester could get no more than two hours of my time. Nor would he get any coffee from me. Hey, the man once declared in writing that I was passive-aggressive. I was merely proving him right.

"You have a splendid memory," I replied with a smile. That, and a good set of patient records.

On the walk over to my little oasis, I described to Fiester its organic beginnings. What had started as a service project by an Eagle Scout had taken on a life of its own. The Finance Committee decided to support him with a brief fundraising campaign that exceeded its goal. A local stone mason offered his time gratis, and the Ladies Flower Guild ensured that something bloomed there nearly every day May through October. The old gals were positively enchanted when yours truly expanded the beds with the sweat of his own brow to plant – what else, tulips. A family-owned funeral home had even contributed two handsome teak benches with discreet brass plaques that identified them as the donors. In the stone nook stood a three-foot, white-marble statue of Mary with palms open at hip level, head slightly tilted, and a serene smile gracing her face as if to say, "I like it when you kids play nice."

Fiester, however, made it clear he hadn't come to play, nice or otherwise.

"Thomas," he began softly, folding his hands in his lap after we'd taken our seats on the bench. "Bishop Sanchez is concerned for your emotional well-being."

Nailed it, I thought to myself, but smiled and nodded.

"The events of the past week could devastate even a strong psyche. I hope you're not following social media on the…ah…controversies."

I tucked my chin up under my lower lip and shook my head. "Nope. In fact, I haven't looked at emails or texts at all today."

"Really?" he said with overdone concern. "Oh, I hope you're not withdrawing again." I sighed. Fiester loved to say "There is no wrong answer," when what he meant was "There is no right answer." If I had said I was following the social media mob, he'd insist I was obsessing.

"Thomas, would you like to come back to therapy? You made wonderful progress back at the seminary but I always thought there was more work we needed to do."

"It's kind of you to offer, Father, but um, I'm doing OK."

"That's great to hear," he said and up went the corner of his mouth again. "Although, any individual – myself included – is unable to accurately assess his own situation. For example, this business Sunday night with the young lady and the police. Which precipitated the," Fiester searched for the right word, "ugliness at the funeral on Wednesday. Before we can effectively deal with the pain generated by those incidents, we must face the biological urges that ignited this unfortunate chain of event."

"I wasn't trying to get laid," I snarled, and glanced at the serene face on the statue. With absolute sincerity, I tapped my right fist to my left breast and said aloud, "Forgive me, *mater benedicta*." And because I just can't help myself, still looking at the figure I hooked my thumb at Fiester. "But he started it."

Fiester glanced from me to the statue and said, "Oh yes. The humor. You and your witticisms," The hint of annoyance in his voice revealed this as a genuine recollection, not something dug out of his notes. "You wrap yourself in them like—"

"Like armor," I interrupted. "That's the word you used back then. Do you remember? You told me to never lose my sense of humor because it was a gift from God. You told me to think of it as angelic chainmail I could always wear close to my skin. I have, and I owe you for that good advice. Humor has been an excellent armor against gossip and self-doubt and –

"– and the black dogs of depression?" he asked. I'm sure my face told him he'd scored a hit. "How are the hounds of hell these days, Thomas?"

"Leashed," I shot back, far, far too quickly. "Anyway, back to Sunday. I've already explained I wasn't soliciting. I was trying to help those women. The bishop backed me up and even issued a statement to that effect."

Fiester nodded at the grass in front of him. "I'm glad you brought that up. This business about a penitent trying to get you to break the seal of the confessional."

"I'm not at liberty to discuss a subject like that until the bishop clarifies what is and is not permissible."

"I know but there's a simple work-around," he leaned sideways to dig into the pocket of his sport coat. "The bishop suggested I serve as your spiritual director during your retreat, if that's acceptable to you." He pulled his hand from the coat pocket and I saw a very familiar roll of fabric.

"Before we start therapy, let me offer you reconciliation and absolution," he said and unspooled a purple stole. The audacity of this little weasel! Using the sacrament to try to place me under his authority.

"I'm very satisfied with Fr. Wulfram as my confessor," I said icily. "Besides, you know it doesn't work like that. I still can't tell you anything about what I may or may not have heard."

"Yes but," Fiester said with sad eyes behind those thick glasses, "if you have already broken the seal of the confessional by sharing information and even evidence with another, this you must confess."

So he knew about the bag with the pills and booze that Mwangi brought back. I stared ahead. If evidence like that can't disqualify Freeman's confessions, then it's excommunication for sure. I slowly lifted my eyes to the face on the statue. There was that faint smile, serene and peacefully confident, which at this moment I found oddly reassuring.

Fiester was giving the gold embroidered cross in the center of his stole the customary kiss before placing it on his shoulders when I said, "You can put that back, Father." My voice held no malice or irritation or anger, but a kind of gentleness and good grace. He turned to me with a startle.

"First of all," I said, "we both know you don't have the power to absolve a priest who has broken the seal. Only the Apostolic Penitentiary in Rome can get a man off that hook. Second, I'm sure even a second-rate canonist could make an airtight case that a confessor-slash-therapist who hears such a confession and uses that information is himself subject to the same charge and," I let it hang, "the same penalty."

I felt a twinge of sympathy for Fiester. The role of hatchet-man didn't suit him, but he lacked the cojones to say "no" to a bishop. "Fr. Fiester," I said with genuine sympathy in my heart, "I'm grateful for your help during those dark days in the seminary. Let's not ruin that appreciation because of politics, internal or otherwise." He opened his mouth, but I kept going. "I cannot be compelled to confess to you. If the bishop insists I go back into therapy, I will obey but only after petitioning for another therapist, even if I must pay for it myself. And yes, he can order me to report to you for spiritual direction or even therapy, but Fred," Fiester's eyes locked on mine at the sound of his name, "is it still therapy if it's done under duress? Does it become something else?"

The man stared at me, but began to roll the stole back up.

"Thomas, I think, I hope, and I'll pray that you change your mind. Because regardless of whatever you think of me, I fear you're in a bad place right now." He craned his head in frustration on that stalk of a neck and looked back at me.

"No one hacked the diocesan computer system," he said quietly. "As soon as the African priest told them your tale, they brought in experts to run scans. No intrusion occurred."

"Then how could he have known what medications you prescribed for my depression?"

"I don't know," he said. Fiester took a deep breath, like a man making a plunge. "I don't know that he did. Thomas, there is no evidence this Penitent exists. The items in the envelope your friend brought back could have come from anywhere. The same is true for those bits of jewelry you showed the auxiliary bishop. They could have come from you. No one, including the canonist, saw this Penitent fleeing yesterday. He found you outside the church in the freezing cold with only your dog and your sister. And discreet inquiries have been made with the police, who told us there are no reports of missing prostitutes, or street people, or unmarked graves or anything like that."

"You're saying I made all this up?"

"I'm saying you and I need to talk. In a structured way, not here like this."

I looked away and saw that the autumn trees had grown dingy in the dimming light. Shadows lengthened on the ground around us, and a chill had returned to the air.

"He's going to do it again," I said. "The Penitent told me he would and he meant it. Maybe tomorrow, or Monday or Tuesday. But he's going to kill again. We can't let him. We can't."

Fiester's hair blew and for a moment, I thought I saw anxiety behind those thick glasses.

"Even if he is real, you can't break the seal by doing something." He turned away and his shoulders dropped as he sighed with a decision. When he turned back to me, he leaned in a bit closer as though we were in a crowded coffee shop instead of a secluded alcove. "Tom, they'll go all the way on this. The bishop, Flannery, all of them. Don't doubt that for a second. Sanchez is too invested in the politics of this issue. He'll excommunicate you just to show everyone he means business."

I looked at the statue but with the sun nearly gone, shadow had veiled her face and her soft smile. Fred watched me expectantly, and I wanted to tell him that I knew, I knew from the deepest wells of my heart that Freeman's confessions were inauthentic. That God had opened a path for me to stop the slaughter of His children, and if I hesitated or refused, my soul was forfeited anyway. Instead, I told him what he wanted to hear.

"Thank you, Fred. You have an annoying gift for bringing clarity to an issue, you know that? That's probably kind of handy for a therapist." He smiled and nodded, but I'm not sure he entirely bought my spiel and meek, little smile. But what else did he have to go on? I gave him another nudge.

"Look, therapy might be a good idea. I'm not sure. Can I pray on it for a day or two and get back to you?"

"Of course," he said with a dip of his head. We shook hands and he chatted about his trip to Greece last summer as I walked him to his car. Already the first handicapped parking spots were occupied for the 5 o'clock Mass, and I spotted Fr. Gannon's Volvo.

"I see my replacement is here for Mass," I remarked to Fiester and explained about Gannon. "If you don't mind, I'd like to avoid any awkwardness so, I'll head back to the rectory."

"Sure, Tom," he said, permission in his tone. "Very understandable."

I nodded my thanks and he headed into the parking lot. I waited a moment, then hiked back across the lawn to cut around the back of the church and avoid any uncomfortable encounters with parishioners.

CHAPTER 37

I prayed myself to sleep Saturday night. Perhaps my guardian angel had gotten a stern reprimand from Michael the Archangel because something fended off the black dogs and I slept like a babe. Long before the first headlights appeared in the parking lot for the 7 a.m. Mass, Bongo and I had made three circuits around the church campus in the cool morning air. By the time the organist arrived for the 10 o'clock Mass, I had prayed the Divine Office; made, consumed, and cleaned up breakfast; and said my two morning rosaries. I did a quick check of my phone to see if Mwangi had called or texted. He hadn't, but Terry had texted several times and Auggie and Jim once each. I couldn't think what to tell any of them, so I replied to none.

Instead I sat in my recliner with a cup of coffee and tried to sort this out. Fiester had said there was no evidence of an intrusion on the diocese computers, and that bothered me. A lot. If Freeman lied about that, what else had he lied about? No. No matter how I looked at it, waiting was no longer an option. Freeman might begin hunting this very night. And my cell phone could ring at any moment with orders to report immediately to the Jesuit retreat house, or far worse, to "report downtown" to the diocesan offices. My fervid imagination painted me walking down East 9th Street wearing only jockey shorts while a mitered Auxiliary Bishop Flannery waddled behind, his crosier clacking on the pavement as he bellowed, *"Excommunicado!"*

What was Mwangi up to, and why hadn't I heard from him? He offered the only glimmer of hope, and as I puzzled about it my phone vibrated in my pocket. Hoping I had somehow telepathically beckoned him to call, I checked and saw it wasn't Mwangi, but the parish IT guy.

"Hey Gary, how are ya?" I asked.

"Good, good, thanks for asking, Father," a tentative note in his voice. "I'm calling to check about a Fr. Gannon—"

"Oh gosh, yeah, I should have warned you," I interrupted. "He's legit, he's going to handle things here while…I'll be gone." Wow did that sting. I hastened to add "On a retreat, I mean. I'll be on a retreat. So yeah, we'll need to switch things over to him."

"Oh…OK," Gary stumbled. "I'll call him back." An excruciating silence descended on us and I desperately scrambled for something to add.

"Hey, Gary, can I ask you a technical question?"

"Sure," he replied, as eager to change the subject as I.

"What exactly is a rootkit?"

"Rootkit? Wow, I don't hear that often from non-techies. It's hacker stuff."

"You mean a program?"

He paused. "More like a suite of programs. Remember in the old cartoons when the burglar tiptoes in carrying a black bag with his tools? A rootkit is a hacker's black bag.

It contains all the nasty stuff to break into systems and create mayhem."

"If someone installed a rootkit on a system, is it hard to find?"

He thought about that. "I don't do software security, but I read about it. You can get a junky rootkit off the dark web for free, or pay a few bucks for something slightly stronger. Those are easy to spot with a memory dump."

"Huh," I said. "What about the other end of the spectrum? Rootkits that are really good."

"You mean like from intelligence agencies or organized crime?"

"Yeah, I guess."

I heard Gary blow out a sigh. "Like I said I have no direct experience, but they say the government stuff is ghostware, nearly invisible. Not only ours and the Russians', but stuff out of Israel, India, China, Iran. Then there are the criminal systems. From what I've read, the programs developed for Eastern European mobsters are a total nightmare. I've never seen one, and I hope I never do. They think that's what shut down the East Coast gasoline pipeline a couple of years ago, remember? Or the ransomware used on airports and medical centers until they pay up? That's really sophisticated stuff. I suppose it's a kind of rootkit, but a rootkit on steroids."

"And if you did that dump thing you mentioned, could you find it?"

"No, no way," he said. "You can bring in all the white hats you want, and give them a year to analyze your system. They won't find it unless whoever planted it tells them where to look."

We chatted a few minutes more, and before the awkward subject of my departure returned, we said goodbye. My coffee had gone cold, but I drank it anyway. Freeman claimed to be a "wizard-level" IT engineer, and even if he was only half as good as he thought, he wouldn't need freebie software. Fiester had said the diocese brought in experts to scan its computer system. Scan. They'd spent maybe a morning investigating, probably checking for one of those bargain-basement rootkits. In which case they'd never find any digital poltergeists Freeman unleashed into the system.

My phone vibrated on the table beside me, and I almost ignored it. Probably another text from Terry. I would have to respond soon or she'd come knocking at the door, but I still hadn't thought up a reply to her inevitable questions. With a sigh, I picked my cell up and opened the texting app.

The text wasn't from Terry, but had a DC area code. I stabbed the screen so hard I almost knocked the phone out of my hand.

"Nuncio agrees. Inauthentic. Formal reversal within a week. Praise God."

I closed my eyes as my mind chattered over and over, "Thank you, God. Thank you, thank you, thank you." I was still on restricted leave and IBS could boot me out of the parish, but there would be no suspension, no laicization, no excommunication. By Friday I'd be in the clear.

A formal declaration of inauthenticity by a papal nuncio meant IBS had two choices: accept the decision and go to the authorities with my report, or oppose the nuncio and kiss goodbye any hope of advancing in the church hierarchy. The Penitent's face came to mind and I muttered, "You're gonna need a new name, Will. You'll look pretty stupid calling yourself "Freeman" inside a prison cell."

CHAPTER 38

Now that my administrative leave would be only temporary, I decided to enjoy it. The Browns had a 4 o'clock game, which left time for a grocery run to pick up such necessaries as light beer and fixins for microwave-nachos. I considered texting the Tulips to see if any of the guys could join me in a small victory celebration, but first things first. The church parking lot was empty, which meant I could have His house to myself to thank Him properly. I grabbed my keyring and headed out.

Some priests, and not a few lay ministers, tend to fill an empty church with clomping footfalls, bangs, knocks and other noise. Maybe the silence bothers them, or it could be asserting one's privilege, like a teen-ager left in charge of the house while the parents are out. Not me. I find solace in silence, and so I tread lightly even in an empty church. Good thing, too, or I would not have heard the soft, female sobbing coming from the office.

I hadn't even gotten into a pew when I became aware of a faint, staccato run of soft crying, gasps and even a low, drawn-out moan. They led me into the church office, where to my astonishment Patty Romano sat in her chair, elbows propped on her desk and forehead pressed against joined fists. She raised her head at the sound of her name, dark eyes brimming and the tip of her nose raw and glistening. I'm not sure what threw me more, the sight of my unflappable office administrator so unhinged or the horror in her eyes and trembling lower lip as she rasped out, "My fault. It's my fault."

I rounded the counter, took a knee beside the chair and tried to throw an arm around her but Patty pulled away, shaking her head.

"What's the matter? What's going on, Pat?"

She kept sobbing, head turned, black hair in my face. I let her continue for a few heartbeats, then rose and said, "I'll get you something." The office minifridge is stocked with bottled water and I grabbed one, twisted off the cap and gently pushed the plastic cylinder into her hand.

"Take a sip," I said, then insisted when she shook her head. Reluctantly Patty took one, then a second, longer sip. The icy water had the desired effect. The tears ceased, Patty blew her nose into a crumpled tissue in her hands, and a bit of her sturdier self returned.

"OK, what's the matter?"

Patty drew a deep breath, and released it with the word, "Bridget."

"Ah no. Was she in an accident? Is she OK?"

Shaking her head, Patty turned to me, eyes moist again. "She's missing."

I reached out and rolled the other office chair over before my legs gave out. "I don't understand. She was here Friday, right?"

Patty nodded. "I just got off the phone with her mom. It's so horrible." She looked at me with pleading eyes. "And I know it's mostly her sister's fault, but it's mine, too…"

"OK, stop. Start at the beginning. What's going on?"

It took a few moments and more sips of water for Patty to collect herself, but when she did it was my office administrator who spoke.

"Do you know about Bridget's sister, Margaret?"

I shook my head.

"She's about five years older than Bridget," Patty said, and looked down into her hands. "They're as different as sisters can be. In fact, I often wonder how much of Bridget's personality is a reaction to Maggs'."

"So not a church-goer," I said. The Mullins consistently attended the 10 o'clock Mass on Sundays, always center aisle, left side, about halfway up. I dimly recalled a younger brother because he'd been an altar server the year I got here, and remembered Bridget talking about an older brother. But I couldn't place a sister.

"Oh, you'd remember her, believe me," Patty said. "One of those troubled ones, you know. Fell in with the wrong crowd in school, a constant heartache to her parents according to Bridget. Drinking and pot, then pills, partying and boys. She left home three years ago and rented a place with another girl. Maggs worked in a tattoo shop and sold homemade jewelry, like pendants and bracelets, but Bridget said she didn't make nearly enough. The girl Magg moved in with," Patty cocked her head. "She made photos and videos to sell online. They call it 'adult content' but you know what I mean," Patty glanced to the side and shook her head. "Bridget said Maggs did a few videos but her brother found out and came down on her hard. Told her she was shaming the whole family, and made her give up the online stuff. But Maggs needed drug money, so…she became an escort.

"I guess there was a fight with the roommate and Maggs moved out last year. She didn't talk to her parents anymore, but kept in touch with Bridget and the boys. One day Bridget said she realized she hadn't heard from Maggs for a while, and her brothers hadn't either. They all tried to reach her but got no response. They filed a missing person's report and passed out flyers with her picture, talked with people she hung out with, but no one knew anything.

"Then after a week Maggs showed up at her brother's apartment. She claimed she'd gone to Denver with some guy, and had lost her phone."

Patty raised both hands. "I'm telling you all this because Maggs has vanished again. The family didn't react at first, but Bridget is really worried. She showed me a recent picture, and that girl looks like somebody in their 40s. Skinny, hollow cheeks, hair all raggedy. Tattoo up the side of her neck, and all kinds of piercings." Patty sighed again. "Bridget thinks the escort service dropped her and she might even be homeless.

"So when she disappeared again, her family thought it would be like last time and Maggs would show up after a few days. But that was three or four weeks ago. Even if she's homeless, Maggs keeps up a burner phone and talks with Bridget a couple times a week. Her brother went to the homeless shelters, but no one has seen her."

Patty's hands rose then flopped back into her lap. "So they started doing the flyers again. Bridget designed a new one and I told her she could use the parish copier," her dark eyes flashed over to me. "We used our own paper and if we needed a new toner cartridge I'll pay–" but stopped when I waved a hand at her. "We did that last week, and the family began posting them on telephone poles and walls and stuff. Then I had to open my big mouth," Patty said, and raised a hand to her forehead.

"What? What was said?"

"They were using a photo from years ago, when Maggs looked better. I told Bridget to use that recent one, but her family said it made her look like a junkie, and who would help look for a druggie? And then Bridget told me they were posting these around here, and downtown by Rocket Mortgage and the casino and Cleveland State. And I said that's dumb because Maggs didn't go to those places, so no one would recognize her. I said they needed to take them, you know, to the rougher places where Maggs did her thing."

Patty's composure began to crumble as her eyes filled with tears. "I thought," she said, and her breath caught in her throat. "I meant for her brother to do that."

"No," I said. "No, Bridget wouldn't. She wouldn't know where to go." But Patty shook her head.

"When I left Friday, she was still here working on filing. I didn't think anything of it. I stopped in today to pick up some things and saw the printer flashing the 'Add paper' message. I put some in and this came out." She held up a sheet emblazoned with the word MISSING at the top, followed by a black-and-white portrait of what looked like a young, tired Tilda Swinton sporting multiple piercings, a lopsided grin, and a tattoo of a star with a broad tail riding up her neck. "See. She made a new flyer with the recent photo, like I suggested. I called her cell but got no answer, so I called their house because they still have a landline. Her mother answered and the poor thing was in hysterics. I could barely make out her words over the crying.

"Bridget went out Friday night to put up more flyers and didn't come home," Patty's breathing became ragged again. "She was gone all day Saturday and doesn't answer her phone. They tried calling the police, but the cops won't take a missing person report unless you've been gone 48 hours. This morning her dad and brother drove into the city to look for her." Tears again slid down Patty's cheeks. "They spotted her car on Superior Avenue by a warehouse. Her dad has a spare key and he found Bridget's purse under the passenger seat, with her wallet inside." Patty nodded her head and began to gnaw on her thumbnail. I put an arm around her shoulder and this time she leaned in. She said something between the sobs but I couldn't make it out.

"What? What'd you say, Pat?"

She pulled back and looked at me from the depths of her anguish.

"I said you know what that means. Someone took her."

CHAPTER 39

I suggested to Patty explanations for Bridget's disappearance that sounded unconvincing even to me. She wiped her cheeks, looked at the clock and got up, saying she needed to get dinner on, but then wondered aloud if she should visit Bridget's mother first. I suggested if she did, she should print out a dozen more flyers to share with the family and possibly the police. Old instincts must have kicked in, because by the time Patty headed to the door she was once again Office Administrator Patty, a manila folder thick with flyers tucked under her arm, and a cell phone pressed to her ear as she gave someone instructions on how to put a roast into the oven.

One of the flyers stayed with me. I folded and stuffed it into my shirt pocket and left for the rectory. The closer I got, the more my steps slowed because I didn't want to go in. I didn't want to do what I knew had to be done. "It'll be fine," I reassured myself as I climbed the steps. "Your mind is playing tricks on you." But I had to check.

Bongo greeted me at the door but sensed my agitation and decided it was best to go elsewhere. I went into my bedroom, warm and bright with sunlight, and sat down at my desk. Before I went through with this, I blessed myself and pressed my lips against clasped hands.

"Dear Lord let me be wrong. Please," I muttered. The flyer flipped open as I drew it from my pocket and I laid it on the desk, smoothing it out. Maggs' image grinned up at me. I opened the wide, flat desk drawer and pulled out the baggie containing Freeman's trophies. Even before I opened it, my stomach began to twist. I slid the nose ring out onto the flyer and used a pencil to nudge it beside the black-and-white image. The small glass chips in the nose ring were light grey on the flyer, not exactly the pale blue on the actual ring. But the Victorian-style mounting matched perfectly.

My gaze wandered to Magg's unhappy eyes and the lopsided grin that seemed to mock, "What are the odds of two women wearing the same weird nose ring? Not good, eh priest?"

Stomach acid erupted into my throat, and I bit it back long enough for a mad dash to the bathroom. My knees hit the floor beside the porcelain throne just seconds before lunch made a return appearance. By the third heave the process seemed finished, so I wiped my lips, slumped back onto my heels, and tipped my forehead against the rim. Well, a voice in my head whispered, at least now you have a face and a name when she visits you in your nightmares.

*   *   *

He'd said he couldn't resume hunting until his wife left.

That would be today, Sunday. But Bridget went missing two nights ago. Surely Freeman wouldn't risk discovery by claiming another victim with his wife still at home, would he? On the other hand, he had left St. Al's in a fury Friday afternoon when I slipped through his fingers. Might his anger and bloodlust have driven him to risk another victim so soon?

I washed my face in the bathroom sink, and lit the black stubs of a triple-wick candle to mask the sour stench hanging in the air. Not trusting my stomach to anything stronger, I filled a dixie cup with water from the sink and returned to my desk to think.

The possibility that Freeman had abducted two sisters in separate, unrelated incidents was too stunning to consider. Surely God would not crush the Mullins family with such a blow. Bridget's disappearance had to have another explanation.

Even if their vanishings were unrelated, I sensed a message in the circumstances. I hooked the nose ring with the pencil and returned it to the baggie, where it slid beside the green ear gauge. Yes, Freeman's incarceration was coming, but not soon enough. IBS could drag his feet in contacting the authorities simply out of pique at being overruled by the papal nuncio. That could give Freeman another week, maybe two.

I looked at the missing woman's face on the sheet before me. A Vatican representative said the seal does not apply, so what's to stop me from going to the police? Sure, I'd pay a price for doing an end-around IBS, and Mwangi might catch blowback for sharing confidential information. But if it gets Freeman off the streets sooner, so what? I was pretty sure Mwangi would agree with me.

When I started thinking of how to do this, though, the idea crumbled. What would I do, go to the cops who locked me up for soliciting and say, "Hey guys, remember me? Maybe you saw me on YouTube." And if I approached the attorney general, or the sheriff's office? I've read and watched and listened to more than my share of police procedurals. They wouldn't much like the implication that a serial killer was slaughtering prostitutes and homeless people right under their noses. And what did I have for proof? A missing person flyer and two pieces of costume jewelry. With glum reluctance I admitted that the bishop probably had the best chance of getting genuine action from authorities.

I looked at Maggs' eyes in the photo. They resembled Bridget's but lacked her honesty and openness. Instead, I saw pain, misery, and suspicion. Wherever the camera had captured her expression, it now reached through time and distance to say to me, "Hey whatever happened to 'Do what you can do?' Or is that only to help the righteous?"

The accusation pressed down like a weight, but in doing so it squeezed out of me a realization. There *was* something I could do: I could go to Freeman. The more I pondered the idea the more it energized me. I could find Freeman, show up on his doorstep. Explain that his confessions had been ruled inauthentic and even now the bishop was handing over evidence and information to the attorney general. I would tell him I was that sudden gust of wind one feels on a hot July afternoon, smelling of rain and jangling wind chimes to warn of an approaching storm. But instead of lightning and hail, this storm would bring black-clad tactical police, detectives in sport coats, coveralled forensic units, and prosecutors in pencil dresses and pinstripe suits. I would be Freeman's very own Jeremiah, prophesizing doom if he didn't repent. Or at least cooperate.

This could work.

I could negotiate with him. Renew my offer to speak on his behalf. Appeal to his cynical nature with this chance at self-preservation. And I hadn't forgotten that fleeting trace of humanity I saw in him Friday in the confessional. It was tiny and overwhelmed but still there. And I believed, I truly believed that charred remnant of decency within him could be nurtured, could flourish, and grow and push back the evil that dominated him.

The thought popped into my consciousness: what if I find Bridget there? I shook it from my head and grimly went down another, darker avenue, a consideration I would not share with Freeman. If I failed to persuade him and he refused my help, there was a way to accelerate his arrest and stop him from carving out fresh sorrows. If the Enemy whispered to him that I had foolishly delivered myself into his hands, and he chose instead to finish what he'd begun at the church on Friday, I would fix it so the cops would know where to search for me.

CHAPTER 40

It only took Google about 30 seconds to find him. There he was on my computer, second from the right among a half dozen snapshots. I clicked on his image and in a heartbeat his smiling, bespectacled face filled my screen, with a caption beneath reading "William Freeman, Senior DevOps Engineer, Alastor IT Solutions LLC." No hotlink to his bio, so I jumped to the "About Us" section on the company's website. It was all marketing blather, with dense lines of copy containing so much computer jargon, acronyms, and brand names it may as well have been written in Mandarin.

Freeman had said he lived in Springfield Township, on 80 acres or so. It took a few more minutes, but his address popped up. Google Maps' satellite screen displayed an overhead shot of a McMansion with fresh signs of construction nearby and lots and lots of trees and fields. There was a greenish-blue oval near the house too big for a swimming pool. This had to be it. No streetscape view was available, probably because the house was too far from the road. I zoomed out the satellite image to find the closest home but had to go so high the image pixilated and I couldn't tell if the nearest structure was a house, a barn, a warehouse or what.

A few more clicks revealed Freeman's home was only

40 minutes from the rectory. That pretty much clinched it. I knew where he lived, how to get there, and I had plenty of time on my hands. No doubt about it, the Holy Spirit had cleared a path for me. I just had to tug on my big boy pants and start moving. But first, some preparations.

I found my small travel Bible filled with post-its, holy cards, and notes scribbled in margins. And yes, from my dresser I grabbed a small bottle of holy water. No garlic or wooden stakes but the sacred water seemed prudent. Look, I have blessed many homes and I firmly believe when done with the sincere participation of the family, such a blessing transforms a home into a domestic church. It fills it with grace and peace.

So if belief and prayer can make a place holy, sin and horrors can make a place profane. If you don't believe that, go visit Auschwitz. Or consider how often the dwellings of serial killers are torn down. You can clean and detoxify all you want, but the funk of evil lingers. Freeman had taken at least one human life at his home and possibly desecrated bodies there before burying them. Through repetition of sin, done willingly and perhaps even enthusiastically, he may have invited a spiritual malignancy to attach itself to that place. If I was going into a dwelling that harbored demons, I would arm myself with faith in God and the spiritual weapons fashioned by the Church.

But should I take a gun?

Holy water might repel a demonic assault, but another knife attack? Not so much. A gun could benefit Freeman in the long run, I argued with myself. If worst came to worst, the sight of a muzzle pointed at him might prevent Freeman from attempting further violence. And if, God help me, Bridget was there as a prisoner, I'd probably need something more than moral appeals to win her freedom.

I went down to the basement and found the Smith & Wesson Victory in its plastic case. Terry hadn't provided ammo but I could pick up a box of Federal hollow points at Walmart. A queasiness rose in my gut at the thought. I've never shot a living thing in my life, not even the crows or rats on the farm. I wasn't sure I could even point a firearm at another human being, let alone pull the trigger. Dad had said a priest has no business with a gun and he was right. What kind of shepherd goes about the Lord's work cocked and locked? A shepherd's defense was his faith in God. And maybe a sling with a handful of pebbles. That metaphor tripped a circuit in my brain. I didn't own a sling, but thanks to dear old Pops, I had my pick from a variety of the modern equivalent. Not one bit lethal, but Freeman wouldn't know that.

I pulled out the tub with all my father's "toy" guns. A little confidence seeped back in as I considered the six shooters and semi-autos in the collection. Some were darned convincing, and a few looked to be the real McCoy, even down to wear marks on the metal from being holstered. But something told me a famous gun probably would work against me. Freeman might laugh at the sight of a priest holding a Colt Peacemaker.

Turning to a table behind me, I saw the Dan Wesson revolver I had left there when target practice was interrupted by Stan Schumacher on Thursday. Now there was a possibility. A modern, chrome-plated revolver with a four-inch barrel, the noses of cartridges visible in the cylinder. That should give Freeman pause. I picked it up and remembered I hadn't unloaded it. Sighting at the paper target across the basement, I used Terry's two-hand hold and fired. An anemic "pfft" and "ping" as the pellet bounced off the table beneath the target told me most of the CO_2 had leaked out. I replaced the near-empty gas capsule with a new one and reloaded the fake cartridges with good Meisterkulgen target pellets.

Aiming again, I slowly released my breath, paused and squeezed. A crisp crack like that of nail gun sounded, and a black hole appeared in the quarter-sized, red bullseye. I repeated the sequence and another dot appeared in the red below the first, close enough to touch. Well, if Freeman got aggressive, I stood a chance. But only if he showed the courtesy to remain stock still while I drew my piece, adjusted my stance, acquired a sight picture, and executed a controlled firing sequence. Then maybe I could pull off a Ralphie and crack his glasses. In the ensuing confusion this parish priest would beat feet out the nearest exit.

The gun and the holy water fit easily into the pockets of my sport coat, and I could carry the bible in my hand. There was one more thing to do. I opened Word on my laptop and typed out a paragraph explaining where I was going and why. I erased the last line, then retyped: "If I disappear, it will likely be at the hands of William Freeman."

I hit the print button, fetched the sheet from the printer in my office and laid it neatly on the keyboard of my open laptop. A bit melodramatic maybe, but who knows what God planned for this imperfect, little priest. And one last bit of insurance was required.

"Hey," I said into my phone.

"What the hell, Tommy? What is going on with you? You had me worried sick. I just about had my car keys in my—"

"T, I have to go somewhere right now. Someone needs me very badly."

"I thought you said you were suspended or something. How do you still—"

"Listen, 'cause I'm almost out the door. Terry, I left something in my office, on my laptop, and I need you to be in charge of it. I'll call tonight to explain everything, but on the off chance that, um…"

"Tommy," the word came out flat and I recognized her cop persona. "Stay there. I'm coming over and we can discuss this."

"No, no. Look, never mind. I'm going right now."

"Tommy, listen to me. You stay right there. I'm on my way, I'm grabbing my purse –."

"Forget I called," I shot back. "Wait a couple of hours and I'll call ya. There's no one here besides Bongo, so you won't be able to get in." The moment I blurted that I realized what a foolish thing it was to say. Terry would take it as a challenge, and not much of one, either.

"Terry, I love you, and everybody else in the fam. Just…be patient," I said and ended the call.

Bongo wandered in and stared at me with those big brown eyes.

"You need to go out before I go?" I asked. "It might be a long time."

For reply the beagle turned a circle and laid down.

"Fine," I muttered. "I'll give you the run of the place but don't piss on my bed. Use the filing cabinet if you have to."

I headed to the back door, flicking off wall switches along the way. With a brisk twist and tug on the door knob, chilly evening air swept in. I set the lock and stopped for a final check, patting my clothing. Wallet. Phone. Car keys. Bible. Holy water. Toy gun.

"Bless me, Lord," I murmured, "for I know not what I do."

CHAPTER 41

The female voice of my GPS announced I had arrived at my destination with more confidence than I felt. Through the trees loomed a two-story monstrosity built to resemble an English manor. Not a single sound, light, or motion came from the structure as I glided along its curved asphalt driveway. You'd think that would calm my jitters, but it didn't. Instead, I kept thinking of Van Helsing arriving at Castle Dracula just as the sun disappears. Which, in fact, it had. Only a furnace-orange glow remained in the western sky, all other quadrants gone purplish black. A decaying jet contrail sketched a pale, wispy streak overhead before disappearing into the gloom. The near-horizon rose in a clumpy silhouette of trees, some already stripped down to skeletal branches. Shadows welled up from the ground on all sides, and in the failing light it felt as though holiness and joy had withdrawn from the world, leaving a shivering void where something wolfish could stalk in.

I parked my Nissan on the far side of a pole barn large enough for four cars and a cherry-picker. It was separated from the house by a driveway at least 60 feet wide. I opened my door, stepped out onto gravel and stood there, sizing up the brown-brick house.

The narrow, asphalt driveway led to the house's

attached three-door garage. A second drive, this one grey concrete, sprouted like a graft from the black asphalt to connect the side of the house and pole barn. A plain, white, single-car garage door stood on the side of the house, matched by a steel entry door with a small square of frosted glass at eye level. A few feet away a large, commercial air-conditioning unit jutted out from the brick wall. If you parked against the brick wall a half dozen dusty, grass-stained push mowers with cardboard tags dangling from the handles, you'd swear it was a repair shop.

Construction must have been recent or the Freemans were taking their time landscaping. A mound of fill dirt taller than me remained beside the back corner of the house, and I shifted uneasily on the gravel. Freeman had boasted how deeply he'd buried his victims. It would take a sizeable hole to produce that much dirt.

The rear of the house ended with an elegant stone patio and elaborate firepit with built-in benches. A lawn as wide as the home ran about 30 yards to end abruptly in knee-high field grass. Another 50 yards beyond, the sky's faint orange glow reflected off a body of water easily two to three acres. I could just make out a short dock and what looked like a small bass boat tied up to it. The opposite side of the pond ended against a sheer cliff of raw earth that rose right out of the water. The former quarry must have gnawed away half a hillside before work stopped.

This place brought back memories of well-to-do neighbors who bought the property next to our family's orchard. Those folks tried hard to wedge a slice of upscale suburbia into the countryside. They had wanted both worlds: sophisticated Saturday night gatherings on the patio with cool jazz, cocktails, and brick-oven pizzas; and on Sundays they'd pull on Duluth-brand jeans, fire up a farm-grade John Deere and use its 72-inch dirt bucket to move four bags of potting soil.

Unlike our old neighbors' place, the Freeman estate wasn't play-acting. It really had a split personality. The frontage feigned an English estate with faux stone facing, multipaned windows, and neatly shaped greenery. The east side of the house, however, was country commercial, complete with gravel, concrete, and wild grass and weeds encroaching on the lawn. Might this simply reflect differing tastes between Freeman and his wife, or was it a hint into Freeman's own personality; a veneer of techno-bourgeois ostentation concealing a more feral nature?

No one seemed to be home, but the house was not deserted. As soon as I shut my car door a cacophony of barks, grunts, snorts, and yowls erupted from above. Freeman's French bulldogs bustled out onto a wooden deck 20 feet in the air and set off a motion-sensor light. I counted three bat-eared, little gargoyles banging against one another. As they barked, they stomped their stubby front legs on the deck like angry toddlers pounding on high chairs.

Since no one responded to this canine alarm system I assumed I had missed him. Though twilight was fast giving way to true night, it seemed too early for Freeman to hunt. Perhaps he was running errands, ghoulish or otherwise.

My breath now condensed on the still air and the cold seeped into my collar, so I considered getting back into my car to wait. Or, a timid voice inside me whispered, we could head back to the rectory, catch the second half of the Browns game, and try again tomorrow. Choice Number 2 sounded very appealing, but before I ran away I had to at least knock. Scuffing across the pavement, I got within five feet of the entry door and its frosted-glass window when a motion-activated floodlight switched on, bathing me in harsh, halogen light. The sudden illumination revealed no doorbell button, so I decided to give a polite knock, send the doggies on the deck into an even greater fury, then call it a night and head back to the ranch. I banged my knuckles against the door with the kind of moderate authority a busy UPS driver might use if he needed a signature. To my dismay, the lockset's deadlatch slid off the plate with a soft click, and the door drifted open.

"Aw c'mon. You've gotta be kidding," I moaned. For a moment I did nothing, just stood there staring at the blackness revealed by the gap. An image rose in my mind of Bridget, bound and blindfolded, lying unconscious on a concrete floor. The security light winked out, I glanced up at a night-hidden heaven and, grumbling "Alright already. I'm goin', I'm goin'," stepped in.

The first thing I did once inside was to feel the wall to my right. There had to be a switch, it's where everybody puts switches. My fingers found nothing and for a moment I wondered if Freeman had rigged the place with indoor motion-sensor lights. Or cameras. The second thought stopped me as my fingers slid against a smooth surface. It was a flat, rectangular toggle switch: press the top for on, the bottom for off. Of their own volition, my fingers pressed the top and LED shop lights winked on, illuminated the entire room in the intense, almost bluish glare hideously mislabeled as "daylight."

I'm not sure what I had expected, but it was not this. The harsh light bounced off white, metal-paneled walls, stainless steel counters and appliances. I was instantly transported to a December day decades ago when my dad took my brother, John, and I to a meat market to process his newly-bagged, white-tail deer. Dad knew the manager and got permission for us to go in the back to see the operation, as long as we didn't touch anything or get in the way. While the dead deer leaked blood in the bed of Dad's F-150, the manager hooked a coat hanger-shaped gambrel into the joints of its back legs. A garage door opened and a forklift rolled out with an electric whine. The manager hooked the gambrel onto a bar across the forklift's tines, the dead deer rose again, and we followed its dangling carcass into the building.

Freeman's processing area was similar, albeit much smaller. Directly across from me a row of cleavers, knives and shearing scissors clung to the wall on a long magnetic strip. A pair of hack saws hung from a hook. Below these a stainless-steel counter with shelving ran six or seven feet, ending in a commercial-grade double sink with overhanging hose & grip nozzle.

To my left ran another stainless-steel counter, this one crowded with small appliances like a meat grinder, sausage stuffer, and vacuum sealer. An inexpensive power washer stood upright against the counter, and beside it a pile of cinderblocks, scraps of two-by-fours, rolls of insulation, heavy gauge chain, and a spool of electrical wire. An open door revealed a cavernous main garage with a red Mini-Cooper almost lost in the shadows at its far end.

Looking up I saw an electronic hoist on a trolley track, and dangling below it a pulley, hook, and gambrel. It hung behind the single garage door and I understood Freeman's set-up. He could back his truck in, attach the gambrel to his deer, hoist it out of the truck bed, and track it over to a large, metal table on wheels. On the concrete floor beneath the hoist ran a narrow, discolored drain grate about six feet long.

To my right a small, silver, walk-in freezer extended into the room. No lock hung from the pull latch, but my gut tightened at the thought of what might be hanging on meat hooks inside. Further down on the right I spotted a door on the wall at the far corner. Let's investigate there instead, I told myself. Besides, if Bridget was in here she was probably on the other side of that door. I timidly called "hello," and got no response. Steeling myself, I walked to the door, turned the handle and stepped in.

I found no captive teen-ager, but did discover Freeman's man cave. The long, rectangular room held recliners, a dorm refrigerator, a gun safe, archery tackle on the walls, several carboard moving boxes, and a 50-inch TV mounted on the rear wall. A braid of cables hung down from behind the TV to a stand filled with cable box, laptop, game stations and electronic gear I didn't recognize.

I left my bible on a stack of boxes, stepped back into the butcher room and wandered a bit. To my many sins I could now add breaking and entering, but I justified it by looking for Bridget, or any evidence of Freeman's murders. A jury of vegans would find plenty here to put

Freeman away for life, but nothing else. Remembering what he'd said about "slicing" a homeless man, I took some tentative steps toward the knives on the wall. They were in easy reach across the countertop, but the temptation to take one for police examination vanished almost as soon as it arose. Which, if any, had he used on his victim? Besides, my job here was not to collect evidence, but to persuade Freeman to give himself up. Go back to the car, I thought, and try again tomorrow.

As I turned, my eyes fell to the metal shelves under the counter. Something odd lay among the boxes of plastic film, gloves, and bottles of sanitizer. Leaning in closer I saw it was a camera tripod. That seemed out of place for a butcher shop, unless Freeman hoped for YouTube fame as an amateur meat-cutter.

I recalled him saying something about using video to lull his victims into thinking they were about to star in homemade porn. The shelves yielded nothing else out of the ordinary, except for a couple of heavy-duty folding chairs stacked against the end of the counter. I tugged the top of one and it moved an inch before catching. I've stacked and unstacked plenty of folding chairs in church social halls, so I knew how to get these rascals apart. I jostled and pulled until one finally lifted free. Dangling on either side were bright silver handcuffs, one end closed around the scratched bracing of the chair and the other open like hungry, skeletal jaws.

I let it drop back into place as an ice ball formed in my belly. "Dear God, those poor people," I whispered. Theories evaporated in the face of stark, ugly reality. This is Freeman's slaughterhouse. Get out of here you little church mouse, a voice inside me said, and run like hell to a police station.

Walking to the door, I reached out and pressed the light switch but nothing happened. Then I remembered you have to hit the bottom part to toggle it off. The room went black in an instant. The butcher shop's bright lights and white walls had made me night blind, and I groped for the door handle. When I discovered it and yanked the door open, I saw only a wall of black. Blinking and rubbing my eyes seemed to help my vision slowly return. I saw the vague shape of the pole barn, and far away twin dots of headlights moving on the road. Of course, as soon as I stepped out the motion-sensor would pick me up and light would return, as would the frenzy of the Frenchies.

My foot had just swung forward when the headlights on the road slowed and turned toward the house.

CHAPTER 42

It was a simple plan. I'd hide in the man cave until Freeman came in and went upstairs to the living area. I'd quietly, very quietly, make my way to the door, step outside, then turn around and bang my fist on it. He'd never know I'd been inside.

I cracked open the man cave's door in time to hear his truck door thump closed in the garage. Freeman said something and laughed. My heart leapt into my throat when a nasally feminine voice responded and another door slammed. It wasn't Bridget's voice, thank God. Maybe it was the wife. Maybe she got sick and Freeman had to pick her up from the airport, again postponing his hunting season.

A third door banged and I stepped back deeper into the room's shadows. Three people now. That scotched everything. Had it been only his wife, I could ask for some time alone with him, but not now. I'd let their little party go upstairs, then sneak out, start the Nissan without lights and quietly glide up his drive to the road. It had been too cold to leave the house's windows open, and they'd probably be talking, maybe laughing, and wouldn't hear the Nissan. I would come back tomorrow.

The butcher shop's brilliant lights flicked on and my narrow door opening offered enough angle to observe

Freeman and his guests. They weren't heading upstairs.

"I seen places like this," the woman said, still out of view. "My cousin works at one down by Morgantown. He used to give us deer meat in the winter."

"You like venison?" Freeman asked.

"Take it or leave it," she said and I caught a whiff of her tantalizing, hypnotic aroma. Marlboro menthol. Maybe Newport.

"I'll give ya some when I take ya back. I got tons," Freeman said. He strolled into view wearing blue jeans and a button-down shirt too tight across the middle. He turned and looked behind him. "How 'bout you?"

The first woman said something in Spanish, and an almost girlish giggle replied. My breath caught, and a pulse started in my throat. They were prostitutes. Two of them. Just like he said he would find.

The female voices continued, one in rapid-fire Spanish and the nasally one much slower. Again, they giggled.

"What's so funny?" Freeman asked, a hint of irritation in his voice that I hoped the women recognized.

"I told her you wanted to give her some meat. She said 'Ain't that why we come here?'"

"She's right, I'm gonna give it to ya both," Freeman chuckled.

Finally the first woman walked into view. I'd put her somewhere in her 40s, though maybe she was younger and had aged prematurely. Dark brown hair hung to her shoulders, and a part on the left side let her bangs sweep over her forehead. Thick eyebrows, little or no make-up, frown lines and a strong jaw gave her a formidable air. The cigarette jutting from her lower lip added to the impression. For a moment I wondered if I was mistaken, because her clothing did not scream "sex for sale." A long, dark-blue, cardigan sweater hung to mid-thigh, beneath which a red and white print dress ended a modest inch or two above her knee. Black tights and dark grey Sketchers completed her ensemble. She could have been the accounts receivable manager at a trucking firm.

The second woman, however, removed any doubt. Girl or teenager might be a more accurate term. Frizzy black hair and deep olive complexion gave her away as an immigrant, possibly Central American. No worry lines marred her rounded features, and she stood several inches shorter than her companion. An unbuttoned, bedazzled jean jacket stopped at her waist, and beneath it what looked like a yellow tube top. Her hips and backside were barely covered by the smallest denim skirt I'd ever seen, but perhaps in a concession to the cold she also wore black legging or yoga pants. Cowboy boots with red firebirds on the sides seemed clownishly large on her petite frame.

They continued chatting, and the tripod opened with a metallic clack as Freeman explained that he wanted to make a video of their adventure. The nasally woman warned that he'd better clear it with "Gee" before posting anything online. "Maybe I'll keep it to myself for a while," Freeman replied and I risked cracking the door open a bit wider.

He bent over the tripod, attaching a cell phone horizontally. The older woman eyed the row of knives on the wall beside them, and muttered something in Spanish to her companion. Freeman seemed too occupied with his role as a cinematographer to notice. He walked the two women into positions facing one another in front of the counter, checked the view from the camera, and moved it back a few feet. When it met his satisfaction, he raised both hands for them to stay where they were.

"OK, I'll get chairs for you guys. Lose the tights and your panties, but keep the rest of your clothes on." He looked at the younger woman. "Take off the jacket, too." The older woman translated and they kicked off their shoes. Freeman pulled the first chair out and set it up behind the older woman. She tugged her tights and green panties down to her ankles, but stopped abruptly.

"No. No, huh-uh. No cuffs. We're not doin' that," she said.

"Oh, don't worry," Freeman soothed. "These don't even work. I lost the key for them."

"Well, since we don't need 'em," the woman turned, picked up the open-ended cuff and swiftly snapped it closed. Before Freeman could stop her, she did the same with the other.

"OK, not a problem," he grumbled after a pause, "but remember, I said this would be a bondage thing. That's why Gee is getting the big bucks. I've got some rope we'll use."

"Sure," she chirped back. "Hey, why don't we do this, it'll be really hot. Why don't you have her tie me up, and I'll play like I'm fighting it, and we'll yell shit at each other in Spanish."

"I like that, that's good," Freeman said eagerly. "Then I come in and tie her up, like I'm breaking it up. I'll get started with her while you watch, then you ask to join in, and we'll take it from there."

"Sounds like a plan," the woman said. "But don't put

no cuffs on her neither. Gee won't like that." Freeman thought about it a second. "The problem is I don't have enough rope for both of you. What about zip ties?"

"OK," the woman said, "but put something under 'em, like a rag or some shit, so it don't cut her."

Freeman nodded and went off to get his supplies while the women spoke softly and quickly in Spanish. For a moment I thought of stepping out and telling them to run for it, but before I made up my mind – or more likely found my resolve – Freeman was back.

They briefly discussed "the scene," then Freeman took his place behind the tripod and watched through the viewfinder as the two women acted out a confrontation. I could only see the younger woman from behind, and apparently the plot called for them to argue, the younger woman to slap the seated older woman into unconsciousness, then tie her up. There was shouting and the younger woman delivered a very fake slap, so lame that Freeman stepped forward from behind the tripod and demanded she do it again. "I can edit it. Let's do a second take." The older woman grinned, enjoying the novelty. They argued again briefly, and this time the slap looked marginally better. The older woman's chin dramatically dropped to her chest, and after glancing at Freeman to confirm it was OK to continue, the younger woman got behind her. I couldn't see what kind of binding she applied, but she made the thin, white roping fly.

"What are you doing, you bitch?" the suddenly conscious older woman screamed. "Lemme go."

Taking his cue, Freeman ran into the scene, grinning from ear to ear. He grabbed the younger woman by her bare shoulders and pushed her back and onto the other chair. Shouting "I'll show you," he jammed his knee into her stomach and roughly pulled an arm behind her. Freeman yanked a long, white zip tie from his trouser pocket and secured her arm with a vicious tug on the plastic. The young prostitute yelped something in Spanish. Freeman grabbed her other, flailing arm, secured it as well, then moved behind her. I watched as he lifted one leg and zip-tied her ankle off the floor and onto the back chair leg.

"Hey, hey," the older woman called to him. "You don't need to do that." She tried to project authority but worry sounded in her voice.

Freeman ignored her and zip-tied the young woman's other leg as well. He stood, panting, took off his wire-rim glasses and wiped the sweat from his face with his sleeve.

"Alright," he said and turned to the younger woman. "I gotta say, even for porn that was bad acting. Your fingers never touched her face, and that wasn't much of a swing. If you're gonna slap someone unconscious, you gotta put your hips into it. Like this." He wound back and whirled forward, striking a blow to the girl's jaw, toppling both her and the chair. She lay on the floor shrieking as the other woman hurled a stream of obscenities. The Frenchies upstairs resumed their muffled barking. Freeman set the girl upright again, and I saw a cruel grin on his face.

"Now, to do a backhand just reverse it. But you still have to use the hips," he said and struck her again, whipping her head to the other side and rocking the chair, but she maintained her balance.

Freeman must have heard the older woman's chair bouncing as she struggled to get up because he spun about and stalked toward her, leaving the younger woman sobbing.

"That was crappy acting on your part, too, bitch. But you're gonna deliver. Lemme teach you what knocked out really feels like."

He didn't make it to her. The sound of my voice held him.

"Stop it, Freeman." Honestly, I don't remember stepping out of the man cave. My recollection picks up with me standing a few feet behind the Latina.

Freeman turned and stared as though I had appeared out of thin air, which it probably seemed I had. His lower lip moved with an unspoken word.

"What the hell are you doing in my house?" he finally demanded, equal parts wonder and outrage in his voice.

"They know," I said. "The bishop ruled your confessions inauthentic and went straight to the cops. I'm surprised they aren't here already."

His stare didn't waver, though a hand twitched. Then his face slowly twisted into very ugly smile.

"No, they're not coming. And they certainly don't bring priests with them."

The young woman called out hopefully "*¿Policia?*" The older woman looked around Freeman and said, "*No. Padre catolico.*"

"*¿Que?!*" the other asked in disbelief, and tried to twist in her chair.

"No policia," Freeman said. "Just a nobody priest. A disgraced priest, in fact." He tilted his head and asked me, "Did you think this would restore you? Not only won't that happen, I've got a great idea." He took a wide sidestep, reached out and pulled a carving knife off the magnetic strip. "What this video needs is another male actor. And we've got a volunteer."

My hand rose on its own accord, and I took a step back. "People know I'm here. If anything happens to me, you're first on the list of where to look. I mean that literally."

He shrugged his shoulders. "I'll say you came here, you were drunk, and tried to talk me into skinny dipping with you in the hot tub. I refused because I don't swing that way, and you left in a huff. Who knows where."

"My car is here. You can't get rid of it that fast."

"I can."

"They'll find it," I warned, shaking my head. "They'll know I was here, and didn't leave. No matter what you—"

"They'll never find the car," Freeman interrupted. He twisted slightly and pointed his finger behind the house. "Cause it's goin' in there. The quarry. That's where I put all my garbage. The others, my wife's stinkin' dog," he waved the knife between the two bound women, "these two," then he pointed the tip at me, "and you."

Understanding and maybe horror must have shown on my face because Freeman's smile got deeper and darker. "You thought I buried the ones I told you about, didn't you? Why should I do all that work when there's a grave a hundred and twenty feet deep right back there."

The Latina paused in her sobbing to fire off some Spanish at her colleague. The older woman's face betrayed no fear, I'll give her that. She simply stared at Freeman, glanced at the line of knives on the wall and replied in a low voice, "*El es un asesino.*" Sobs welled up again from the younger woman, and I didn't need a translator to understand her whimpers of "*No, no, por favor, amado Dios, no.*"

"Well," Freeman said. "Like they say in Hollywood, time is money," and took a casual step toward me. I jammed my hand into my jacket pocket and pulled out the Dan Wesson. The revolver gave the most satisfying, gratifying series of realistic clicks when I thumbed back the hammer, and the cylinder rotated those fake cartridges in a menacing clockwork motion.

Freeman froze.

"Shoot," the older woman shouted. "Blow his freakin' brains out!" Freeman straightened up and took a step back.

"Let 'em go, Will," I said. "And you and I will talk this out. There's still a door open for you. There's a way out of all this. I can help you."

"Just shoot the bastard!" the prostitute shrieked. She bounced on her chair a couple of times. A white snake of rope dropped behind her, curling and lashing against the chair leg, then a second end dangled.

"He's not," Freeman said quietly. The tip of the carving knife in his hand wiggled as he adjusted his grip. "He's not gonna shoot anybody. It's not in him."

To hold him at bay, I raised the gun in a combat stance, left hand tight around the shooting hand, thumbs crossed, and tried to center the front sight on the left lens of Freeman's glasses. But I've never pointed a gun at a human face, and I kept looking off the sight and at his eyes. I saw the skin around them crinkle as he squinted.

"What kind of gun is that? What's in the barrel?" he

asked.

You're not a tactical shooter, I heard Terry's voice far away in my mind. And a thought answered the memory: no, I'm a lights-out shooter.

I spun to my left, sighted, and squeezed the trigger. The revolver went off with a full charge of compressed air, meaning it gave an anemic crack no louder than a flyswatter hitting a countertop. The pellet pinged off the wall a good inch from the light switch.

"It's a BB gun," Freeman laughed out of my line of sight. "A goddammed BB gun! Of course. A candy-ass like him wouldn't carry a real gun."

You're not a tactical shooter, you're a bulls-eye shooter, I reminded myself and corrected my stance. Standing erect, I turned my body at a right angle to the target like every movie duelist you've ever seen. I put my left hand in my trouser pocket, and with my right thumbed the hammer back again, muzzle held high and extended out. Slowly the front sight slid down and settled into alignment with the rear sight as I softly released my breath through parted lips.

"What are you doing?" Freeman scoffed. "The garage opener is over there if that's—" he caught himself as he realized what I was attempting. But I'd already begun the slow squeeze and the trigger broke cleanly, my sights didn't waver, and the pellet flew true to the bottom of the light toggle.

Darkness swallowed us and the young woman screeched. The night blindness I'd experienced earlier probably shocked Freeman and his intended victims. I didn't have a plan beyond shooting out the light, but in fairness to me, it's not like I had time to think this through. So I stood there, at a loss, when I heard the women shouting in Spanish, another shriek, metal chairs banging on the pavement, a sudden bellow from Freeman, and more rapid-fire Spanish.

Do something, dumbass, my brain screamed. All I could think of was to rush Freeman, get the knife out of his hand, and maybe get on top of him. Improvisation is not my strong suit.

I lumbered toward where I thought he might be, my arms extended, the pellet gun still in my right hand. Shrill Spanish phrases continued to fly through the darkness and the girl gave a yip. As I closed in, someone banged into my right shoulder, spinning me into something that tangled my legs and I fell hard on my left shoulder. Scrambling to my knees, I heard the door open behind me and turned in time to see the outdoor overhead light flash on and two barefoot women rushing down the driveway, the younger one bent over because her wrists were still zip-tied to the chair she carried on her back. The older woman ran completely free and a few yards ahead, holding what was probably a cell phone to her ear. Where she had hidden it, I try not think about. Then the door swung shut, cutting off all light save for a dim glow in the frosted window.

That left me in the dark with a killer. It was quiet except for the muted commotion of the Frenchies upstairs. I had dropped the pellet gun when I fell, but that was OK since it wouldn't do much good against a carving knife. I gingerly felt my way forward and my hand touched fabric. Holding my left forearm in front of my face in case something pointy and sharp came my way, I patted forward and felt what I knew to be

Freeman's back. He lay flat on the ground, and when I put a hand where his shoulder should be, it felt warm and sticky. He gave a faint groan, somewhere between "Ow" and "Ah."

Assuming his threat potential to be significantly diminished, I got up and went to the wall to turn the lights back on. After a few fumbled attempts I found the switch, and when the LED glare returned, I saw that the light switch was smeared with blood. Looking at my right hand, I knew why. I turned and gasped.

Freeman lay on his belly, right leg pulled up under him. A dark red puddle pooled around his shoulder, and a pencil-wide stream of blood led to the metal grate in the floor. Cautiously, I stepped closer and looked beyond his hunched back. The handle of a meat cleaver jutted from the juncture of Freeman's neck and shoulder.

I stepped over the tripod laying on the floor and tried to raise him up, at least into a sitting position. He groaned and a sudden pulse of blood flowed higher on the side of the cleaver blade. I set him back down and knelt beside him. Somehow my cell phone was still in my inner jacket pocket, and I called 911.

"There's a man here, badly injured. He bleeding," I stammered to the dispatcher's question as to the nature of my emergency. "Send an ambulance. And police."

The dispatcher fired a lot of questions at me and later, when I heard my answers on the recording, I really couldn't blame the police for their reactions. All I do remember is reciting Hail Marys as I pressed my hands against the wound in Freeman's neck to try to slow the bleeding. Close to the blade his flesh felt warm, but when I touched his hand, it was ice cold.

It seemed only moments before lights flashed through the door's small window. I got up, walked over, and pulled the door open. Standing in the doorway, I waved one hand over my head while using the other to shield my eyes from the glare of the headlights.

"He's in here," I yelled as a car door opened and closed to a renewed chorus of barking. "Man, you guys are fast," I babbled. "I just got off the phone." The overhead sensor picked up motion and flicked on yet again. The vehicle in the drive was not a police car or ambulance, but a blue Ford Escape. And it wasn't a cop walking toward me.

"Tommy," Terry said, staring in horror at my bloody hands made even more lurid by the headlights of her car. "Oh my god, are you hurt?"

"No, I'm fine," I said.

"But your hands…"

"It's not mine," I said glancing at them, and made a quarter turn toward the room. "It's that guy's," I added with a flick of my head toward Freeman's prone body.

When I turned back to my sister, her jaw was hanging open a little and her eyes said it all.

I was in a hell of a lot of trouble.

CHAPTER 43

"He's not bleeding as much now," I said over my shoulder to Terry as I knelt beside Freeman. The dogs upstairs had gone quiet, and in the silence the prone figure' breathing came in shallow wheezes. "If I keep the pressure on, he'll last until the squad gets here, right?"

My sister said nothing. After deciding I wasn't Fr. Jekyll and Pastor Hyde, she'd followed me in, gingerly stepping around the debris on the floor. She kept fingertips tucked into her armpits, gently rested her back against the edge of the stainless-steel counter, and stared with an unsettling calm at Freeman's inert form. I leaned in and used my fingertips to gently press flesh against the cleaver in hopes of stopping the bleeding. Freeman's eyelids remained closed, his forehead and cheeks white as talcum powder, and lips pale to the point of translucence. As I pressed, I gave Terry a very condensed version of the whole story, beginning with his first visit to my confessional and finishing with her arrival. She took it all in without a word. I glanced at Terry, then at the man below me. I've sat beside dying patients in hospitals and hospices, and Freeman's face had that same awful stillness.

"He's not gonna make it, is he?" I asked.

Terry glanced at the glistening line of blood that

ended at the drain. "Probably not," she said without a trace of emotion.

"Ok," I replied. "I'll keep the pressure on until the EMTs show, but I've got to say the prayer for the dying for him."

"You said he's a serial killer. And was gonna kill you and those women, too."

I closed my eyes and focused. Usually I read the words from a booklet or my phone, but I'd done it often enough that it seemed like it would come to me. Most of it, at least. I switched hands, freeing my right to bless myself.

"In the name of the Father, and of the Son, and of the Holy Spirit."

"Tommy," Terry said sharply. "We need to talk before the cops get here."

"I commend you, my brother William, to Almighty God, and entrust you to your Creator. May you return to Him who formed you from the dust of the earth."

"Come on. You can do that later."

"May Christ who died for you admit you into his garden of paradise. May Christ, the true Shepherd, acknowledge you as one of his flock. May He forgive all your sins, and set you among those He has chosen. Amen."

I opened my eyes and saw no change in Freeman. Terry, however, was shaking her turned head in annoyance. Since high school I had called that her "I-can't-even" look, and it certainly applied here.

"What? What did you want to tell me?" I asked.

She kept that head shake going for another heartbeat or two, then glared at me. For a second, I thought she wasn't going to talk. Slowly, over-pronouncing each word, she said, "Keep your stupid mouth shut."

"No, this has to come out. There are families—"

"Oh, it'll come out, believe me Tommy. You wanna say prayers? Offer one now that no reporters are listening to their scanners."

OK, that got my attention.

"This is what you're going to say the cops. This sentence, and not one syllable more. You got that?"

I nodded.

"This is what you say: Sir, I will cooperate fully with your investigation after I have conferred with my attorney."

I shook my head. "I don't have a lawyer."

"I'll get you one, dummy. I know a bunch. But Tommy, I know how this is gonna play out because I've done it myself. They'll try to buddy you into talking, or they'll bully you into talking. They may even say they called the bishop and he gave you permission to talk. It's all bullshit. The law allows them to lie to get information. From the cops' point of view, you're the likely perp and the easiest way to close this case. You literally have his blood on your hands. If you talk to them without a lawyer, I guarantee they will maneuver you into statements that make you look guilty."

She must have seen the doubt and resistance in my face.

"You will help them, Tom, I promise. But you have got to get an attorney first. You've got to have one present when they interrogate you. They'll call it an interview, but believe me it's not, it's an interrogation. You gotta keep your mouth shut until you talk to a lawyer. Promise me, Tommy."

"Ok, Ok, I promise."

Terry's shoulders heaved with a sigh, and she leaned herself off the counter. "I'm going outside to make some phone calls. If we're lucky I'll reach some lawyers before it turns all red and blue outside."

"Lawyers, plural? You really think I'll need more than one?"

She was already walking, scrolling on her phone. "One for you and one for me." Terry looked my way and shook her head dismissively again. "This is a crime scene, Tommy. And there are three people here: you, me, and a soon-to-be dead guy. We're both gonna be suspects."

"Oh my God," I moaned. "I didn't mean to drag you into this. I shouldn't have left that letter."

"What letter?"

I stared at her. Terry's finger was flicking slower now as her eyes bored in on her screen.

"The one I left for you on my computer," I said. She shrugged her shoulders.

"You didn't go to the rectory?"

"Waste of time."

My mouth fell open. "How did you know where—"

She jabbed the phone and put it to her ear, holding the other hand up to silence me. I wasn't having it.

"T, how did you know I was here?"

"Apple Air Tag. Inside your passenger door panel. If you've heard a rattle, that's what—Hey, Melvin, how's my favorite flattop? Good, good. Hey look, sweetie, I gotta be quick. I got a client for you, and believe me, you are gonna love this guy."

CHAPTER 44

Terry was wrong. I wound up with two lawyers instead of one.

She was right about the cops, though. Freeman's house is in a township, so the first to show up were county deputies in black SUVs with "Sheriff" spelled out in two-foot gold stencils. The EMTs arrived shortly after, and I said a deep prayer of gratitude when they wheeled out Freeman on a gurney with an oxygen mask on his face instead of a sheet. It was hard to see because red and blue lights strobed the night, and the squad car in which I sat had its cabin light on, turning the passenger window into a mirror. I would have shaded the light but my wrists were manacled behind me.

The deputies in their light-grey campaign hats did not like me lawyering up as soon as they walked in the door, but I got an appreciative nod from Terry. No matter how frequently and sincerely I said, "Sir, I *will* cooperate with you *fully*…" the second part of that statement always pissed them off. They stopped talking to me directly, but the communication did not end. They spoke between themselves loud enough for me to hear remarks like, "Lawyered up already? Oh yeah, he's our guy," and "There's kinky shit in there. Bet it was a lovers' quarrel," and "It's like I tell my wife, this is why I don't go to church anymore." My calf cramped up and when I asked the red-headed cop in the front seat if I could to step out to walk it off, he shook his head without a word. Then he got out and stretched.

Long after the ambulance raced off with Freeman, they hauled me out of the backseat to get my car keys and to put me in another car for transport. There were at least six units there, including two with the township name on it. An older cop grabbed my elbow and began walking me, and I saw Terry talking with two of the cops. One gazed down at her phone while the other examined the contents of her wallet. She glanced my way, our eyes connected but neither of us made any sign. Three more cops approached Terry's group, one clutching something in his hand. They huddled around it like referees examining a replay screen, and one of them motioned Terry away. But she must have seen something because as they stuffed my head under a squad car roof, she turned fully to me and flashed a thumbs-up.

At the station two cops led me into a small, white room with a tiny table and three plastic chairs, the classic interview room seen in every TV cop drama. As they uncuffed me, a portly, uniformed officer stepped in to hand me a can of lukewarm Mountain Dew. Then all three left my little cell. I sat alone for what seemed a long time, but it was impossible to say since they'd taken my phone and of course, there was no clock in the room.

The door finally opened and the chubby cop entered followed by a tall, dark-haired man with glasses. He wore a North Face fall jacket, denim jeans and carried a black leather portfolio zippered shut.

"Are you Melvin?" I asked.

He blinked and shook his head. "Tom O'Reilly." He stuck out his hand and I shook it because, well, that's what you do. "I'm an attorney, and our firm is on retainer for the diocese of Cleveland."

"I was supposed to get a lawyer named Melvin," I said.

"You have a personal attorney?" he asked, surprised.

"No, my sister handled this. She called him—" I stopped. Ah, I saw what was going on. Mr. O'Reilly nodded to the cop who left and closed the door behind him.

"I signed in as your attorney, but I can withdraw that or work as co-counsel with whomever you appoint attorney of record."

"Who contacted you?"

"My boss," he replied as though I were an 8-year-old.

If this was a trick to irritate me, it worked. "How could the diocese know so quickly that I was here?" I didn't even try to keep the scorn out of my voice.

He shrugged. "I dunno. I woke up to a phone call with instructions to get down here and speak with you ASAP. Look, this is going to be a very, very short meeting. The diocese wants you to know," he paused for effect and it worked. I practically fell into him listening. "The papal nuncio has ended the debate. The Penitent's confessions are inauthentic, and you are free to cooperate with police."

A wry smile twisted my face. "Nice try, Mr. O'Reilly. Or is it Detective O'Reilly? I'm not falling for it."

His lips parted and he stared in wonder at me. The guy was a marvelous actor. "This is legit," he said. "It's not whatever you may be thinking."

I smiled and shook my head, waving my hands in front of me as I backed up and sat down. "I'm not talking to anyone until I see Melvin."

"Melvin who?" he asked.

It was with some embarrassment that I realized I didn't know if "Melvin" was the attorney's first or last name. The first red and blue flashing lights – "cherries and berries" Terry had muttered into her phone – appeared on the road in front of Freeman's house before she explained anything more to me. I looked at O'Reilly and shrugged.

He stared at me a second and abruptly flipped a hand in the air. "Fine, works for me," he said, and turned. He knocked on the door and it opened instantly. "I'm going home and getting back into bed. Good luck, Fr. Pastor."

The cops' attitude toward me continued to improve. First, they asked if I wanted another pop, or if I was hungry. They asked if I needed to use the restroom, which I did. No one handcuffed me, held my elbow, or stood beside me at the urinal. And I noticed they'd begun calling me, "Father."

Melvin, or I should say Mr. Melvin Crumwell, Esquire, arrived about an hour later, which gave me time to realize what a butthead I'd been. The cops could not have known about the confessions, or that there had been a tussle over their authenticity. Mr. O'Reilly had to have been who he said he was. I never learned how the diocese found out so quickly I was in custody, but speculation centered on a township cop who also happened to be a deacon at his parish.

As soon as this second attorney walked in, I understood Terry's "flattop" joke. In strolled a thin, youthful Black man in a sharp grey suit with a pencil-eraser haircut so flat he could carry a tray on it. His dark eyes peered intently at me through stylish black glasses as he introduced himself in a smooth, professional patter.

"First, there was a guy here earlier—" I started to say.

"O'Reilly," he cut in. "Yes, I saw his name on the ledger and texted him. You gave him a good laugh. Since he's already signed in we're listed as co-counsel, but we'll work that out. You think of me as your counsel of record."

"Not to be difficult," I said, "but my sister set this up so, I don't know what payment arrangements you guys made. I have very limited assets…"

Crumwell nodded, maybe a little impatiently. "I'm doing this pro bono," he said and flashed a professional smile that belonged on a politician's webpage. God makes use of us all, I guess.

"This room is fitted with recording equipment, so we'll go to another where we can consult privately," he said.

The police took us to another room very much like the first but larger, with a conference table in the middle. For a second time that night I related my experiences with Will Freeman, while Crumwell scribbled furiously with what I think was a Cross Townsend rollerball, though I couldn't be sure. Nice ink flow, it didn't make a scratching sound. At the end, he sat back and tapped the pad with the Cross.

"You never heard names used for either of the women Freeman brought to the room?"

"No."

"Could you identify them from photos?" he asked. I

thought about it and shook my head.

"The older one, maybe, but I was focused on Freeman. The other was a Latina, but she had her back to me ninety percent of the time, so definitely not for her."

Crumwell nodded. "They're the only ones who can support your story. And one of them had to have been the assailant who chopped Mr. Freeman. Give me a moment, I'm going to speak to the detectives and find out what they're considering in terms of charges."

Without further discussion, he got up and left the room. A uniformed cop came in and escorted me back to my interview room. Crumwell got my mind chewing on the word "charges" and I fiddled with my empty pop can for a time, then decided to follow St. Francis de Sales' sage advice and retreat into prayer. It was, of course, the correct thing to do and as often happens a kind of meditative peace descended on me. Grace flowed so abundantly I didn't notice Crumwell re-enter the room.

"Father Pastor? I'm sorry to interrupt your prayers," he said courteously, "You'll be happy to know the police are not bringing charges against you, and are very eager for your assistance."

I smiled, still suffused with the peace of Christ from my prayers. If Crumwell had told me this great news any other time I probably would have whooped or shouted for joy. Now I simply accepted it as another example of God's infinite mercy. I should have enjoyed the moment and kept my mouth shut.

"Did they find the women? Are they OK?"

Crumwell shook his head. "They just started looking. But if, as you said, one was on a cell phone, they probably got someone to pick them up. A pimp, maybe.

They could conceivably be out of state by now."

"Why did the police wait so long to look for them?"

"All they had was your word for it. But if I may say so," the politico smile flashed again, "your guardian angel was on duty tonight, Father Pastor. Freeman's phone recorded everything until it was knocked over. Including his admission of killing and disposing of bodies in the quarry. My understanding is they've contacted a diving club to provide a submersible drone to check it out."

My grace-high was wearing off very fast now, but I clung to the hope of bringing some good out of all this. "After I help the police, is there any chance I could visit Freeman at the hospital when we're done? Just to talk to him."

Crumwell stared at me, then shook his head. "I'm sorry, reverend, I thought you'd heard. He expired enroute to the hospital."

CHAPTER 45

When I think of January in Northeast Ohio, I think in terms of white and grey, numbing cold, and wind with teeth. Maybe nostalgia edits our memories, but those impressions were embossed in my youth and they've stuck. Nothing at all like the present conditions, brought to us courtesy of climate change. Dormant lawns blotched yellowish-green. Dreary skies and damp air, eternal puddles, and sodden clumps of decaying leaves clustered under dripping shrubs. This isn't January. This is limbo.

I tried to keep Bongo on the grass and off the sidewalk where his paw might pick up a rare salt crystal left from a scattering many days ago. The afternoon air no longer showed my breath, and the leaden sky overhead threatened rain instead of snow. The top two buttons on my peacoat were open, and it'd been so long since I'd worn gloves I couldn't recall where they were.

Bongo heard Terry first. I'd been ruminating on something – I do that a lot lately – and didn't notice my sister's Ford in the parking lot. All I know is Bongo's leash went taut and he began dragging me backwards. That's when I saw Terry waving at me from her car and my goddaughter, Cammie, get out on the passenger side. I dropped a half-smoked cigarette, crushed it under my shoe and toed the butt into the less conspicuous edge of the lawn.

"Hey Bongo. Heyyyy boy," Cammie called in that sing-song soprano girls use to wind up a dog. Bongo responded on cue and pulled me across the pavement toward them.

"What brings you guys out here?" I called, staggering behind the straining beagle.

"Bonnngooooo," Cammie called. She still looked every inch the moody teen, but the delightful kid I treasured in my heart tumbled out of her mouth as dog and girl greeted each other.

"Uncle T, can I take hero dog for a walk?" Cammie asked, holding her hand out for the leash.

"Sure. Just make sure he's back by Memorial Day. Or the Fourth of July."

"Hear that, Bongo? D'you hear that? You're my baby now," she said and looped the leash over her wrist. She took off at a trot across the pavement with that numbskull loping alongside, long ears flapping and a goofy beagle grin on his face.

Terry locked her car (in an empty church parking lot. Sheesh.) and we slowly followed the laughing teen and dog.

"So how you doin'?" she asked.

"I'm fine," I said, hands in my coat pockets. I wasn't particularly interested in discussing my state of mind, so I nodded to the pair far ahead of us. "How'd you coax the old Cammie out of Brooding Gen Z over there?"

My sister chuckled. "I dunno. Suddenly I'm not so lame anymore. I must have evolved."

I smiled. "Yeah, before you were nagging mom. Now

you're celebrity bad-ass mom."

"I still nag," she protested. "Not as much, I don't need to. And I'm no celebrity. Just a minor player in this cluster you-know-what."

"Do you think the *Dateline* people will use your interview?" I asked.

"Parts of it, maybe. I hope not. They made me do that thing where I walk along the street, pensively looking away from the camera. It was during the warm spell last month, and my fall jacket is all ratty so I wore a heavy sweater instead. I probably look like I weigh 500 pounds."

"Nah, 450 tops," I said and got a backhanded smack in my ribs. "I suppose IBS will be the star. Did you know he was on the *Today Show*, and even had an interview with a British production team?"

"About this stuff?" Terry asked, then saw the sour look on my face. "Sorry, that was dumb."

"I would've thought he'd had his fill with all the newspapers and local TV," I grumbled. "Ya know, at one point I think the guy would have happily handed me over to the Inquisition, but now I'm probably one of those things he thanks God for every night. He wanted publicity, and boy howdy, he got it."

We both fell into an awkward silence, which didn't bother me but must have gotten to my sister. From out of nowhere she asked, "Hey, how's that college kid doing? The one that works for you. Is she OK?"

"You mean Bridget?"

Terry nodded.

"God is good," I said, grateful for a positive topic. "She's fine, all things considered. Went back to classes when the semester started last week."

"I heard they found her in a hospital."

"Sort of. Metro had her as a Jane Doe for almost three days."

"What happened?"

"The way I heard it, she was posting flyers in a bad part of the city and had just gotten back into her car when some bag-lady came up to her, knocked on her window. She told Bridget that Maggs was in an alley just a block away. Maggs was her sister."

"One of those...?" Terry tailed off.

"Yeah," I said. "In the quarry. Anyway, Bridget went with this woman, but some guy popped out of nowhere and she realized it was a set-up. So she ran for it, turned a corner of some building and boom, fell down a stairwell and hit her head. Whoever chased her must have taken her cell phone, but didn't see her keys or they would have gotten the car, too.

"Somebody found her and called it in. They took her to Metro and put her in the ICU with a severe concussion. She was unconscious with no ID so, she became Jane Doe Number 8. Her family started calling hospitals on Sunday, somebody at Metro put two and two together, and they identified her that night. I guess she just woke up after that."

"Geez," Terry said. "And she's OK now?"

"Yeah, crazy right? She was home a couple of days later. Doctors say no long-term effects."

"It's a blessing," Terry murmured. "For the family, I mean. They lost one kid, thank God they didn't lose a second."

I hadn't heard the word "blessing" come out of my

sister's mouth in years, maybe decades, and I gave her a quick glance.

"Yeah," I said. "Bridget even made it to her sister's funeral. Good turnout, too. 'Course, I couldn't help wonder where were all these people while Maggs was alive, when she needed support. I almost said that in my homily, but for once kept my big, fat yap shut."

Terry seemed to be studying the pavement as we walked.

"Hey, while we're on the topic, the *Dateline* producer keeps pestering me to get a meeting with you. I've told her twice to pound salt, but ya know, she might have a point."

"Nope, nope, nope," I said, and swung my head for emphasis. "Keep tellin' her no. I want nothing more to do with it. I just want – I pray for – anonymity again."

Terry gave an exasperated sigh. "T, I don't know if you'll ever get that. Remember when you were the 'pervert pastor?' I checked and YouTube hasn't pulled that video. So maybe it's a good thing the media turned you into the 'pistol-packing priest who helped catch the Cleveland Quarry Killer.' You shouldn't run away from that—" I looked at her, maybe a bit too abruptly. She ducked her head and brought it up with a shake. "I'm not saying boast about it or anything. Just...acknowledge it."

The temper came out of nowhere. That's happened a couple of times in recent weeks, but even I was unprepared for the flare-up.

"Benefit from it like everybody else, huh?" I snarled. "IBS is stretching his 15-minutes of fame as far as he can." My hands flew out of my coat and waved about, but I couldn't stop them. "That hooker who put the cleaver into Freeman's neck is now the self-proclaimed spokeswoman for sex workers, thanks to your pal, Melvin. And look at you, your daughter thinks her mom is The Equalizer or something. Hell, even the damned dog is a hero.

"Forget it, I'm not joining that parade," I spat, struggling for control. "The biggest damned failure of my life, and people want me to celebrate it."

I'd probably taken at least three steps before I realized Terry wasn't beside me anymore. When I turned, I saw her with hands – no, probably fists – pushing the pockets of her coat down to the point the fabric strained on her shoulders.

"What the hell is the matter with you, Tommy? You talk like he was some little innocent who lost his way. He was a freakin' killer." A hand shot out of her coat and jabbed a finger into her chest. "I saw the evidence, even the home security video that caught him tossing that poor little dog in its cage into the water." Terry took a step forward like she was about to deck me.

"And goddammit, Tommy, I saw the drone videos. Not the edited stuff, I saw the raw footage. I saw his victims. I wish to hell I never talked the cops into letting me see it. I'll never get that out of my brain."

"I don't wanna hear it," I said, shaking my head.

"Oh, you're gonna hear it, alright. I saw them, Tom. I saw all nine, not three like he lied to you. I saw them down there in the dark, chained to those cinder blocks."

"I know, I know, I know, I know," I flustered, trying to wave her off.

"He ran the damned chains through their rib cages,

through their freakin' rib cages, Tommy," Terry nearly
shouted. "And he stabbed each of 'em dozens of times, to
let the gases out so they wouldn't bloat and float free. But
ya know what the coroner said? He didn't need to,
because the weight of the water at a hundred feet would
have held those bodies down. And it's so cold down
there, they hardly decayed at all. Not even the first one,
the kid. Her eyes were open. You know how I know that?
The light from the drone bounced off them. Made 'em
glow, like she was awake down there, chained in the
dark."

"Alright, stop it," I demanded.

"No, you stop it, Tommy," she demanded and
stomped a foot for emphasis. "You stop feeling sorry for
that son of a bitch. He played you. He played you like a
fiddle. He didn't care about his soul because he didn't
think he had one. His wife told the cops he laughed at
religion. He probably learned just enough about
confession to torment some poor, dumb priest. You were
a toy to him. Another notch on his gun."

I glared at her but that's never had any effect on my
sister. She jabbed that finger at me.

"And you stop this bullshit that the devil or some
demons made him do it." There must have been
something in my face, because she backed off a little.

"I'm not, I'm not sayin' that wasn't part of it. My god,
how could there not be evil in this? But dammit, Tommy,
even if there was some demonic – I don't know what,
that's your area, not mine – but even if there was, he had
free will, didn't he? He could have said no at any point.
And you tried. You tried to reel him back." She shook
her head. "He didn't want to come back, Tommy. He

didn't want the light. He wanted the dark. Well, he's got plenty now, doesn't he?"

I saw her look past me, then back at my face, and her eyes became watery. "And who knows, maybe he's become one of those devils himself because he's still got it in for you. He still has his hooks in you." Terry's voice caught for a moment. "I don't want him dragging you down. I don't want you in that dark water, Tommy. You hear me? Talk to somebody. Talk to another priest. What about your buddy from Africa?"

"He's back there," I said sourly. "In Kenya. For now. He'll probably end up in Rome. Probably become pope, God help us all."

"They have phones in Kenya, Tommy. And there's this incredible new thing now, it's called the Internet."

"I've talked with him," I told her. "And T, I'm goin' back to therapy. That's what the Wolfman wants," I saw the puzzlement on her face. "It's a nickname, he's a priest and my confessor. I'm getting help on this, Terry. It's just hard. Really, really hard."

Terry looked past me and wiped her eyes quickly. I turned to see Cammie and Bongo heading back towards us.

"I'll tell her to go play with the dog some more," Terry offered.

"Nah, I've got to get over to the church," I said and spread my arms like wings. She huffed and shook her head, but did the same. Sometimes a hug does amazing things for a person. "I'm doin' better than you think, Terry," I said softly into her ear. "Really, I am."

She stepped back and looked at me skeptically. I smiled and said, "Hey, you free tomorrow morning?"

She nodded. "Wanna launch bullets down at the gully?"

She seemed taken aback. "Is that a good idea?"

"Sure," I said. "A little cordite therapy might do me some good. Besides, I'm lookin' forward to another free meal at Nemo's after I whup your butt."

She shook her head, but came in for another hug and we held each other tight.

"Gross," came a voice behind us. "I thought priests aren't allowed to even touch a woman."

I turned toward Cammie.

"Hey, I can hug family. C'mere, I'll show ya." And just like in the old days, I got to hug my goddaughter. It felt great, and when I opened my eyes, I saw Bongo laying on his side, tongue lolling out of his mouth as he panted.

"Geez, what'd you do to my dog?"

*   *   *

I owed Cammie big time. After they left, Bongo and I headed into the confessional and he trotted straight to his small blue and white bed, circled it twice and flopped down. His brown eyes closed and soft snores rose from him before I'd finished my first prayer.

My watch showed it was nearly 3 p.m. I got up to flip the wall switch for the green bulb outside my door that signaled my confessional was open for business. But before I did, I reached into my shirt pocket and drew out a thumb-sized figurine of a lamb. It had arrived a week before Christmas in a small Federal Express box that contained an even smaller, brown cardboard box with the label ExpressCourier and an address in Kenya. I turn the lamb upside down, knowing what was there. I wanted to see it again. I wanted to feel the warmth of Mwangi's friendship in the small, blue handwriting inside the base: Jn 17:12.

Looking at the tiny ceramic creature, I whispered the verse softly to myself: "While I was with them I protected them by your name that you have given me, and I kept them safe. Not one of them was lost, except the one destined to be lost, so that the Scripture might be fulfilled."

I place the lamb on a shelf in the shadow of some boxes where only I can see it from my chair. Glancing down at the table beside me, I considered the figurine of the Good Shepherd leading several smiling sheep.

"You couldn't save Judas," I said, "so why do I feel such guilt at having lost this one? I know what You're telling me. I can't save them all, and to think I can is folly and sinful pride."

I looked at the serene, patient face of the porcelain savior. "But forgive me, Lord, I still intend to try."

Turning, I reached out and with a quick motion flipped the switch on. Then I sat down to await the next penitent.

The End

ACKNOWLEDGMENTS

This book, like anything else I have accomplished over the years, would not have been possible without my beloved partner and wife, Deb.

I am grateful to my daughter, Dally, a successful author and better writer than her old man. She reviewed and improved my manuscript, then cajoled this grumpy Boomer into the mystifying world of self-publishing.

My nonconformist son, Ben, encouraged me to take a new direction after the semi-traditional face-plant that is one's first novel. Ever true to his nature, Ben liked the first one better.

I am blessed with beta readers who provided patience, support and constructive criticism: Paul Herold, long-time friend, mentor and one of the keenest wits I know; Marian Badaczewski, a role model in so many ways who made time in her busy life to apply her analytical mind to this project; and Ann and Tony Sutphin, dear friends who gently exposed unnoticed plot holes and proved to be frustratingly good copy editors.

The cover of this book was designed by David Flynn, graphic artist and professor of practice in art at The University of Akron. Thank you, David, for the generous loan of your talents.

During the writing of this book I leaned heavily on expert advice to lend credibility to the storytelling. My thanks to Dr. Michael A. Fistek, DO Internal Medicine, whose knowledge resolved plot problems in this and other works, and who graciously does not wince at my sometimes ghoulish questions.

I also want to extend my deep thanks to two men who were vital to the creation of this story. Fr. Raymond P. Guiao, S.J., president of St. Ignatius High School in Cleveland, OH, who kindly guided me all the way to the Vatican in search of an authority on the seal of the confessional. Rome referred me to an outstanding resource in my own backyard, St. Mary's Seminary. There I gained the invaluable help of Fr. Gary D. Yanus, judicial vicar, Diocese of Cleveland, and for many years a key faculty member at St. Mary's. Fr. Yanus patiently shepherded me through the ins and outs of the seal, the legalisms of excommunication, and away from embarrassing inaccuracies, inconsistencies and misconceptions.

Finally, I want to thank all the parish priests encountered in my lifetime. They inspired the writing of this book. Most were good men, some were great, and a few not-so-good. They are ordinary people leading extraordinary lives, and their self-sacrifice, service to others, and devotion to a mystery beyond human comprehension is worthy of our respect and admiration.

ABOUT THE AUTHOR

David Nypaver is an erstwhile journalist, PR flack, ad copywriter, and speechwriter. He and his wife, Deb, reside in Uniontown, Ohio, with their dogs, Belle and Otto.

Made in United States
Orlando, FL
05 August 2024

49948119R00176